Tobia:

SAP Small Business One

Tobias Lombacher

SAP Small Business One

A hands-on guide to install and configure SAP Small Business One

VDM Verlag Dr. Müller

Impressum/Imprint (nur für Deutschland/ only for Germany)
Bibliografische Information der Deutschen Nationalbibliothek: Die Deutsche Nationalbibliothek
verzeichnet diese Publikation in der Deutschen Nationalbibliografie; detaillierte bibliografische
Daten sind im Internet über http://dnb.d-nb.de abrufbar.
Alle in diesem Buch genannten Marken und Produktnamen unterliegen warenzeichen-, marken-
oder patentrechtlichem Schutz bzw. sind Warenzeichen oder eingetragene Warenzeichen der
jeweiligen Inhaber. Die Wiedergabe von Marken, Produktnamen, Gebrauchsnamen,
Handelsnamen, Warenbezeichnungen u.s.w. in diesem Werk berechtigt auch ohne besondere
Kennzeichnung nicht zu der Annahme, dass solche Namen im Sinne der Warenzeichen- und
Markenschutzgesetzgebung als frei zu betrachten wären und daher von jedermann benutzt
werden dürften.

Coverbild: www.purestockx.com

Verlag: VDM Verlag Dr. Müller Aktiengesellschaft & Co. KG
Dudweiler Landstr. 99, 66123 Saarbrücken, Deutschland
Telefon +49 681 9100-698, Telefax +49 681 9100-988, Email: info@vdm-verlag.de

Herstellung in Deutschland:
Schaltungsdienst Lange o.H.G., Berlin
Books on Demand GmbH, Norderstedt
Reha GmbH, Saarbrücken
Amazon Distribution GmbH, Leipzig
ISBN: 978-3-639-13681-4

Imprint (only for USA, GB)
Bibliographic information published by the Deutsche Nationalbibliothek: The Deutsche
Nationalbibliothek lists this publication in the Deutsche Nationalbibliografie; detailed
bibliographic data are available in the Internet at http://dnb.d-nb.de.
Any brand names and product names mentioned in this book are subject to trademark, brand or
patent protection and are trademarks or registered trademarks of their respective holders. The use
of brand names, product names, common names, trade names, product descriptions etc. even
without a particular marking in this works is in no way to be construed to mean that such names
may be regarded as unrestricted in respect of trademark and brand protection legislation and
could thus be used by anyone.

Cover image: www.purestockx.com

Publisher:
VDM Verlag Dr. Müller Aktiengesellschaft & Co. KG
Dudweiler Landstr. 99, 66123 Saarbrücken, Germany
Phone +49 681 9100-698, Fax +49 681 9100-988, Email: info@vdm-verlag.de

Copyright © 2009 by the author and VDM Verlag Dr. Müller Aktiengesellschaft & Co. KG and
licensors
All rights reserved. Saarbrücken 2009

Printed in the U.S.A.
Printed in the U.K. by (see last page)
ISBN: 978-3-639-13681-4

Table of contents

List of figures

List of tables

List of formulas

Introduction

Mid-size companies sized with up to 300 employees are today in a very complicated situation today, regarding which enterprise software is most suitable for their company . This uncertainty is due to the rising number of small software companies that offer enterprise software as well as the uncertainty about the future development of the company. Since a few years the big enterprise companies like SAP or Microsoft have begun to discover the mid size business and recognize the potential in these markets.

SAP has introduced Small Business One as the mid-size version of their enterprise management system which allows these companies to handle their business. Small Business One is easier to configure and covers around 70 percent of the mid-size business needs without additional customizing. In case the business grows and the company needs to switch to an extended version the transfer from Small Business One to the more advanced systems in the SAP family is a small step. The reason for this is that the underlying structure and technology is implemented to match the whole family.

This diploma thesis will show a typical implementation situation for a midsize company with about 25 employees and its main area in the service business. The described situation will match for many mid size companies and can be adapted easily to others. Also some special requirements that come into existence for a company acting as reseller and service provider will be described.

This thesis will start with the overall demands that where requested by Alfing Corporation. A detailed description of the individual situation and the resulting requirements is given in each chapter. Each of the chapters will describe also the implemented solution. The corresponding setup procedures are specified in the appendix.

Plymouth, January 2007   Tobias Lombacher

1 Alfing Group

The Alfing Group is a machine and part supplier delivering parts and turnkey solutions to the worldwide automotive industry. The Alfing Group itself consists of three subsidiaries located in Aalen, Germany. For the North American market an additional facility exists that provides installation and service for this area. This is also the company that is implementing Small Business One.

The following chapters will give a short description of each subsidiary and their products.

1.1 Maschinenfabrik Alfing Kessler GmbH

The Maschinenfabrik is the main company. It was founded in 1911 by Karl Kessler. Since then the company delivered crankshafts for aircraft engines.

Since the 1920s Alfing started to manufacture large crankshafts for maritime diesels, locomotives, construction vehicles, generator sets, gas engines, mining equipment, aircraft engines and other applications.

In the beginning of 1932 Alfing increased their engagement in the smaller crankshaft market. Since then, Alfing crankshafts have been used in Zeppelin airships and smaller aircraft engines. After World War I Alfing focused on the development of automotive crankshafts for high performance engines. A milestone in the development of automotive crankshafts was the 1932 Mercedes Benz SKL, equipped with an Alfing crankshaft, which was the first car crossing the finishing line at the Berlin Avus.

Since then Alfing crankshafts have been well known for their reliability and performance. Even today Alfing is often the 100% supplier for high-performance crankshafts in the racing and sports car industry.

The manufacturing process for crankshafts made it soon necessary to invent some special hardening equipment. This was in 1952, when another special division of Alfing was established, the construction and manufacturing of induction hardening machines. Today this equipment is delivered worldwide to automotive suppliers.

Some typical crankshafts and hardening machines built by Alfing can be seen below.

Figure 1-1: Alfing crankshaft

Source: Alfing Corporation

Figure 1-2: Alfing hardening machine

Source: Alfing Corporation

1.2 Alfing Kessler Sondermaschinen GmbH

The Alfing Kessler Sondermaschinen GmbH was founded in 1938. In the beginning Alfing Kessler Sondermaschinen was specialized in the production of aircraft propeller hubs.

Soon the objectives changed and Alfing started producing specialized milling machines for the automotive industry. Especially during the 1970s Alfing Kessler Sondermaschinen became famous for their high quality and durable transfer lines. This tradition lasts until today and is gaining its momentum high in the development of linear motor driven machining centers.

Today Alfing supplies standard milling machines, as well as transfer lines to many customers in the automotive industry. Alfing is very specialized to provide turnkey solutions for its customers. Therefore a good service is one of the essentials that must be offended.

In the last years the business on the machine market decreased and many machine builders where not able to stand the pressure forcing them into bankruptcy. Today Alfing is one of the last independent machine tool builders for the automotive industry worldwide.

The next images show some pictures of machines and parts manufactured on Alfing machines.

Figure 1-3: Alfing machine examples

Source: Alfing Corporation

Figure 1-4: Alfing part examples

Source: Alfing Corporation

1.3 Alfing Kessler Montage Technik GmbH

Alfing Kessler Montage Technik GmbH was founded in 1981 as the third division of the Alfing Group. The company is specialized in assembly and automation equipment for the automotive industry. The product program consists basically out of three main areas, the nut runners, assembly machines and the automation equipment.

While the nut runners are one of the standard products, manufactured in batch production, the assembly and automation equipment is customized for the specific demands of each customer.

Specialized in the automotive industry, the automation equipment is often used as a complement to the Alfing transfer lines and milling machines. The assembly machines could be arranged before or beneath the milling equipment.

The next figures show some of Alfing's products.

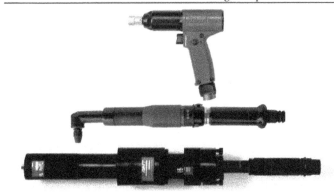

Figure 1-5: Alfing nut runners

Source: Alfing Corporation

Figure 1-6: Alfing assembly machine

Source: Alfing Corporation

Figure 1-7: Alfing automation equipment

Source: Alfing Corporation

1.4 Alfing Corporation

Alfing Corporation is the US subsidiary of the Alfing Group. It was founded in 1992 and established itself since then as a major supplier to the automotive and other large scale manufacturing industries.

Since its foundation Alfing Corporation has sold over 200 manufacturing systems, special purpose machines and machining centers throughout the United States and Mexico. Also the complete service from installation until disassembly is provided from there.

From their office in Plymouth, Alfing Corporation provides the North American, Canadian and Mexican customers with complete product support. This includes sales, service, spare parts, project management, simultaneous engineering and system integration.

The main goal for Alfing Corporation is to build up long lasting relationships with customers and provide them with complete and flexible solutions.

Figure 1-8: Alfing Corporation in Plymouth

Source: Alfing Corporation

1.5 Organizational charts

Alfing Corporation is the connection point between the North American customers and German companies, which is illustrated in the figure below:

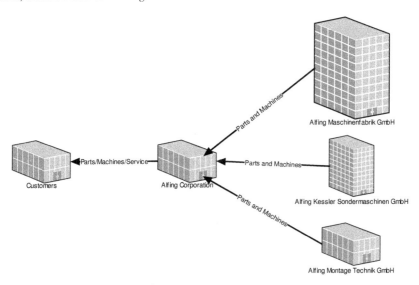

Figure 1-9: Alfing Corporation's Role

Source: Self

This picture shows how Alfing acts as a reseller between the customer and the German company. The black lines symbolize the deliver of goods and service from Germany to the North American customer.

The main role for Alfing Corporation is to forward goods to the customer and provide after-sales service. In special cases the service is also carried out by German technicians.

The financial organization of Alfing company can be seen in the figure below:

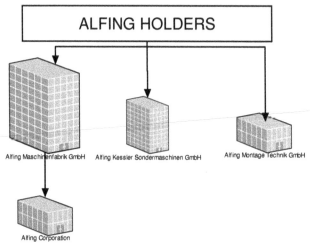

Figure 1-10: Organizational chart

Source: Self

The complete Alfing group is held by the members of the Alfing and Kessler family. Each of the subsidiaries is directly responsible to them. Only Alfing Corporation has a special role. Located directly beneath the Alfing Maschinenfabrik it is reporting only their profit and loss statements to it and not directly to the Alfing holders.

The following chapter gives a description of the initial situation and the goals which had to be achieved. A detailed overview of each functionality within the company will be given afterwards.

2   Initial Situation and objectives

When Alfing Corporation started in 1992 the accounting department was shared with two other companies located in the same building. The accounting system was a single user system called Open Systems. This system was only used to record the financial transactions of the companies. All other business was managed externally in Microsoft's Office package.

With today's number of transactions and the growing number of employees the accounting system became the bottleneck of the company. It tied also a lot of work capacity because every invoice and inventory transaction had to be recorded twice, in the departments as well as in the accounting. Regardless of this it became very hard to keep an overview about all documents and its location on the file servers. After visualizing this situation it shows up the following way:

Figure 2-1: Workflow within Alfing Corporation

Source: Self

This figure can be described as followed. Each department had its own workflow which was executed internally. After the internal working procedure was completed all information had to be transferred into the accounting department to provide be processed there and provide information for the management. The results of this working procedure were that a lot of transactions had not been recorded correctly or with differences to its original, which tied up a lot of energy. One of the main issues was the year-end closing which was always a very difficult procedure because the inventory in the accounting, the manual records and on the shelf didn't match together. Also the management did never exactly know what was happening in the company as long as the information was not transferred into the accounting. And even then did the accounting reflect only the information which was available there and the management had to ask especially for it. Therefore was accounting the center of the complete company. Additional information, for example outstanding deliveries, actual quotes or others, was not accessible.

Parallel to this situation an independent development took place in Germany. The main companies introduced SAP to manage their transactions. Alfing Maschinenfabrik uses this system to record all of their transactions, while Alfing Kessler Sondermaschinen GmbH and Alfing Montagetechnik use SAP for financials and PENTA for their production management. The previously described software infrastructure is illustrated in Figure 2-2: Software Environment.

This was the initial situation when Alfing Corporation decided to switch to a new enterprise system which provides a multi user environment and can be integrated flawlessly within the German companies. This was also the main decision to work with SAP's Small Business One. The main objective was to have the SAP system running within Alfing Corporation itself. The integration with the German companies is planned in future and not part of this diploma thesis.

The main objective covered by this diploma thesis is to introduce SAP Small Business One into the working environment of Alfing Corporation.

Based on the aspect of a multi-user system which integrates all company departments some additional goals could be defined:

- Reduction of the paper trail
- Improve of the workflow within the company
- Integrated inventory management
- Improve the accessibility to the companies data
- Reduce the work for the accounting department
- More transparency for financial transactions
- Improve of service and machine management
- Application of a corporate identity which shows up in every document.

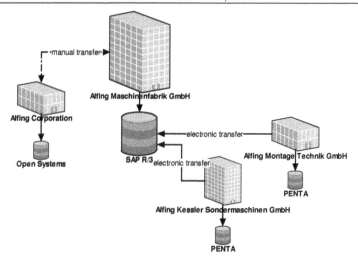

Figure 2-2: Software Environment

Source: Self

The following chapters will provide some basic information about the business workflow in Alfing Corporation and determine a functional overview. A detailed description of each department and its difficulties is provided in the corresponding chapters.

3   Business Process

A business process is basically a specific event in the chain of structured business activities. Within Alfing Corporation the following chain of activities could be determined.

Figure 3-1: Business process

Source: Self

This basic workflow shows the different level of business activities which happen within Alfing Corporation, starting with the sales and customer relationship management and ending with the accounting. Based on this information a more detailed flowchart of the process can be developed:

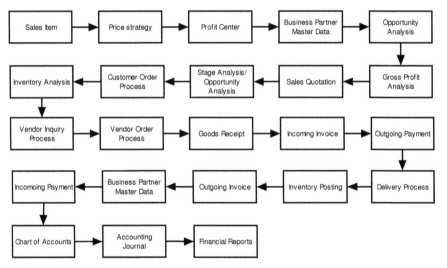

Figure 3-2: Process flow chart

Source: Self

This process flow chart can be rearranged depending on specific working procedures or the business area. It is remarkable that no production department shows up within here, which is related to the fact, that Alfing Corporation has no own manufacturing facility.

After rearranging the previous figures and matching them with the integrated modules of Small Business One a functional overview can be retrieved. Based on this functional overview each of the department's work habits have been analyzed and overdone.

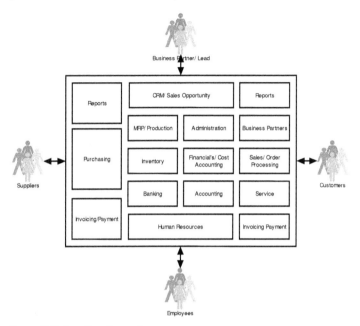

Figure 3-3: Functional overview

Source: According to SAP

This figure shows each of the modules and its connection to the different surroundings of Alfing Corporation. The arrangement is made in the way that inside tasks are located in the center, while functions with connection to outside surroundings are located at the borders.

The subsequent chapter will provide an overview about the functional structure of Alfing Corporation, followed by the costs for the complete implementation process.

4 Organization structure

The following chart shows the organization structure of Alfing Corporation. Remarkable is the very flat structure without any hierarchical expansions.

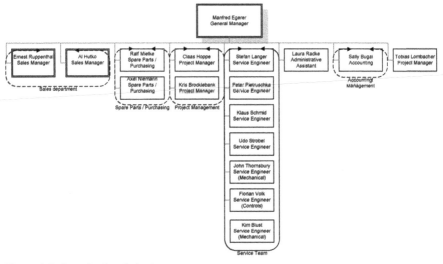

Figure 4-1: Organizational chart

Source: Alfing Corporation

Based on the previously collected information and some additional knowledge provided in subsequent chapters it is possible to generate different views to the company, based on their internal structure.

For SAP's grown up system exists a special way how to show a companies structure which is shown below. This structure does not directly apply to Small Business One but it provides a very well overview why it is shown here.

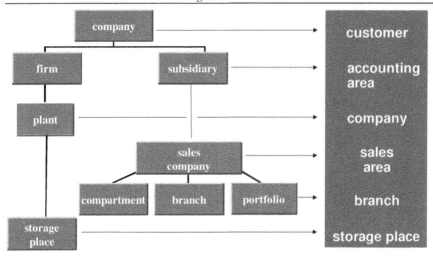

Figure 4-2: Organization units of SAP

Source: SAP Kompetenzzentrum Passau

The customer is the highest ranked organizational unit. It is a closed unit with view on the data structure and its own master records. From the view of business administration shows the customer up as the top-level of a company which can consist out of several legal independent subsidiaries.

The accounting area reflects the smallest unit which makes it own balances sheet. The accounting area has its own balance sheet and profit and loss statement. From the view of business administration is an accounting area one legal independent subsidiary within the company.

The plant is the central unit of the logistics. A plant is containing the area of production, the material management and the sales as a unit of delivery. One accounting area can contain several plants which means that all transactions are shown in the balance sheet of the related accounting area.

The sales area is the highest ranked area within the sales of a company. This area is responsible for the sales of goods and service of the company. A sales area can have several related plants from where they deliver goods. The below oriented structures in compartment, branch and portfolio allow to separate some fields of the sales area. The following figures illustrated the view of the different company areas on Alfing Corporation.

4.1 Financial view

The financials of the company has a profit performance, cost accounting, credit controlling and an accounting area. The portfolio for the financials shows up in four different categories each of them separately.

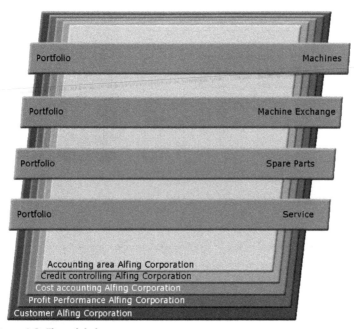

Figure 4-3: Financial view

Source: adapted from ShoeFa documentation

The Maschinenfabrik does not show up here due to the reason that Alfing Corporation acts independent from its mother company and has only to report their profit information to it.

The basic structure is to start with the customer Alfing Corporation. The profit performance is the area which measures the profit and loss, while the cost accounting calculates the sales prices. The credit controlling is the area where the monetary financials of the company show up. The accounting area itself is the area where the book-keeping is executed. The portfolio lines up the different areas which are separated within the financials.

4.2 Sales view

The view from the sales side shows up slightly different and is basically separated by its areas.

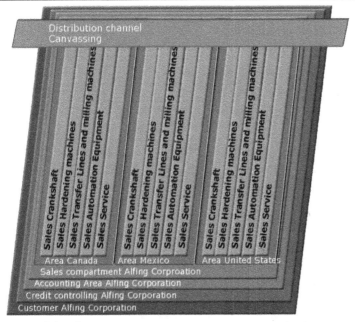

Figure 4-4: Sales view

Source: adapted from ShoeFa documentation

The sales view has basically the same areas as within the financial view with its credit controlling and accounting area.

The base description of this figure is basically the same as above in the financials view. The sales area itself includes the different areas which are Canada, Mexico and United States. Within each of the sales area are the different sales groups included. It is remarkable that these sales areas show up different than in the financials view. The distribution method is only a canvassing direct to the customer.

4.3 Logistic view

The view on the logistic side shows the particular storage locations and its organization.

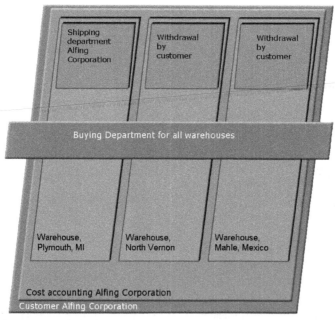

Figure 4-5: Logistic view

Source: adapted from ShoeFa docuemntation

The logistic view of Alfing Corporation is basically simple and contains mainly the different ware-houses. The crossbar shows that only one buying department manages all warehouses within the company. The smaller boxes on top symbolize the shipping department, which is Alfing Corporation itself and for consignment warehouses the customer.

The following figure can be derived directly from theses overviews and provide the following picture.

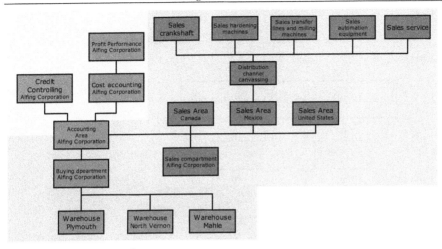

Figure 4-6: Complete overview

Source: adapted from ShoeFa documentation

The following chapters will provide some background information about the initial costs and the necessary expenses to keep a SAP system running.

5 Cost

The costs of a new software system can be split into two main parts, the implantation costs and the operating costs.

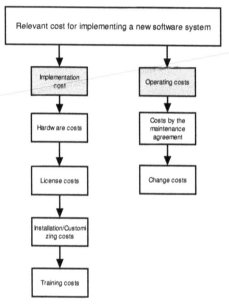

Figure 5-1: Implementation costs

Source: Self

The implementation cost contains all costs which are one time expenses while the operating costs include the costs which have to be calculated to keep the system running.

5.1 Hardware requirements

Small Business One is a strictly based Client/Server system. It needs a server where the main application and database management system is running and a client where the data input is made. According to this the hardware costs can be split into server and client.

5.1.1 Server

The hardware requirements of the server depend mostly on the number of clients using the system. Based on suggestions of SAP and their experience the following hard- and software had been bought by Alfing Corporation:

Server	
Operating System	Windows 2003 Server
Database Management System	Microsoft SQL Server 2005
CPU	4 Processor System
RAM	8 GB Ram
Free Disk Space	150 GB
Network	UTP-RJ45 Connections
Price:	$14,895

Table 5-1: Server configuration

Source: Computer Divisions International

After running the system for a longer period it showed that it has at least enough performance to run up to 30 users at the same time.

5.1.2   Client

The client side has fewer efforts. SAP suggests at least the following configuration:

Client	
Operating System	Windows 98/2000/XP
CPU	Pentium III, Mhz 450 and above
RAM	128 MB RAM
Free Disk Space	> 500 MB Free
Network	UTP-RJ45 Connections
Software	Internet Explorer 5.5 and above

Table 5-2: Hardware Requirements Client

Source: SAP

It turned out that those requirements are the absolute minimum for the client side and not very satisfying. In a multi tasking environment with several applications running and working with add-ons the RAM and CPU should be at least tripled.

Due to the reason all computers in the office met those requirements no further expenses had to be made for this.

5.2 License cost

For Small Business One exist two different types of license, the professional and CRM license.

The professional license has access to all modules of SAP, while the CRM license is restricted to the modules without accounting transactions. Based on the license information of SAP (see [12] **SAP (January 2006):** *License Guide.* SAP Library.) and the users' responsibilities the number of licenses could be determined to:

User	License	CRM	Professional	Price
(Manager)			X	$ 3187.50
Manfred Egerer		X		$ 1875.00
Ralf Mielke			X	$ 3187.50
Claas Hoppe		X		$ 1875.00
Kris Brocklebank		X		$ 1875.00
Allen Hutko		X		$ 1875.00
Laura Radke		X		$ 1875.00
Sally Bugai			X	$ 3187.50
Tobias Lombacher			X	$ 3187.50
Stefan Langer		X		$ 1875.00
Peter Pietruschka		X		$ 1875.00
Klaus Schmid		X		$ 1875.00
Udo Strobel		X		$ 1875.00
John Thornsbury		X		$ 1875.00
Florian Volk		X		$ 1875.00
Kim Blust		X		$ 1875.00
Ernie Ruppenthal		X		$ 1875.00
TOTAL		**13**	**4**	**$ 37125.00**

Table 5-3: Licenses

Source: Self

This list shows each user, his license and its price. At the end of the table the total is provided. The manager license is necessary for special setup and configurations. Additional licensing for add-ons provided by SAP is not necessary.

5.2.1 CrystalOne License

The CrystalOne is a third party tool used by Alfing Corporation to generate reports. The licensing costs sum to:

- CrystalOne Report Interface $ 500
- Crystal Report Writer $ 575

The Report Writer is only necessary if it is intended to generate or modify reports.

5.3 Installation/ Customizing cost

The suggested hour package which had been bought by Alfing Corporation planned 120 hours for the software implementation. The whole package price was $16,000. This covered customizing as well as training. It turned out that at least twice the hours would have been necessary.

5.4 Training cost

See chapter 5.3 Installation/ Customizing cost.

5.5 Maintenance cost

The maintenance cost of Small Business One is connected to the number of licenses. It is calculated as 17% per anno from the cost of licenses. The maintenance covers software updates, patches and basic software support as well as access to the Business One forum in the internet. For Alfing Corporation the yearly maintenance is $ 6311.25 for all licenses.

5.6 Change costs

These are costs to modify the basic system and for third party add-ons. The change costs can't be calculated in advance and they become only necessary in case of extended modifications.

5.7 Summary of costs

Based on the previous information the total costs for Alfing Corporation can be estimated to:

Costs	One time	Annual
Hardware Costs (Server only)	$ 14,895.00	
License Costs	$ 37,125.00	
Crystal Report	$ 1,075.00	
Implementation/Training	$ 16,000.00	
Maintenance		$ 6,311.25
TOTAL	**$ 69,095.00**	**$ 6,311.25**

Table 5-4: Total cost

Source: Self

Additional costs have to be calculated for the network infrastructure, the client computers and for the backup solution. Because each of these preconditions existed these costs are not indicated here.

5.8 Conclusion and problems

The initial cost for appropriate hardware and software is reasonable and realistic. The hardware requirements for the client stations should be calculated generous, depending on the number of add-ons that will be in use.

A problem of the user based licensing mechanism is that it results in very high costs for each individual. A missing feature is the possibility to buy temporary licenses which can be assigned to subcontracted workers or external auditors.

Due to the reason the service contract includes only the update delivery without the installation it gets very expensive. The experience shows that a monthly update has to be calculated. The update procedure on the server side works well, but not the client. The reason for this is that only a system administrator can update the clients. This procedure took Alfing Corporation usually up to three full days for all users. Working with policies couldn't be applied to make this work.

The estimated time for the implementation and training was not enough. Without doing most things internally it would have taken at least twice the time.

The following chapter will provide an overview about the executed implementation steps and the tasks performed during each period.

6 General Roadmap

The general roadmap scheduled four main steps, each with a specified time period:

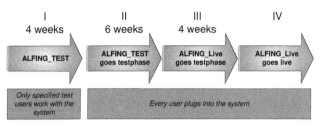

Figure 6-1: Roadmap overview

Source: Self

- ALFING_TEST
  This phases was to setup the basic functionality. The master data for all other modules where set during this time, too. Only a specified number of users where allowed to work with the system during this time. This database was the basis for a blank ALFING_LIVE database.

- ALFING_TEST goes testphase
  During this phases the users where practicing their daily task in the system. The main intention was to test and customize the system to specific needs. All approved configurations where transferred into the ALFING_LIVE database.

- ALFING_LIVE goes testphase
  At this time the daily transactions where performed in SAP and in Open Systems. The intention was to monitor any discrepancies and solve them.

- ALFING_LIVE goes live
  This was the last and final step. At this point all transactions took place in SAP. The old system was switched off.

6.1 Conclusion and Summary

It was very successful to start the basic configuration with some selected users. This phase took about four weeks which was absolutely necessary to get the basic configuration running.

The testphase was helpful providing the users the possibility to transfer training lessons into a working system. It helped also to retrieve additional information about missing functionalities and test several modules. This phase turned out to be the most important for the implementation of additional options.

Running both systems parallel during a certain period of time showed discrepancies and helped to fix them. This phase was initiated after a month end procedure and all data of this procedure was transferred into the system. After the next month the ending balances of Small Business One and Open Systems where compared.

The live phases itself was very unspectacular due to the previous testing. Only minor adjustments of forms and reporting features became necessary.

The complete run-off procedure in about 14 weeks was very strictly organized and had not many space for delays. The time for importing items and business partners is not included here. Depending on the complexity and the complications of the import it can take up to another four weeks.

Another very time consuming part is to generate the forms and print layouts. The time which is necessary here depends mainly on the complexity of the forms and reports. It takes also a lot of time to test the functionality of the forms and reports. This can be done very well during the test phases by several users.

The following chapter will provide some basic administration before the financials and cost accounting is discussed.

7 Administration

The administration chapter will cover especially the licensing mechanism of SAP and the applied concept for Alfing Corporation. The administration is located inside the company without further connection to outside business.

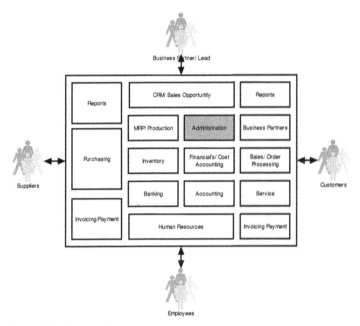

Figure 7-1: Functional overview

Source: According to SAP

7.1 Initial situation

As mentioned in the initial chapter 2 Initial Situation and , Alfing Corporation shared their accounting department with two other companies Bohle Inc. and Berger LLC. It was considered to transfer those companies also into Small Business One and keep sharing of some employees. To keep them strictly separated, which is necessary due to their legal form, made it necessary to create different databases:

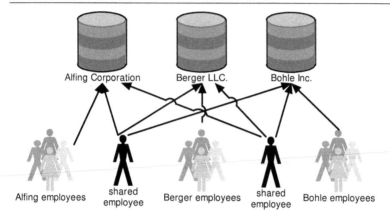

Figure 7-2: Database accessibility

Source: Self

The goal was to transfer this structure into an licensing mechanism which allows to buy only single licenses for the shared employees.

7.2 Licensing and access

SAP's licensing mechanism is based on three levels. The general application license, the user license and the user login. Each of them referring to each other.

7.2.1 Application license

The application license determines the level of access a company has to the Small Business One system. It can be divided into four different types. Each of those addresses different company profiles.

- SAP Business One application license
  necessary for using the SAP Business One application.

- SAP Business One Software Development Kit (SDK) license,
  required for developing add-ons and doing major changes within the forms.

- Add-on solution license
  to distribute add-ons to customers. Working as named-user model, which allocates licenses per user name.

- Data Interface (DI) Server license
  necessary to manipulate the SAP Business One database by using SOAP messages. It is the same as the DI API , but for multiple connections. It is determined by the number of CPUs in the DI Server. Unlimited users can connect to one license.

The necessary type of license for Alfing Corporation is the SAP Business One application license. This is the typical end user license for users without intention to develop third party add-ons.

7.2.2 User license

The user license of SAP follows a named-user model. This means the license is allocated per user name. Each of these user licenses can be one of the listed types:

- Professional
  includes all of the SAP Business One forms.
- CRM license
  - either as sales and contact or as
  - service management module
- Add-On Basic license
  includes forms that do not require a license key

The Professional license allows access to all modules of Small Business One without restrictions. The CRM licenses allows access to some basic modules without financials and banking. A CRM is the minimum license necessary to log into the system. The add-on license alone can't be used to work with the system. It grants only access to additional packages which are provided by SAP.

The licensing options are not connected to a specific company database, which allows to share licenses between several company databases.

7.2.3 User authorizations

The user authorization is the last level and it allows authorizing or restricting users from several forms. A user authorization is limited by the users' license. The different restrictions are:

- No Access
  the user is not able to open the form. This makes it also impossible to view the data
- Read   only
  the user can open the form in read only mode. He can view and browse the information, but is not able to apply any changes.
- Full
  the user can open the form and change, add and delete data.

The user authorizations can be distributed on group and user level.

7.3 Applied licensing

With the previous knowledge the following licensing structure could be set up:

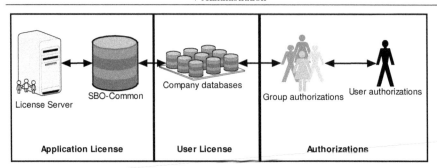

Figure 7-3: Licensing at Alfing Corporation

Source: Self

The license server manages the user and application licenses. The SBO-Common database contains the operating system of Small Business One which is licensed by the application license. The company databases are directly connected to the SBO-Common database which distributes the users license from the licenses server to the company database. Based on the company database applies the user authorization which allows different access levels to each database. This setup allows a very secure environment and the management of different companies sharing users.

The following chapters focus only on Alfing Corporation regardless of the other companies. Within the following chapter the accounting setup, which is the basis for every company, will be discussed.

8 Accounting

The accounting configuration is the basis configuration which contains all important financial settings like currency, chart of accounts and tax setup. Without this basic setup the system is not operable. The location of the accounting in the functional overview can be seen below.

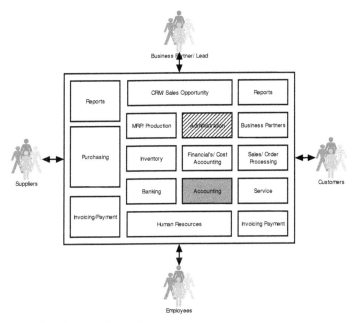

Figure 8-1: Functional overview

Source: Self

These initial settings are very important and should be made very carefully because many of them have influence to nearly all functional aspects of the application. This can be how information is stored, verified, accessed or manipulated. Some of these settings are fixed as soon as the first transactions take place. Therefore a careful configuration is absolutely necessary because it can result in impenetrable problems.

The following chapter will discuss the initial settings which where necessary for Alfing Corporation.

8.1 Chart of Accounts

The chart of accounts is an index of all general ledger accounts used by the company. The chart of accounts keeps track about every posting transaction carried out in the system. Without the chart of accounts no transactions can be made in the system.

The chart of accounts can be divided into two different main areas. Accounts which show up in the balance sheet as a one time statement at the end of the year and the accounts which keep track about the daily monetary transactions which show up in the profit and loss statement. The profit or loss of this statement is transferred at the end of the period into the balance sheet.

The balance sheet shows all assets and liabilities of a company. In detail it follows the subsequent structure.

ASSETS	LIABILITIES
CURRENT ASSETS	CURRENT LIABILITIES
INVESTMENTS	LONG-TERM LIABILITIES
PROPERTY	EQUITY
OTHER	
TOTAL	TOTAL

Figure 8-2: balance sheet

Source: Self

- Assets: entries which show the tangible and intangible properties (Vermögen)
- Liabilities: debt the company owns others (Schulden)
- Equity: the values of the shares issued by a company (Eigenkapital)

The profit and loss statement contains only the revenues and expenses of a period which will result in profit or loss which is transferred into the balance sheet.

- Revenues: which is the income of a business (Ertrag)
- Expenses: costs incurred in the performance of a job or a task (Kosten)

The account itself is indicated through an account code, an account description and information that determines the category of each account.

8.1.1 Initial situation

The above described structure is fixed and has to be transferred one by one into the system. Only the number of sub accounts and the level of detail can be determined individually by each company.

The previous chart of accounts was an approved and reliable structure. It was easy to handle but not very detailed.

A specialty related to Open Systems was that the determination of each transaction was made by its description. The system itself did not separate invoices from general ledger entries or other documents.

8.1.2 Realized solution

Alfing Corporation decided to transfer the chart of accounts without further modifications into Small Business One. The reason for this decision was that the chart of accounts was successfully proofed. A minor adjustment was to remove separate accounts for each technician and manage them by the cost accounting in the new system. A further description of this modification is given in the chapter 9 Cost Accounting. Other adjustments where not requested or applied.

After clearance the following chart of accounts had to be transferred into the financial module:

No.	G/L Account	Name	Group
1	1000-00-00	Petty Cash	Assets
2	1003-00-00	Comerica Bank - Payroll	Assets
3	1004-00-00	Comerica Bank - Checking	Assets
4	1005-00-00	Comerica Bank - Money Market	Assets
5	1006-00-00	LBBW-USD Account	Assets
6	1007-00-00	LBBW-EURO Account	Assets
7	1009-00-00	Cash Holding	Assets
8	1114-00-00	Loans Receivable	Assets
9	1120-00-00	Accounts Receivable - Trade	Assets
10	1121-00-00	Accounts Receivable - AKS	Assets
11	1122-00-00	Accounts Receivable - MAFA	Assets
12	1123-00-00	Accounts Receivable - AMT	Assets
13	1124-00-00	Accounts Receivable - AKS Commissions	Assets
14	1125-00-00	Accounts Receivable - AMT Commissions	Assets
15	1126-00-00	Accounts Receivable - MAFA Commissions	Assets
16	1130-00-00	Advances - Employees	Assets
17	1135-00-00	Notes Receivable	Assets
18	1140-00-00	Advances to Vendors	Assets
19	1210-00-00	Prepaid Insurance	Assets
20	1220-00-00	Prepaid Taxes	Assets
21	1229-00-00	Prepaid Expenses - Other	Assets
22	1230-00-00	Prepaid Expenses - Security Deposits	Assets
23	1310-00-00	Leasehold Improvements	Assets
24	1320-00-00	Machinery & Equipment	Assets
25	1330-00-00	Furniture & Fixtures	Assets
26	1340-00-00	Vehicles	Assets
27	1410-00-00	Accumulated Depreciation - Leasehold Improvement	Assets
28	1420-00-00	Accumulated Depreciation - Machinery & Equipment	Assets
29	1430-00-00	Accumulated Depreciation - Furniture & Fixtures	Assets
30	1440-00-00	Accumulated Depreciation - Vehicles	Assets
31	1510-00-00	Machine Inventory	Assets
32	1511-00-00	Spare Parts Inventory	Assets
33	1920-00-00	Organization Cost	Assets
34	1921-00-00	Accumulated Amortization	Assets

Table 8-1: Assets

Source: Chart of Accounts

No.	G/L Account	Name	Group
35	2010-00-00	Accounts Payable - Trade	Liabilities
36	2014-00-00	Accounts Payable - AKS Machines	Liabilities
37	2015-00-00	Accounts Payable - AKS	Liabilities
38	2016-00-00	Accounts Payable - MAFA	Liabilities
39	2017-00-00	Accounts Payable - AMT	Liabilities
40	2020-00-00	Accrued Payables	Liabilities
41	2030-00-00	Notes Payable - Vehicles	Liabilities
42	2060-00-00	Advances From Customers	Liabilities
43	2110-00-00	Social Security Withheld	Liabilities
44	2111-00-00	Federal Tax Withheld	Liabilities
45	2112-00-00	State Tax Withheld	Liabilities
46	2115-00-00	401-k Withheld	Liabilities
47	2116-00-00	Health Savings Account Withheld	Liabilities
48	2121-00-00	State Unemployment Tax Payable	Liabilities
49	2122-00-00	FUTA Payable	Liabilities
50	2125-00-00	Sales Tax Accrual (, Alfing)	Liabilities
51	2126-00-00	Use Tax Accrual (, Alfing)	Liabilities
52	2250-00-00	Accrued Commissions	Liabilities
53	2260-00-00	Accrued Wages	Liabilities
54	2270-00-00	Accrued Taxes	Liabilities
55	2280-00-00	Accrued Interest	Liabilities
56	2290-00-00	Accrued Expenses	Liabilities
57	2310-00-00	Security Deposits	Liabilities

Table 8-2: Liabilities

Source: Chart of Accounts

No.	G/L Account	Name	Group
58	2910-00-00	Common Stock	Equity
59	2920-00-00	Paid In Capital	Equity
60	2950-00-00	Retained Earnings	Equity

Table 8-3: Equities

Source: Chart of Accounts

No.	G/L Account	Name	Group
61	3001-00-00	Sales - Machine Exchange	Revenues
62	3002-00-00	Sales - Machines	Revenues
63	3003-00-00	Sales - Parts	Revenues
64	3005-00-00	Sales - Service	Revenues
65	3007-00-00	Commission Income	Revenues

Table 8-4: Revenues

Source: Chart of Accounts

No.	G/L Account	Name	Group
66	4001-00-00	Cost of Sales - Machine Exchange	Cost of Sales
67	4002-00-00	Cost of Sales - Machines	Cost of Sales
68	4013-00-00	Cost of Sales - Parts	Cost of Sales
69	4015-00-00	Cost of Sales - Service	Cost of Sales
70	4030-00-00	Freight	Cost of Sales
71	4032-00-00	Customs	Cost of Sales
72	4034-00-00	Commissions	Cost of Sales

Table 8-5: Cost of Sales

Source: Chart of Accounts

No.	G/L Account	Name	Group
103	8155-00-00	Discounts - Earned/Lost	Other Revenues and Expenses
104	8160-00-00	Interest Earned	Other Revenues and Expenses
105	8165-00-00	Interest Expense	Other Revenues and Expenses
106	8170-00-00	Sale of Asset - Gain/Loss	Other Revenues and Expenses
107	8175-00-00	Other Income	Other Revenues and Expenses
108	8176-00-00	Admin & Engrg Income	Other Revenues and Expenses
109	8177-00-00	Rent Income	Other Revenues and Expenses
110	8195-00-00	Federal Income Tax	Other Revenues and Expenses
111	9999-00-00	Suspense Account	Other Revenues and Expenses

Table 8-6: Other Revenues and Expenses

Source: Chart of Accounts

No.	G/L Account	Name	Group
73	8001-00-00	Salaries	Expenses
74	8010-00-00	Advertising Expense	Expenses
75	8020-00-00	Auto Expense	Expenses
76	8035-00-00	Contributions	Expenses
77	8040-00-00	Depreciation Expense	Expenses
78	8050-00-00	Dues & Subscriptions	Expenses
79	8060-00-00	Admin & Engrg Expense	Expenses
80	8065-00-00	Insurance - General Business	Expenses
81	8066-00-00	Insurance - Workmens Comp	Expenses
82	8067-00-00	Insurance - Employees	Expenses
83	8070-00-00	Insurance - Shipping	Expenses
84	8075-00-00	Miscellaneous Expense	Expenses
85	8080-00-00	Office Supplies	Expenses
86	8085-00-00	Professional Fees	Expenses
87	8090-00-00	Outside Services	Expenses
88	8095-00-00	Repairs & Maintenance	Expenses
89	8100-00-00	Relocation Expense	Expenses
90	8102-00-00	Rent Expense	Expenses
91	8105-00-00	Shop Expense	Expenses
92	8110-00-00	Shipping Supplies Expense	Expenses
93	8115-00-00	Taxes - Payroll	Expenses
94	8120-00-00	Taxes - State & Local	Expenses
95	8121-00-00	Taxes - Single Business Tax	Expenses
96	8125-00-00	Telephone Expense	Expenses
97	8130-00-00	Trade Show Expense	Expenses
98	8135-00-00	Travel Expense	Expenses
99	8136-00-00	Meals & Entertainment Expense	Expenses
100	8140-00-00	Utilities	Expenses
101	8145-00-00	Pension Expense	Expenses
102	8150-00-00	Currency Exchange	Expenses

Table 8-7: Expenses

Source: Chart of Accounts

The numbering of the accounts follows this guideline.

- 1510-00-00 = account number, 4 digits or more
- 1510-00-00 = account segmentation
- 1510-00-00 = category as additional divider

The improvement which applies from now on anyways is that SAP separates the transactions automatically into their specific documents. This makes manual general ledger descriptions useless.

8.2 Tax setup

The tax setup is necessary to tell the system the tax rates and the tax accounts that have to be determined.

8.2.1 Initial situation

The tax system in the United States has three levels. The state taxes, the county taxes and the city taxes. The state taxes must be applied for all deliveries within one state. Deliveries to other states do not apply for state tax. The second level is the county tax which applies within specific regions. The third level is city taxes. Those taxes apply on city level and mainly in big cities. Each level is based on the other which leads to tax on tax calculations.

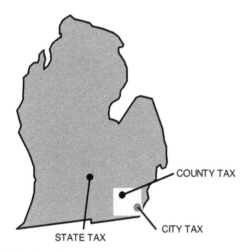

Figure 8-3: Tax levels

Source: Self

All of the taxes apply in the following order STATE, COUNTY, CITY. The calculation is made as tax on tax. See Table 8-8: Tax on Tax for an example.

Description	Amount
TOTAL	$100.00
STATE TAX 10%	$10.00
SUBTOTAL	$110.00
COUNTY TAX 5%	$5.50
SUBTOTAL	$115.50
CITY TAX (20%)	$23.10
ENDTOTAL	$138.60

Table 8-8: Tax on Tax

Source: Self

For Alfing in a business to business environment those taxes apply only for incoming invoices, if specified, or for goods sold to individuals. All other transactions must advise zero taxes.

The previous software system allowed managing taxes manually on document level. This made it possible to apply individual taxes very flexible.

8.2.2 Implementation to SAP

Small Business One does apply taxes based on tax indicators. These tax indicators specify the calculated the tax amount. Due to the reason the tax field is a mandatory field in each document a special tax rule had to be set up to apply zero taxes.

To apply the tax rates on state, county and city level those levels where created in the system. Those will be collected into specific tax codes which can be applied in documents. Based on the arrangement of the tax codes and its percentage the system calculates the taxes and applies them to the corresponding general ledger account.

This is illustrated in the following figure.

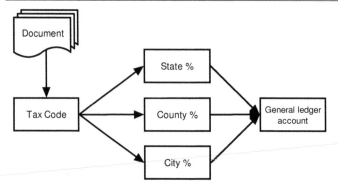

Figure 8-4: Tax code appliance

Source: Self

Because Alfing Corporation is working also with different currencies an individual currency setup had to be made. This will be discussed in the following chapter.

8.3 Currency

The currency setup specifies the currencies that are used internally by the system and available for document processing.

8.3.1 Initial situation

The previous software system allowed only US-Dollars as currency. The problem resulting out of this is that a difference between the local currency and the foreign currency comes into existences due to the staggering exchange rate.

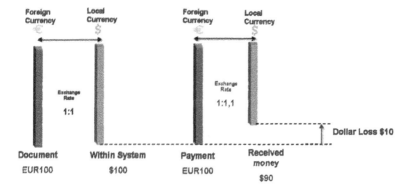

Figure 8-5: Exchange loss

Source: Self

In the example the applied exchange rate during document creation was 1:1 which is stored in this way within the system. When the customer pays the exchange rate is different and results in a loss of $10. This loss has to be accounted to the exchange difference account. The previous system had no automatic exchange system which made it necessary to calculate the difference and account it manually to the specific accounts. The daily exchange rate had to be recorded manually on the document and in an addition to an Excel spreadsheet to keep this information for future purpose.

8.3.2 Objectives

The objective was to have a fully automated exchange management system. This included the management of different currencies and exchange differences within the software system. Another request was to record the applied exchange rate for each document and built an exchange rate history. Automatic exchange rate retrieval was requested, too. Based on this information the setup of SAP could be started.

8.3.3 Solution in SAP

SAP's currency management system differentiates between different currencies classes, which are:

- Local currency: (LC)
  Currency in which the company reports to local authorities.

- System currency (SC)
  Allows to display accounting reports and balances in the system currency.

- Account currency (AC)
  Allows to set a default currency for an account or on document level.

Responsible to report to the US-Authorities, Alfing's local currency was set to US-Dollars.

The outstanding decision was if the system or account currency should be changed to match the German mother company. It was chosen to keep also US-Dollars.

Additional setup had to be made for the account currency which is used for documents. The next figure shows the business relations of Alfing Corporation with its countries. Based on this figure the necessary account currencies could be determined.

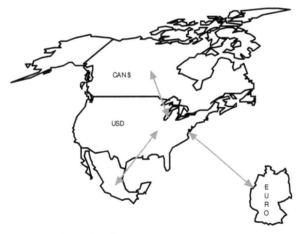

Figure 8-6: Business locations

Source: Self

It can be seen that Alfing Corporation has business with Germany, Canada, Mexico and within the United States. The currencies used in these countries are:

- US-Dollars (also for Mexcio)
- Canadian Dollars
- Euro

Setting those account currencies allows Alfing Corporation the automatic exchange management of documents.

Exchange rate differences apply now automatically based on the daily exchange rate and exchange differences are accounted automatically to the corresponding general ledger accounts. This functionality is illustrated below.

The right side show the documents balance within the accounting system. The initial balance is 100 in foreign (FC) and in local currency. The revalued balance which arrives at payment is only 90 in local currency which leads to an automatic revaluation of 10 to the exchange rate difference account. The automatic revaluation is always calculated based on the difference of the initial exchange rate and the actual exchange rate.

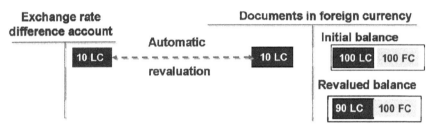

Figure 8-7: Exchange difference accounting

Source: Self

The automatic exchange rate update could not be realized because of a missing interface in Small Business One. Therefore the exchange rate will be entered on daily basis by the accounting department.

The following chapter provides an overview about posting periods and its related tasks.

8.4 Posting periods

Posting periods are exactly defined time ranges where transactions take place. Each document or transaction has to take place in its corresponding period. The accounting regulations do not allow entering transactions in past or future periods. The government regulations specify that a posting period can last up to 53 weeks. The starting and end point can be defined freely; neither the taxation will take place on 31st of December. The posting period defines the start and end of fiscal transactions within the system. The posting periods for Alfing Corporation correspond with the calendar year and they are divided into twelve months. Each of those periods has to be closed itself. This is known as month-end closing. After twelve periods the year-end closing has to take place. Alfing Corporations fiscal year starts on 1st of January and ends on 31st of December. This is the same period used by the German companies.

8.4.1 Previous situation

In Open Systems every previous period had to be closed before a new one could be opened. This made it impossible to enter actual documents if a previous month was still open. The reason for this behavior is a result of the batch oriented structure of Open Systems. Another disadvantage of this system was that a previous month couldn't be reopened to add additional documents. This lead to the point that the month-end closing took usually place until the mid of the next month until all documents where collected and entered into the system. Until this date no documents related to the actual period could be entered into the system. This resulted in a summary of problems:

- Discounts on invoices couldn't be earned.
- Interests had to be paid
- Customer invoices couldn't be initiated
- Transactions where recorded manually and transferred later into the system
- Checks couldn't be deposited
- Financial information was never up to date, for example cash flow ….
- Additional work for the certified public accountant
- Delayed tax reports to the government

Those where the main problems resulting out of the delayed month end procedure.

8.4.2 Objectives

Based on the previous described situation the requests to the new system could be clearly defined. The main request was to have an accounting system which allows entering all transactions in time. This made it necessary to have the possibility to switch between different periods and to close them as necessary.

8.4.3 Implemented solution

SAP's accounting system is a real time and online system. The main difference compared with Open Systems is that no special closing procedures are necessary. As soon as the accounting is completed a period can be locked, either at the real month-end or several weeks later. It is also possible to reopen the period and apply modifications. It is only important to keep in mind that the reporting has to be redone and verified by the certified public accountant.

The following figure shows the three states and its specialties.

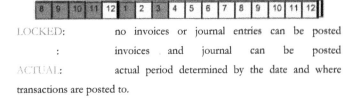

LOCKED:	no invoices or journal entries can be posted
:	invoices and journal can be posted
ACTUAL:	actual period determined by the date and where

transactions are posted to.

Figure 8-8: Periods

Source: Self

Switching between periods is done automatically by the system depending on the actual date. It allows also to switch manually between several periods until they are locked out by the accounting department.

The accounting system itself references to three different period indicators which are posting date, value date and tax date. This allows that documents can be posted in periods even if their value dates are not within the posting period.

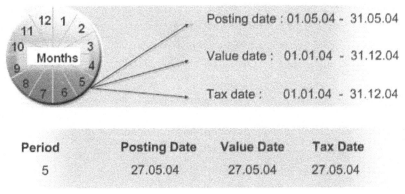

Figure 8-9: Dates

Source: SAP

The posting date specifies the date when the document is entered into the system. The value date and the tax date are used for calculation of exchange rate, taxes. Those dates do not necessarily have to match the posting date. This and the possibility to switch between the periods allow proceeding at the month-end without a special closing procedure.

For the financials of Alfing Corporation result the following consequences:

- Discounts on vendor invoices can be applied
- Invoices can be paid in time
- Cash flow and financials reflect the true values

- Every transaction can be recorded directly in the system without manual paperwork.

Some further conclusions can be found in the following chapter.

8.5 Summary and Conclusion

All financial basis information, like the chart of accounts, could be transferred directly into SAP. The applied chart of accounts is very basic and a big improvement would be to extend it with additional accounts. This would ensure future compatibility and allow a better view on the company's financial structure.

The taxation rules could be applied very well. In comparison with the old system it needs more administrative work but it is more user friendly and secure for usage by every user.

The automatic currency and exchange management improves mainly the document management and allows easy handling by users. Due to the reason the currency management system is extended to all modules it applies for internal transactions as well as banking.

The highest benefit for Alfing Corporation is that transactions are now recorded in time without waiting for the month-end closing. This results in improvement of the financial situation and an up-to-date financial basis. From the management's side of view it allows better planning and helps to recognize upcoming problems.

After completion of this task we can look at several cost accounting methods that will be used within Alfing Corporation.

9 Cost Accounting

Cost accounting is an additional way to separate costs that are spread over several accounts in the general ledger. Generally exist two ways to separate financial transactions in SAP, profit centers and projects.

A profit center in SAP is a separate business area within the company reporting its revenues and expenses. A profit center can include direct and indirect costs.

The project management in SAP is designed to monitor larger key projects and retrieve knowledge about the economic success of each. In the projects all costs are accounted as direct costs to each project.

Costs and revenues included in a project can be also distributed to several profit centers. This allows monitoring the projects and profiting centers separately.

Looking in the functional overview the cost accounting is located internally within the company.

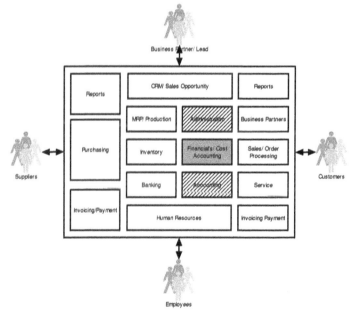

Figure 9-1: Functional overview

Source: Self

The following chapter will discuss the different cost accounting methods and their implementation within Alfing Corporation.

9.1 Initial situation and objectives

Alfing Corporation did not use either profit centers or project codes, neither had they clear objectives what had to be monitored. After several discussions it was determined that monitoring the technicians and machines would be the areas of interest.

The machine monitoring should provide a profit and loss of an overall machine life while the technicians should be monitored for a certain period of time.

Based on the initial definitions it comes very clear to use technicians as profit centers and the machines as projects.

A technician includes several direct costs like car lease and expenses. Also some indirect costs like office rent, utilities and others which have to be calculated to the technicians' expenses or revenues. The machine costs instead are only direct costs. This includes spare parts, service hours and retools engineering which can be calculated directly to a particular machine.

9.2 Profit Center

The profit center setup was driven by the idea to make technician to one profit center. This made it necessary to create the following profit centers.

Profit Center	Name	Sort Code
KB	Kim Blust	100
SL	Stefan Langer	200
PP	Peter Pietruschka	300
US	Udo Strobel	400
JT	John Thornsburry	500
FV	Florian Volk	600
KS	Klaus Schmid	700

Table 9-1: Profit Centers

Source: Eigene Darstellung

The next step was to find several costs and revenues that apply for a technician and define the distribution rules for the indirect ones'.

The next figure shows the typical cost and revenues that apply for the technicians.

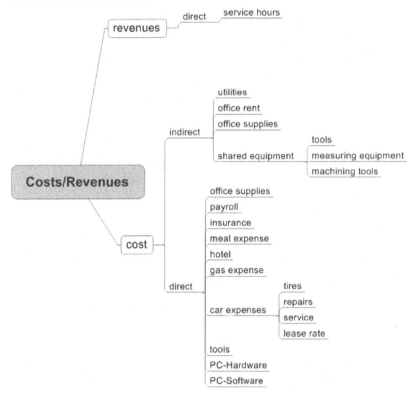

Figure 9-2: Cost/Revenues

Source: Self

All direct costs and revenues of each technician are applied directly to the created profit centers.

The indirect cost could have been distributed by several keys, for example the rent by the space of each one's office, but it was not applied due to management decision. Because the technicians are up to 95% of their time out of the office this distribution method has its limitations but can be accepted under the circumstance that nearly everything is indicated directly through expense reports.

9.3 Projects

The projects will act as collecting point for all direct machine costs which will result in a profit and loss statement on machine level.

9.3.1 Objectives

The initial goal was to gather knowledge about each machines profit and loss during its whole lifetime. This comes close with the total cost of ownership that appears during a machine's lifetime. The main difference is that the maintenance cost executed by customers personal is not included there.

Alfing Corporation's definition of machine lifetime starts with the day it is delivered at the customer's plant. The costs for installation and run-off are already calculated directly to the machine as long as they are not included in the initial contract. A machine lifetime ends after retooling, rebuilding or disassembly of the machine. Each of these operations initiates a new project number or closes one. Some typical costs and revenues during this lifetime are service hours, spare parts, training and others.

9.3.2 Implemented solution

The initial idea was that each machine is represented by one project number. Each service hours, part and other things should be accounted directly to this number.

The first problem was that customers order sometimes spare parts without referring to a specific machine number. This is related to the central buying departments that process each plant's demand.

Secondly it turned out that some costs can't be allocated directly to a project. For example training for technicians or a customer which is done mostly for several machines. This would apply also for technicians' expenses due to the reason they work on several machines at one day. An idea would have been to use the profit centers instead of the project, but the distribution rules do not allow changing often. Every time a distribution rule is changed it will update all its previous records to the new distribution keys which would jeopardize the complete system.

Splitting the originating cost or calculate distribution rules which would represent true values would have been to difficult. The solution of this issue was to create lead projects which will collect all indirect costs. Each of those lead projects will cover one customer plant. This was decided due to the reason that it can be easy determined from the shipping address of parts and to the fact a technician is working only in one plant a day.

Those lead projects will cover revenues and expenses which can't be distributed to machine level directly. The transactions on those projects will be distributed after a certain time to each machine. The distribution key that is used will be determined at this point. All costs and revenues that can be allocated directly to a single project will be distributed this way. It is always necessary to keep in mind that the applied cost distribution method has its limits and can cover only a certain level of detail.

The subsequent figure shows project structure which was realized.

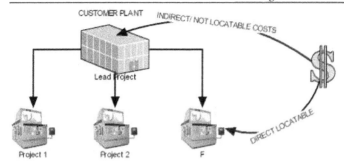

Figure 9-3: Project structure

Source: self

The main advantage of this solution is the easy handling for both sides, the technicians and the people working in the office.

The problem that can result out the lead projects is that most records will be kept under the lead project instead on machine level. This has to be monitored as soon as the system is running and maybe revised.

In addition to the machine and lead project one general project had been created. All costs and revenues that can't be located directly will be applied to this general project. Some items applied to this project are payroll, office supplies, heat, electricity, computer hardware, software and others. In future several projects for internal affairs can be introduced to track for example the complete hard- and software that is bought during a period

9.4 Summary and conclusion

The project codes and profit centers offer a great variety of cost accounting which provides a very detailed view about profit and loss of each one. The applied methods allow monitoring projects and profit centers during their entire lifetime, for certain periods and actual states. This helps to detect abnormalities and make adjustments in time.

A supplemental functionality of the applied structure is the ability to detect often failing parts and weak points of machines and assembly groups. This will allow to improve the overall product quality and in conclusion the customer satisfaction.

Looking at the sales side of the company the project accounting can provide good arguments in customer negotiations and it can help to focus core competences in successful business areas and discover new capabilities.

After the cost accounting is done we will take a look at the banking and the applied modifications and improvements.

10 Banking

Banking keeps track about the complete financial transactions of a company. This includes incoming and outgoing payments via several payment methods like electronic funds transfer, checks and cash or by credit card. In the functional overview the banking comes nearby the accounting.

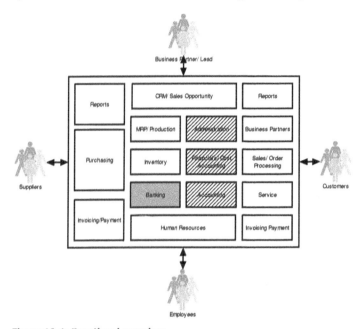

Figure 10-1: Functional overview

Source: Self

The following chapter will provide an overview about the previous situation and the applied solution.

10.1 Initial situation and objectives

Initially the complete banking was managed in Open Systems which provided many of the necessary functionalities. The main issues had been always the same as described in the period's setup.

10.1.1 Payments

All outgoing payments where made once a week. The software allowed to apply a payment runs which collected all due invoices and listed them for payment. This list could be adjusted and applied which created the checks.

The incoming checks where collected from Monday to Friday. On Friday the checks where deposited and bank statements of the last week collected. The reconciliation took place by means of the bank statement which advised the cashed and deposited checks. The reconciliation was done manually by checking the bank statement against a list with all checks.

The following list provides information about the applied payment methods.

- Outgoing checks
  invoices from vendors within North American/ Canadian and Mexican markets
  payment checks for expenses and payment roll. In special cases a confirmed check.

- Incoming checks
  invoices to customers. Often paid as partial payments.

- Electronic funds transfer
  only used for invoices from vendors located in Europe. Payment either in USD or EURO

- Petty Cash
  used for payments up to $100

- Credit Card
  used for expenses, credit card invoice paid as outgoing check.

- Exchange payment
  used for exchange payment between Alfing Germany as vendor and Alfing Germany as customer. Balanced through an special exchange account.

The request was to transfer this workflow without further changes into the new system. In addition to this an automatic payment system which is able to handle partial payments and installments had been requested. Discounts on incoming and outgoing invoices should be applied automatically, too.

The credit card management had to be overdone also. Further information is given in chapter 10.3 The simulated payment means that the check is printed and stored for documentation purpose within Alfing Corporation.

Credit card management.

A special functionality which had been asked for are the exchange payments. All invoices between Alfing Corporation and Alfing Germany had to be excluded from payment runs. Only a manual release function should allow running those payments. This is due to the reason that these payments are executed only once a quarter or less.

10.1.2 Banking

The banks of Alfing Corporation are located in different locations in North America and Germany and they are managed in different currencies.

The following table shows the bank accounts and the currencies they are managed.

Bank	Country	Currency	Account
Commerica	USA	USD	1063105314
Commerica MM	USA	USD	18050813740
LBBW	GERMANY	EUR	1522745
LBBW-US	GERMANY	USD	7482026647

Table 10-1: Bank accounts

Source: Alfing Corporation

A special account is the money market (MM) account which is a special savings account with higher interest rats and a minimum balance requirement. This account has a limit of six transactions per month. The advantage is that a money market account is insured by the Federal Deposit Insurance Corporation (FDIC) who pays in case the bank is going out of business.

The problem with Open System was that foreign currencies couldn't be managed. This made it necessary to transfer every bank statement manually and apply the exchange differences to separate accounts.

The main request was to manage each bank account in its local currency and apply the daily exchange rate during the creation of payments.

10.1.3 Exchange payment

A specialty of Alfing Corporation is the exchange payment. This comes into existence because Alfing Germany acts as vendor and customer for Alfing Corporation. A typical vendor task would be parts deliveries for Germany to Alfing Corporation while a typical customer task would be that Alfing Corporation provides service hours for Alfing Germany.

Because of the strict separation between the vendor and customer accounts in Open Systems it became necessary to initiate exchange payments. An exchange payment balanced the vendor and customer account over an exchange account and applied the difference as outgoing or incoming payment.

The subsequent figure show the principle workflow which applied.

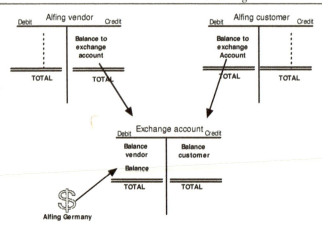

Figure 10-2: Exchange payment

Source: Self

The problem was that the exchange account did not provide enough transparency for the auditing procedure. This made it necessary to change this behavior.

10.2 Implemented solutions

The basic requests could be transferred very well into the system. The setup of the different bank accounts and their currencies could be integrated in the banking module. An additional feature which was implemented is that payment methods are linked directly to business partners now. This avoided the manual selection and reduced mistakes. The payment methods itself where transferred directly to Small Business One with two additions, outgoing hold and incoming hold which will be used for the quarterly exchange payments with the German mother companies.

The following figure illustrates the default appliances which are in the system.

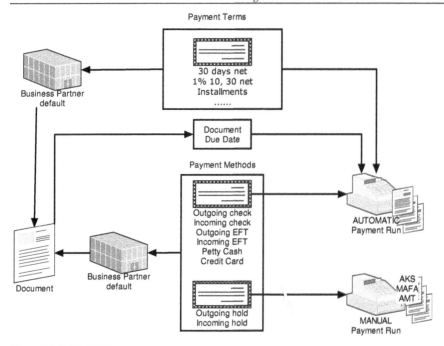

Figure 10-3: Payment

Source: self

It can be seen that the payments methods and terms are linked into the document, based on each business partner's defaults. All of those payments are included in the automatic payment run, but the outgoing and incoming holds which need a manual payment run. The automatic payment run determines the due documents by the payment term and the documents due date. Based on the information from the payment method will be chosen which method applies. The manual payment run is not related to payment terms and automatic due date calculation.

A big change was made in the internal handling of the incoming and outgoing payments. All payments will be applied as soon as they arrive and transferred to special holding accounts. As soon as the execution is confirmed through a bank statement the payment will be cleared from the holding account and transferred to the general ledger account.

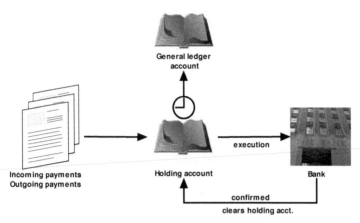

Figure 10-4: Holding accounts

Source: self

The advantage is that incoming payments can be applied as soon as they arrive and show up as received payments: For outgoing payments it allows to see future payments. This provides real time information about the company's financial liquidity. All customer statements reflect the actual balance without delay.

The exchange payments where overdone to make the whole process more transparent. The exclusion of those payments from the weekly payment routine was described above. The next step was to eliminate the exchange account. Because Small Business One does not allow merging customer and vendor payments the workflow will apply the following way:

Every time an exchange payment becomes necessary two payments, one from the vendor and one from the customer account will be made. Those payment checks will be kept and never transferred to the bank. The difference will be balanced by a separate document which payment will be executed. See Figure 10-5: Exchange payment for illustration.

This process allows clearing the customer and vendor accounts and it had been approved by the certified public accountant to fulfill auditing requirements.

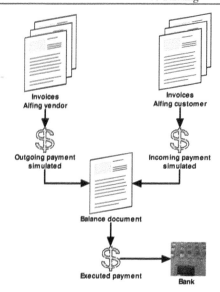

Figure 10-5: Exchange payment

Source: self

The simulated payment means that the check is printed and stored for documentation purpose within Alfing Corporation.

10.3 Credit card management

Alfing Corporation has one company credit card which is shared by several people in the office. To understand the difficulty it is necessary to understand the functionality of a credit card.

All things bought with a credit card are invoiced from the suppliers to the credit card company which pays them. The credit card company itself invoices the credit card holder (here Alfing Corporation) at the end of the month about the overall payments which where applied.

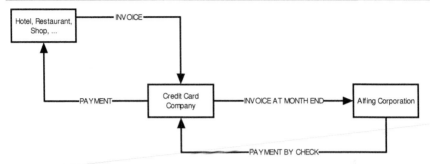

Figure 10-6: Credit Card Payment

Source: Self

10.3.1 Initial situation

After receipt of the credit-card-invoice it was handed to everybody in the company who had to approve his own payments. After all line items on the credit card had been approved the invoice returned to the accounting department and the payment was made. Due to the long approval procedure Alfing Corporation had to pay interests very often. Another difficulty was that people didn't approve all of their payments which lead to further delays. Additional to this comes that in future the profit centers and projects have to be specified, too. Therefore a new and faster solution became necessary.

10.3.2 Implemented solution

The initial idea was that every user will enter his transactions directly as invoice into the system. This didn't work due to the restrictions of the CRM-Licenses. In addition to this the accounting department liked to adjust the general ledger accounts in some cases.

A practical solution was to have everybody entering their payments as purchase orders into the system. This allows adjusting general ledger accounts and it is possible to create this document with the CRM-Licenses. The accounting department will create afterwards the invoices based on those purchase orders. The disadvantage of this procedure is that the financial information is updated only after creation of the invoice.

An additional feature which was applied is that everybody can attach the original receipt as a scanned or printed PDF document to the purchase order. This allows the accounting department to retrieve additional information and provides good documentation.

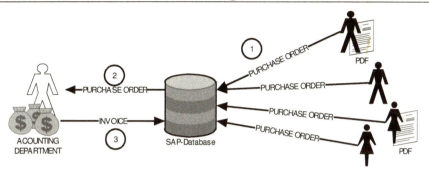

Figure 10-7: Credit card processing

Source: Self

Especially the processing of credit card invoices will be improved with the realized workflow. This allows payments in time and avoids interest payments. Another advantage is that everybody enters information in time which allows prediction of the credit card invoice at the end of the month. The additional PDF documents allow further information without having to keep paper documents.

10.4 Summary and future improvements

Transfer of the banking processes from Open Systems could be done very well. The basic process will remain the same as before. Especially many small details could be improved.

The main enhancement for the payment system is the holding account which leads to better planning abilities. Also an up-to-date cash flow will be shown in the system. Another improvement is the ability to manage installments by their due dates. Other changes to incoming and outgoing payments allow now to separate between payments on hold and payments to be executed.

A future improvement can be switching from checks to electronic funds transfers. This would speed the complete process up and provide more flexibility. Especially payments in advance could be applied much faster. The reason why this couldn't be realized is primarily due to the missing infrastructure of the banks and the suspicion of the companies to use this transfer method.

With all of this information the basic functionality of the accounting and financial system of Alfing Corporation is ready to work. The next step is to integrate the inventory and all external departments.

11 Inventory management

The inventory management was the most important area for Alfing Corporation. This is due to the reason that nearly every sales, purchasing or service operation refers to the inventory and effects it.

The inventory management can be split in two sub parts which are

- Stock valuation   covering the item values
- Inventory   covering the number of items

The main task for an inventory management system is to keep track of incoming and outgoing items. All stock values must be recorded together with the inventory changes.

One part of the inventory management is the physical inventory. The physical inventory can be executed as annual or permanent inventory. The inventory itself shows the number of parts kept actually on the shelf.

Beneath the inventory itself the inventory management has to keep track about the actual stock values. The stock value shows the amount of money which is represented by the actual number of items on the shelf. This information is kept in accounting. Stock values are important because the tied up capital could be invested and the company could earn interests for it. As soon as the possibly earned interests are higher than the profit of sales goods it isn't worth to keep stock anymore. There are several other objects like cost for the warehouse, storage capacity or the others that can make the decision to reduce or avoid inventory.

The following functional overview shows the inventory located internally. It is also the backbone for all transaction on the sales and purchasing side.

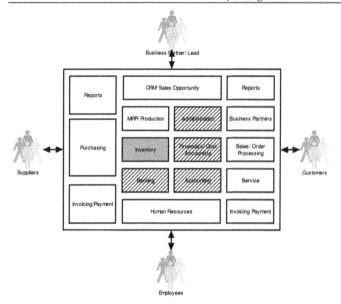

Figure 11-1: Functional overview

Source: Self

The next chapter describes the initial situation for Alfing Corporation, followed by several basis decisions which lead to the implemented solution.

11.1 Initial situation

The previous stock management system was based on Excel and Open Systems. The stock value was kept in Open Systems, while the inventory and the stock value were kept in Excel.

Keeping stock values in Open Systems was necessary because they affect all financial figures of the company which where reported monthly to the certified public accountant. Those values where kept as one overall sum and not broken down on item level. The Excel spreadsheet kept track about the actual number of items and the broken down values. All data management was done manually in this system.

Resulting from this separation the following workflow applied:

For every shipped part the shipping documents where created in Word. Stock value and the inventory was taken out and a copy of this documents handed to the accounting department. The accounting department created the invoice and decreased the stock value.

For receipt goods applied the opposite procedure. Every receipt of goods was recorded in the Excel spreadsheet with number and value. The records in Open Systems where updated after receipt of the vendor's invoice.

The below figure illustrates the process for a delivery to an Alfing customer

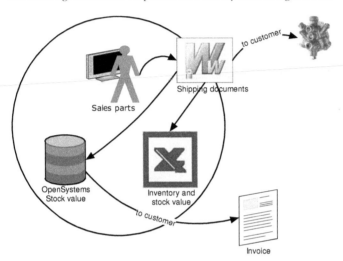

Figure 11-2: Customer delivery

Source: Self

The physical inventory which took place at the end of the fiscal year showed usually great discrepancies between Excel and Open Systems. Even the Excel spreadsheet itself showed differences between the recorded parts and the counted parts on the shelf. This was related mainly to the reason that parts where shipped without recordings which bypassed the complete workflow. All those discrepancies had to be adjusted until they matched. Having an up to date and exact stock value during the year was always kind of guessing.

Another problem was that no storing locations or warehouses where recorded. This made it hardly possible to access parts without the responsible storage manager who knew the storage location.

The targets for the stock management system could be defined based on this situation.

11.2 Objectives

The main objective for the stock management system was to keep the stock value and the inventory in one place. This must eliminate the discrepancies between accounting and material management. In consequence the doubled work for accounting and shipping would be removed.

In conclusion, the whole process of invoicing and shipping had to be integrated into the stock management system. The goal was that every inventory transaction either incoming or outgoing effects the stock value and the inventory together. The subsequent documents had to be initiated in their correct order which ensures that all following processes take place in the correct manner.

Deliveries without stock quantity should not be permitted which avoids bypassing the inventory.

Automatic ordering procedures, triggered by a certain stock amount, where not requested. A worthwhile reason can't be seen either, because Alfing has no typical stock parts that need to be refreshed regularly.

Storage of item descriptions, item numbers, manufacturers, storage places, values, sales prices, purchasing prices, storage places and packing units where other important demands. Detailed description is not provided due to its simplicity.

A specialty for the storage locations became necessary because Alfing Corporation has several commission warehouses at customer plants.

Part lists with assembly structures where not required. The price strategy will be discussed in chapter 12 Price strategy.

Generally the complete workflow had to be transferred from manual recordings to an electronic process increasing the transparency and the accessibility of the inventory and their corresponding documents.

The initial decision which had to be made was the stock valuation method. This will be discussed in the next chapters before the implemented inventory solution is described.

11.3 Stock valuation method

The intention of a stock valuation method is to estimate the correct values of the stored items. In reality exist several different ways to do this, each matching different market criteria, and in the end with the purpose to determine the actual market value.

Looking at the previous stock valuation method turned out that no clear regulations could be determined. A mixed valuation method is not allowed by the government which made it necessary to make the decision for one method and apply it.

The valuation methods offered by SAP are the following ones:

- Moving Average,

- First In – First Out or

- Standard Price

Each of these stock valuation methods has different attempts and is calculated in different ways. The following chapters will discuss the advantages and disadvantages of each method until the final decision is described.

11.3.1 Moving average method

The moving average system calculates the stock value based on single transactions. This means that every item transaction triggers the recalculation of the stock value, including selling as well as buying operations. The overall value is calculated as average price from the same items.

A description of the applied procedure is given below:

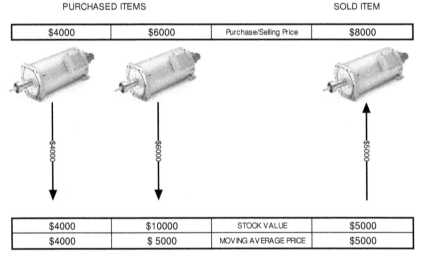

PURCHASED ITEMS			SOLD ITEM
$4000	$6000	Purchase/Selling Price	$8000
$4000	$10000	STOCK VALUE	$5000
$4000	$ 5000	MOVING AVERAGE PRICE	$5000

Figure 11-3: Moving average calculation

Source: Self

The first part is bought for $4,000 increasing the stock value by this amount. The second item is bought for a price of $ 6,000. The average stock value is calculated as average price which is the total of the buying prices divided by the number of items. In the example the moving average price is $10,000 divided by 2 pieces which results in $ 5,000.

Moving average calculation applies generally by the following formula:

Moving Average $= \dfrac{i_1 + i_2 + \ldots + i_n}{n}$
Moving average calcualtion 11-1

with i_n =item purchase price

n= number of parts

Selling the item decreases the moving average price and the stock value by the same amount. In the example the part is sold for $ 8,000. The stock value decreases by $ 5,000 and the resulting profit is $ 3,000.

The moving average method is suitable for businesses with high price fluctuations because it provides a realistic picture of the actual stock value any time, regardless of falling or rising prices. Stock revaluations are not necessary when choosing this stock valuation method.

11.3.2 Standard price method

The standard price valuation method assumes a constant item value, regardless of the purchase price. The same item is always valuated with its standard price. The difference between the standard price and the purchase price has to be written off. This has to be done through the price variance account in the general ledger.

According to the figure below, the initial definition after buying the first item was a stock value of $ 4,000. This stock value will be kept, ignoring that the second item costs about $ 6,000. The $ 2,000 price difference between the stock value and the purchase price is distributed to the price difference account. If the item is sold for a price of $ 8,000 the stock value decreases about $ 4,000. The difference is calculated as profit.

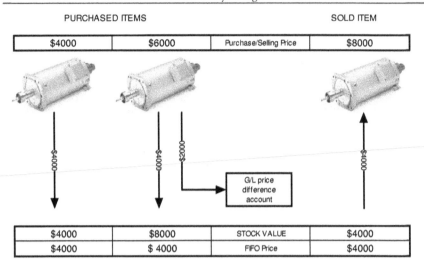

PURCHASED ITEMS   SOLD ITEM

$4000	$6000	Purchase/Selling Price	$8000

G/L price difference account

$4000	$8000	STOCK VALUE	$4000
$4000	$ 4000	FIFO Price	$4000

Figure 11-4: Standard price method

Source: self

Using this system makes it necessary to revaluate the prices more often and correct the stock values based on those amounts. The advantage of this method is that fixed standard costs are assigned to the item which allows easy calculation.

11.3.3 First in – First out

The First in – First out (FIFO) method records purchasing prices in the order they get in. When the item is sold the same order applies. The value of the oldest part in stock applies to the sales price.

This method is the most common method due to the idea that the oldest good should go out first, while the newest remain in stock.

PURCHASED ITEMS   SOLD ITEM

| $4000 | $6000 | Purchase/Selling Price | $8000 |

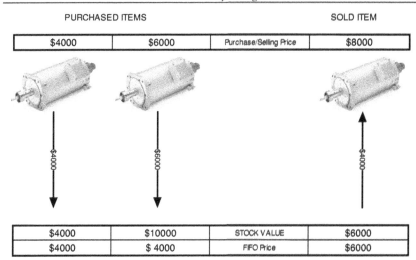

| $4000 | $10000 | STOCK VALUE | $6000 |
| $4000 | $ 4000 | FIFO Price | $6000 |

Figure 11-5: FIFO calculation method

Source: self

Buying the spindle for $4000 increases the stock value about the same amount. Buying the next item for $6,000 increases the stock value about this amount while the FIFO price remains unchanged. Selling the item takes the oldest out of the stock. It decreases the stock value about its purchasing price ($4000). The new price of the item will always be the purchase price of the oldest item remaining in stock.

The risk of this valuation method is that long stored goods, having low purchase prices, are sold to actual prices which increase the income for tax calculation.

11.3.4 Effects

This chapter explains the effects resulting out of different stock valuation methods, especially the effects on company's income and its results.

Pretending the beginning inventory of a company is 15 units with a cost of $1,000/each results in the total stock value of $ 15,000. Within the next three months the company buys goods to the below specified costs. This results in a total increase of 30 pieces which equals an amount of $60,000.

Month	Units	Costs/each	Total value
Beginning Inventory	*15*	*$1,000*	*$15,000*
January	10	$1,500	$15,000
February	10	$2,000	$20,000
March	10	$2,500	$25,000
TOTAL increase	**30**		**$60,000**

Table 11-1: Inventory transactions

Source: Self

After those transactions a total of 30 parts is sold for $ 3,000/each. The inventory decreases to the starting level of 15. Depending on the sock valuation method the cost of goods sale and the income of the company vary. This can be seen in the next table.

Managing method	AVERAGE	STANDARD	FIFO
Beginning inventory value	$15,000	$15,000	$15,000
Sales (30 units, each $3,000)	$90,000	$90,000	$90,000
Inventory (beginning and end)	15 pcs	15 pcs	15 pcs
Ending inventory value	$25,000	$15,000	$35,000
Cost of goods sale (COGS)	$50,000	$60,000	$40,000
Income	$40,000	$30,000	$50,000

Table 11-2: Income calculation

Source: Self

The additional calculations for the different methods are listed below.

Average:

The cost for one unit is calculated by:

$$\frac{15 * \$1,000 + 10 * \$1,500 + 10 * \$2,000 + 10 * \$2,500}{45 pieces} = \$1666,67 \text{ per unit}$$
Average 11-2

This results in a inventory total of:

$1666.67 * 15 \text{ units} = \$25,000$
Average stock 11-3

Standard:

The ending value of the standard valuation method is calculated by:

$1,000 * 15 \text{ units} = \$15,000$
Standard value 11-4

FIFO:

The FIFO stock calculates to the following amount:

$10 \text{ units} * \$2,500 + 5 \text{ units} * \$2,000 = \$35,000$
FIFO value 11-5

COGS:

The cost of goods sale (COGS) is calculated via the next formula:

beginning inventory + net purchases - ending inventory = cost of goods sale
COGS 11-6

11.3.5 Results

The comparison of different stock valuation methods turns out that the FIFO method advises the highest income, followed by the average and the standard method. For the first sight the decision would be to choose the FIFO method because it will increase the income. A closer look shows that a higher income will result in higher tax rates of the government. From this point of view the standard method would be the best decision.

Based on this information basis the certified public accountant was introduced to prove several tax minimization strategies which can be applied for Alfing Corporation. It turned out that the FIFO method will allow Alfing Corporation to apply several tax minimization strategies which are not available in the other methods. Additional to this most goods within Alfing Corporation are sold in a short time range which reduces the need for revaluation and reflects the true values very well. This made the decision to apply the FIFO method for the inventory valuation.

After these basis definitions the following chapter will cover the inventory structure which was implemented in SAP.

11.4 Realized inventory structure

Before SAP was introduced by Alfing Corporation a inventory structure with several levels did not exist. Developing a complete new inventory structure helped Alfing Corporation to manage their inventory.

Referring to the initial situation several warehouses and items had to be managed by Alfing Corporation. From this point of view a two level structure, warehouse and items, would have been enough. The problem of the two level structures is that accounting information has to be determined either for warehouses or on item level. The warehouse level was not detailed enough while the item level made it necessary to determine general ledger accounts for every single item which is created. This would make it very uncomfortable and error-prone.

Therefore the decision was made to introduce a three level structure, warehouse, group and item, with the idea to determine the general ledger accounts on group level. This structure makes the whole process error-proof and easy to handle.

The next figure shows the planned structure with warehouse, item group and item level.

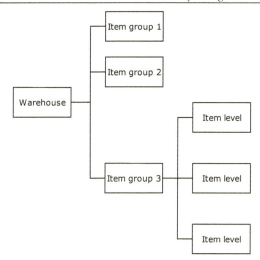

Figure 11-6: Inventory structure

Source: self

Each of the groups has its assigned general ledger accounts. Looking from the financials side on this inventory structures draws a different picture:

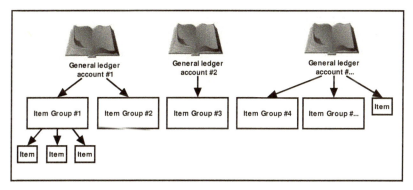

Figure 11-7: General ledger determination

Source: self

Each item group has its assigned general ledger accounts, neither it is also possible to overwrite those and assign items directly to general ledger accounts. The warehouses do not show up from the financial side of view. This is due to the reason Alfing Corporation does not have different general ledger accounts for separate warehouses.

11.4.1 Warehouses

This chapter reviews the warehouse setup required by Alfing Corporation. It is the first level in the inventory structure. A warehouse is a location where parts can be stored and withdrawn.

Alfing Corporation has its main warehouse in Plymouth. Additional to this exist two additional warehouses at customer locations.

- 01   Alfing Corporation
- 02   Metaldyne North Vernon
- 03   Mahle Mexico

Those additional warehouses, North Vernon and Mahle, are consignment warehouses. The functionality of a consignment warehouse is illustrated below:

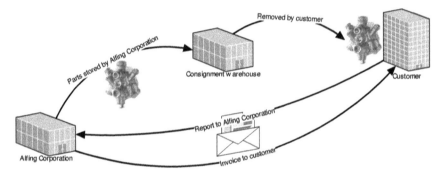

Figure 11-8: Consignment warehouse

Source: Self

The items delivered to those warehouses are managed by the customer. The material itself is still property of Alfing Corporation but the customer has direct access to it. Every time a item is withdrawn by the customer this is reported to Alfing Corporation. Based on this information the invoices is created by the shipping department of Alfing Corporation. Once a year a physical inventory takes place at the consignment warehouses to verify that the inventory numbers are correct. This structure could be implemented directly into Small Business One by creating several different warehouses. Items can be transferred into those warehouses and withdrawn as used.

The warehouses have no separate accounts in the general ledger and need no separate groups.

11.4.2 Item groups

The item groups exist to sort the parts in several categories. Each of the item groups can be linked directly to its reflecting general ledger accounts. The determination which item groups are necessary and need to be created is described in the following chapters.

11.4.3 Initial situation

Initially was no group level existent. Within Open Systems the general ledger accounts had to be determined by the accountant for every invoice manually. This made it very flexible but also error-prone and very unhandy for the common user. Without items defined the reporting capabilities of the system had very strict limits. To improve the reporting and the user friendliness the groups had to be defined.

11.4.4 Implemented solution

The determination of the different groups was made by its role in the general ledger.

Looking at the expenses and revenues in the general ledger allowed determining four main groups:

- Machine exchange (account 3001 and 4001)

The Machine exchange is the general ledger account with the least number of transactions but the highest amount.

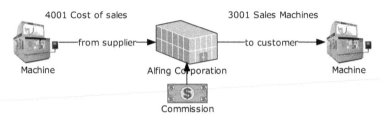

Figure 11-9: Machine exchange

Source: self

For a machine exchange Alfing Corporation handles the negotiation process in corporation with Germany until the order from the customer is placed. For every order that is placed Alfing Corporation gets a commission based on a fixed percentage. This percentage varies depending on the German mother company it is related to.

- Spare parts (account 3003 and 4013)

This account is the most common group for Alfing Corporation. It is also the group with the highest number of transactions.

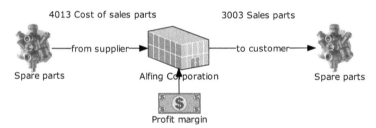

Figure 11-10: Spare parts

Source: self

The main difference between the machine exchanges is that Alfing Corporation calculates its own profit margin, which is not a fixed percentage of the total. The spare parts bought by Alfing Corporation can be delivered from several different suppliers and they are not necessarily from the German holdings. Depending on the buying price and the sales price the profit margin can increase or decrease.

- Machines (account 3002 and 4002)

  The name of this account can be misleading. This account contains engineering tasks which are provided by Alfing Corporation directly to customers.

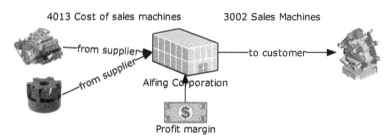

Figure 11-11: Machines

Source: self

Alfing Corporation supplies several engineering tasks to their customers. This includes retooling, rebuild, project management and some other operations. On the sales side this shows up as single package to the customer. For the buying side of Alfing Corporation several suppliers show up.

- Service (account 4015)

  The service group covers all service hours executed by Alfing Corporation.

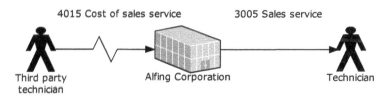

Figure 11-12: Machines

Source: self

The service is executed usually by Alfing Corporation's own technicians who show up as sales service.

Occasionally a third party technician executes repair work at Alfing Corporation which will show on cost of service.

Those are only the main groups which can be determined directly out of the general ledger. Besides exist several other accounts which cover the expenses of Alfing Corporation. The detailed list is shown in Table 8-7: Expenses and Table 8-6: Other Revenues and Expenses. It is not necessary to generate groups for every general ledger account but for some, mainly as soon as they are used more often and cover several things.

After observation and looking at previous transactions it was agreed to add some additional groups. Some of them will cover only single general ledger accounts while others will cover several accounts which made it necessary to determine the accounts on item level. The main advantage in this case is that the reporting allows monitoring groups even if they are spread over different accounts.

The following list provides an overview about the created groups and some of its corresponding items. The agreement is that each blue box symbolizes the created group with its items beneath. The yellow highlighted box shows the corresponding general ledger accounts.

- Miscellaneous:

    This group was created for all things that can't be added to one of the other groups.

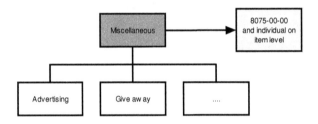

This is mainly the group which will cover several different and individual items which happen occasionally and have no need for separate item groups.

- Office supplies:

  This category is used for office material, software and hardware which are not an asset.

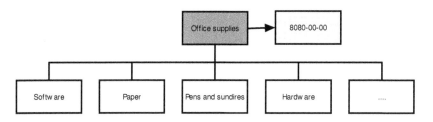

- Repairs/ Maintenance:

  This is a category for special repairs which are not covered through service. Those repairs take place within the Alfing shop or through some third party suppliers.

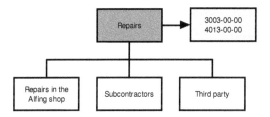

The accounting information here shows two accounts which are related to the reason that repairs can be expenses and revenues.

- Travel Expenses:

  This is used for travel expenses or for travel related expenses.

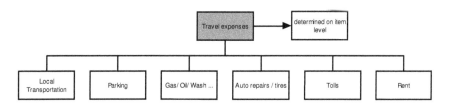

The travel expenses where sort into a group to have better reporting functionality, neither most of them have to be determined on item level.

- Meals/ Entertainment:

  This group is used for food allowance, hotels and customer entertainment.

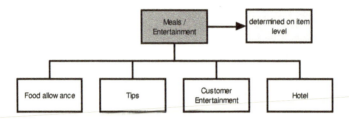

  Here applies the same condition as above, advanced report functionality but general ledger accounts determined on item level.

- Sales Quote

  This category is used for generic items that are used only for the negotiation procedures.

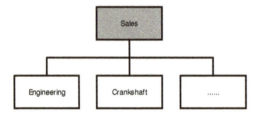

  This category will never affect the general ledger because they are transferred into one of the other groups before they are accounted. All of them have basically management functionality as long as it is not worth to create items in the database. During a negotiation process those things change so often that it makes no sense to create items which will never be used.

- Fixed Assets

  Fixed assets are purchased items that are neither sold, nor used in production as raw material. Instead they are used internally for daily use in the company. For Alfing Corporation are three asset groups, each containing several items existing.

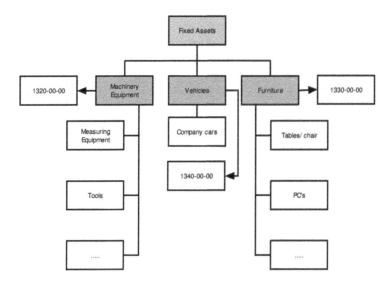

Those main groups cover most occurring situations for Alfing Corporation. Additional specifications will be determined on item level or by creation of separate groups.

The main advantage of this solution is that each user can create new items by order them into one of the main groups without hesitating the accounting department. Supplementary features are the easier document creation and better report functionality.

The following step refers to the item level and creation of the item master data.

11.5 Item Master Data

The item master data is the place where all individual item data is stored and located. The item master data contains individual parameters for single items.

The main objectives where to store:

- Item group and number
- Item description (in local and foreign language)
- Storage place

- Packing Unit
- Part Picture (if applicable)
- Manufacturer
- Manufacturer part number
- Prices
- And some additional

To avoid that all data had to be imported manually a list of parts from each of the German holding companies where requested as Excel spreadsheet. The preparation and import of those data is explained in the appendix.

Due to the reason that most parts are received directly from the German mother companies it was decided to keep their part numbers instead of introducing new ones. The intention was to reduce maintenance and improve compatibility.

Assembly and subassembly structure shouldn't be stored in the database. This decision was made to keep the database small and because it is not necessary for Alfing Corporation.

Because each of the German companies different numbering system for item it became necessary to examine them to see if there are any conflicts between the different numbering methods.

11.5.1 Alfing Kessler Sondermaschinen GmbH

Alfing Kessler Sondermaschinen's numbering system is based on part numbers. The part numbers equal the drawing numbers and they are assigned in sequential order. The numbering format consists of seven digits with a leading zero.

0632105 = spindle holder   **Part numbering 11-7**

Machine numbering is different and contains additional information.

The main part is a four digit code indicating the unique machine number, followed by a character specifying the project type and two digits for the revision.

3730N00   **Machine number 11-8**

The character code changes depending on the actual machine status.

- 3730N00   =   New machine
- 3730U00   =   Rebuilt or Retooled machine.

The last two digits show the revision of the rebuilt.

- 3730U00   =   first rebuilt, retool
- 3730U01   =   second rebuilt, retool

The machine number will be used within Alfing Corporation as project number, too. See further chapters for detail.

11.5.2 Maschinenfabrik GmbH

The crankshafts of the Maschinenfabrik will not be managed within the item master data because they are not sold directly through Alfing Corporation.

The hardening machines instead had to be managed in the item master data. Its numbering consists of six digits.

632105 = electrode   **Part numbering 11-9**

The hardening machines itself have a numbering system that starts either with 21 or 22 and a running number beneath.

21.xxx   new machines
22.xxx   reconstruction   **MAFA numbering 11-10**

Those numbers do not collide with the AKS numbering system.

11.5.3 Alfing Montage Technik GmbH

Alfing Montage Technik uses, like AKS, a seven digit number system for their parts. Instead of a zero they use a seven as leading number.

7002903 = transducer   **Part numbering 11-11**

Machine assemblies are completely integrated in this numbering system. Comparison with both systems shows that no collusions apply between those three numbering systems.

11.5.4 Alfing Corporation

The manual numbering system of Alfing Corporation had different formats which where not in numerical order. This drove the decision to redo the numbering system and introduce a complete new one. The numbering starts with a leading "AC" followed by six digits.

AC000000 = Alfing Corporation item   **Part numbering 11-12**

This allows separating them easily from the other companies. The first weeks of usage turned out that it could be helpful to introduce some customer related numbering system in future. This will be examined on going.

The final decision was to import the individual numbering systems of each company in the system and redo the internal numbering of Alfing Corporation to the described one.

11.6 Summary and Conclusion

The introduction of an integrated inventory management was the most important part for Alfing Corporation. Small Business One allowed to realize the discussed structure and improved the parts handling within the complete company.

The separation between stock values and inventory could be broken up and merged together which will ensure an up to date and exact matching inventory. Discrepancies between stock values and numbers are not possible further more. The complete integration in the document creation allows automatic release and receipt functions which allows an up to date inventory and minimizes the risk of inventory manipulations. This improvement will be recognized especially during the year-end closing and when the annual inventory takes place.

The functionality of the integrated release system is illustrated below. For the goods receipt procedure applies the same process but vice versa. Instead of a withdrawal and decrease of the stock value happens a increase of the value and inventory.

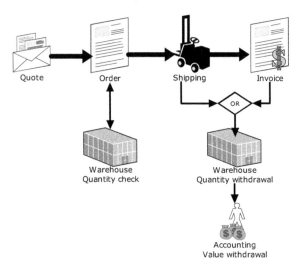

Figure 11-13: Shipping process

Source: self

Advanced reporting makes it possible to track parts, their storage location and supplier numbers. The integrated price management system, discussed separately in 12 Price strategy, completes the inventory and allows to assign prices and build a history.

11.7 Future improvements

Future improvements which will turn out won't be limited to the inventory system itself but the overall business of the company.

After intense usage often failing and requested parts can be detected and kept on the shelf for fast availability and delivery. This will have direct influence to the customer relationship management and the customer satisfaction. Contrary the less needed parts can be reduced or sort out which will help to improve the cash flow and reduce the loss due to deducted parts.

As soon as all parts are seduced and their storage locations monitored in the system they can be located more easily and shipped faster. Also the dependence on certain persons is reduced by using this functionality. An automatic system working with barcodes would be additional but not necessary.

Calculation of the turnover rate allows Alfing Corporation now comparisons with other companies in the same business area which can an indicator for the stock management.

Within the upcoming section the price strategy and price management of Alfing Corporation will be discussed.

12 Price strategy

Pricing strategy is one element of the marketing mix, consisting out of the four p's which are product, pricing, promotion and placement. Within the functional structure the pricing is allocated nearby the inventory but has direct connections to the vendor and customer side.

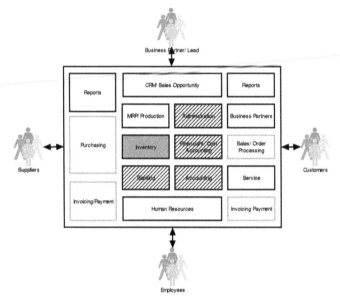

Figure 12-1: Functional overview

Source: Self

Prices are usually set by the law of supply and demand. For the price calculation of a company it is necessary to consider many influences to determine suitable prices. Influence factors that apply are quantity breaks, specific quotes, competitors, fixed and variable costs, profit margins as well as implications of the pricing strategies. Law regulations, for example against price dumping, can apply also in some cases.

The basic law of supply and demand works mainly for regular markets with a polypoly structure. For Alfing Corporation this applies especially for selling new machines.

The spare parts business, which is the main business for Alfing Corporation, has a different structure. This is due to the reason that many parts are individually manufactured or only available by a small number of suppliers. This leads to an oligopoly or monopolistic structure where the laws of supply and demand apply only partially. Especially on monopolistic market the prices for goods can be calculated only by profit, regardless of other influence factors.

The next section will provide information about the initial situation in Alfing Corporation and their requests to price management system.

12.1 Initial situation

Alfing Corporation managed their prices partially in Excel spreadsheets. Additional pricing was kept in Open Systems due to the created invoices. In most cases the pricing information was not up to date and reliably enough to initialize a new quote to the customer, which made a request Alfing Corporation's supplier necessary.

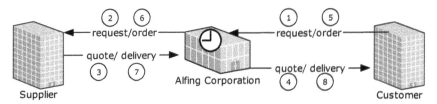

Figure 12-2: Quotation workflow

Source: Self

Requesting a new part started from the customer, was processed in Alfing Corporation, that requested a quote from the supplier and all the way backwards to the customer. In case of an order the complete workflow had to be repeated for order and delivery. Processing this workflow is very time consuming especially under the point of view that customer need parts very quickly due to production stops.

Analyzing this process turns out that mainly an up to date pricing information would allow to speed up the processing. Another way is to keep often necessary parts on stock, as mentioned in the last chapter which is very hard to realize due to the great number of different parts.

12.2 Objectives

Initially requested was a price management system that allows differentiating between customers and vendors. Derived from this comes the petition to manage purchase prices and sales prices for goods. Setting two price lists referring to each other allows also calculating the profit margin on each item.

Another request was to manage base price lists, special customer prices and quantity based discounts. Special prices based on specific date ranges became not necessary.

Tracking previous purchase and sales prices was asked for, too.

Because of the different currencies used by Alfing Corporation the price lists had to be able to manage local as well as foreign currencies.

12.3 Implemented solution

The implemented solution consists out of eight different price lists referring to each other

- Special price list   (customer and vendor)
- Item group discount prices   (customer and vendor)
- Quantity based discount price list   (customer and vendor)
- Base price list   (customer and vendor)

Every time a document is created the price lists will be checked against the customer/ vendor in a specified order. As soon as an applicable price is found it will be applied. If no corresponding special price is found the price form the base price list will be used (see Figure 12-3: Price list structure).

In addition to those price lists exist two, separate price list to track the last purchase and last sales prices. Those prices are updated with the last prices that where applied in any document which refers to accounting. Inquiries, quotes and orders do not update these prices.

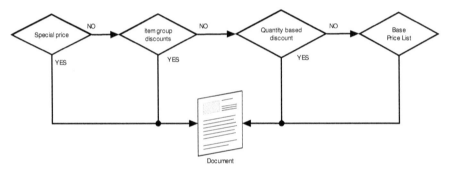

Figure 12-3: Price list structure

Source: Self

The requested price history will built through transferring all evaluated prices into a separate table. Additional reporting allows a price history by item or by customer from this table and the database.

12.4 Summary and conclusion

The realized price management system fulfills all requests of Alfing Corporation. With the four level structure a very detailed price policy is applicable on business partner and on item level. The main advantage for Alfing Corporation will be the speed up of the inquiry/quotation process. The old pricing information was not imported due to the untrustworthily data source.

An additional improvement which could be realized was the possibility to make bulk adjustments to price lists which allows to update complete price lists on a certain calculation basis.

As an overall conclusion results a more transparent and easier applicable process. This ensures that workload can be distributed between departments without problems.

A missing functionality in Small Business One is an integrated cost calculation module which would allow calculating sales prices assemblies based on estimated costs. This does not apply for Alfing Corporation as reseller but for other business areas.

The internal structure of Alfing Corporation business basis is reflected within the previous chapters. The next chapters will start to apply this into the outside structure of Alfing Corporation.

13 Purchasing

The purchasing manages and controls the whole purchasing process. It includes negotiations as well as order and invoice processing. Looking at the functional overview shows that it is located in direct contact with suppliers.

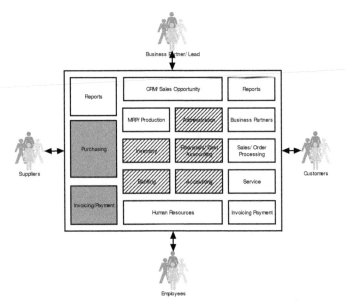

Figure 13-1: Functional overview

Source: Self

Purchasing stays close to the inventory management because it references on the items. The next chapters will cover some specialties of the purchasing process within Alfing Corporation and the applied process.

13.1 Initial situation

Initially the complete purchasing process had been managed by one department within Alfing Corporation. All necessary documents, like inquiries, orders or quotes where processed in Word. Inventory data was managed in Excel as described in chapter 11 Inventory management.

The difficulties resulting out of this process where that outstanding tasks like inquiries, deliveries and orders had to be monitored manually. In addition all corresponding documents had to be created manually. As soon as the vendor's invoice had been received, it had to be verified by the responsible buyer and afterwards forwarded to the accounting department which transferred the data into Open Systems and initiated the payment. This made the whole process very unhandy and error prone.

Due to the manual management a history, any reporting functionality wasn't available either. This made it impossible to track outstanding deliveries easily and check for its state.

13.2 Objectives

In conclusion with the inventory and based on the previous described situation the defined main objective was to have an automatic document managing system which integrates all necessary purchasing documents. For a usual purchasing process the following documents are necessary:

- Inquiry
- Purchase Order
- Goods receipt / Goods return
- Invoice / Credit memo

Additionally was requested to move as many documents as possible from the paper into electronic stored documents. This implicates especially vendor documents.

Obviously the management of different currencies, freight, tax and other basic functionality had to be applicable for each document, too.

Processing documents had to apply also to the integrated project management and profit center, as discussed previously in 9 Cost Accounting.

13.3 Solution

With the integrated functionality of Small Business One it is possible to manage the below listed documents:

- Purchase Order
- Goods receipt / Goods return
- Invoice / Credit memo

Due to the integrated inventory the goods receipts and goods returns effect the inventory. The price lists apply to each of the documents automatically. Confirmed invoices are passed into the payment system of the accounting department which initiates the payment. Partial payments and installments are applied there, too

13.4 Problem

The main problem that turned out was that Small Business One has no ability to manage inquiries in the system. This means that each inquiry has to be processed outside and the purchase order created afterwards within SAP.

Because this was not acceptable it became necessary to implement a inquiry solution in SAP which allows to manage inquiries. Initial requests to the supply company and SAP to create this functionality as separate module where denied due to several reasons. Developing a complete new module on its own was not possible for Alfing Corporation due to the high costs of the Software development kit and the short time range.

Based on this information it became necessary to find a solution which is realizable with the integrated functionalities and transferable to SAP.

The next chapter will describe the necessary functionality of the inquiry module and the implemented solution.

13.5 Inquiry Process

An inquiry process has the aim to find the best supplier fulfilling requested conditions. Those conditions can vary depending on the individual situation. Some of them can be delivery time, availability, price and quality as well as some others. Typically a customer inquiry leads to several inquiries to Alfing suppliers.

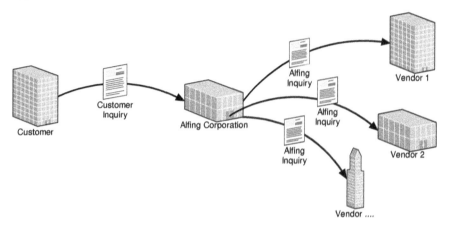

Figure 13-2: Inquiry procedure

Source: Self

Depending on customer requests and the suppliers offers Alfing Corporation makes its selection of the vendor and quotes the customer. After receipt of the customer order an order to the selected vendor is placed.

Out of those process result different demands to an inquiry process which have to be implemented. To gather an overview about the demands of Alfing Corporation a brainstorming session was started which returned the following results.

13.5.1 Demands to Inquiry management

The following demands to the inquiry management could be established by the buying department.

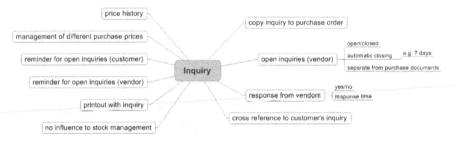

Figure 13-3: Demands to inquiry management

Source: Self

Based on this information a search for active principles was started, which is illustrated in the next chapter.

13.5.2 Searching for active principles

Searching for active principles brought the following suggestions. All of them where collected without judging them by their possibility.

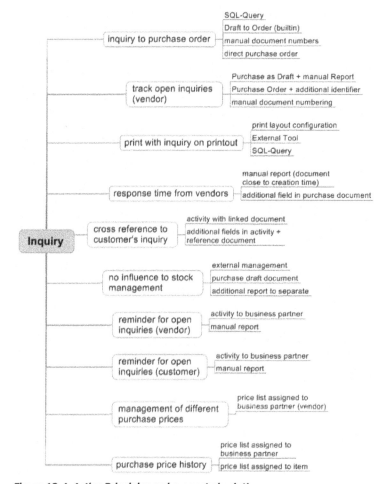

Figure 13-4: Active Principles and suggested solutions

Source: Self

Starting from the left are shown the base request, their active principles and the suggested solutions. Based on this information a comparison of their advantages and disadvantages could be started.

13.5.3 Comparison of the active principles

This chapter picks each of the suggested solutions showing the possible advantages and disadvantages of each one. Based on this information, the decision of the implemented solution had been made. It turned out that some active principles are not suitable and can't be used while others fit very well.

13.5.3.1 Copy inquiry to purchase order

SQL Query

Advantage	Disadvantage
Very flexible	Hard to maintenance
Additional functions realizable	Error prone
Highly automatic	Support is difficult through third party (avoided)
	Changes in the fundamental system architecture

Table 13-1: SQL Query

Draft to order (builtin)

Advantage	Disadvantage
Builtin function	No document numbering for drafts
Very secure	Difficult to manage the inquiries
No influence to stock management	Impossible to reference and link

Table 13-2: Draft to order (builtin)

Manual document numbers

Advantage	Disadvantage
Easy to track and separate	No backchange to automatic (primary) numbering system
	Different number formatting
	Mistakes during number input
	Documents can be lost

Table 13-3: Manual document numbers

Direct purchase order

Advantage	Disadvantage
Fit into numbering system	No separation to inquiry
Document can be referenced	Influence to stock management
Very compatible to the software system	Manual management

Table 13-4: Direct purchase order

13.5.3.2 Track open inquiries

Purchase as Draft & manual report

Advantage	Disadvantage
No influence to stock management	No document numbering
Easy to track	Report difficult
Close out not so important	

Table 13-5: Purchase as Draft & manual report

Purchase order & additional identifier

Advantage	Disadvantage
Strict separation	Needs extra field for identifier
Good handling in reports	Influence to stock management
Document has unique number	Manuel document close out important

Table 13-6: Purchase order & additional identifier

13.5.3.3 Print inquiry on printout

Print Layout Designer

Advantage	Disadvantage
Built in solution	Configuration hard
Cheap solution	Inflexible
	Maintenance complicated

Table 13-7: Print Layout Designer

External Tool

Advantage	Disadvantage
Better configuration	Expensive
Easy to adjust	Training necessary
More options to configure	
Use for other reports	

Table 13-8: External tool

SQL-Query

Advantage	Disadvantage
Flexible	Maintenance is complicated
Complex information procedure realizable	Hard to create
	Unsecure

Table 13-9: SQL-Query

13.5.3.3.1 Response time from vendors

Manual Report

Advantage	Disadvantage
Less maintenance because document has to be closed	Information depends when document is closed

Table 13-10: Manual Report

Additional Field

Advantage	Disadvantage
Information quality is good	Additional manual interaction from user necessary

Table 13-11: Additional Field

13.5.3.4 Cross reference to customer inquiry

Activity with linked document

Advantage	Disadvantage
Built in function	Only one link to a document possible

Table 13-12: Activity with linked document

Additional fields

Advantage	Disadvantage
More documents	Configuration difficult
Flexible solution	

Table 13-13: Additional Fields

13.5.3.5 No influence to stock management

Purchase draft document

Advantage	Disadvantage
Built in solution	Document has no number
Information is in the system	
Access for everybody	

Table 13-14: Purchase draft document

External Management

Advantage	Disadvantage
Easy to handle	Less information
	Only local accessibility
	Manual transfer into the system

Table 13-15: External Management

Additional report to separate

Advantage	Disadvantage
Separate open inquiries and open items	Influence to other reports (builtin)

Table 13-16: Additional report to separate

13.5.3.6 Cross Reference to customer's inquiry

Activity with linked document

Advantage	Disadvantage
Built in function	Only one document possible
	No backtrack from invoice

Table 13-17: Activity with linked document

Additional fields in activity + reference document

Advantage	Disadvantage
Flexible	Needs extra configuration
Individual configuration to specific needs	SQL-Queries necessary
Fulfill the efforts	Additional Input

Table 13-18: Additional fields

13.5.3.7 Reminder for open inquiries (vendor)

Activity to business partner

Advantage	Disadvantage
Integrated in the system	Additional activity for each inquiry
Automatic reminder	

Table 13-19: Activity to business partner

Manual Report

Advantage	Disadvantage
	No regular runs are done
	Additional setup

Table 13-20: Manual Report

13.5.3.8 Reminder for open inquiries (customer)

Activity to business partner

Advantage	Disadvantage
Integrated in the system	Additional activity for each inquiry
Automatic reminder	

Table 13-21: Activity to business partner

Manual Report

Advantage	Disadvantage
	No regular runs are done
	Additional setup

Table 13-22: Manual Report

13.5.4 Decision

After weighting all advantages and disadvantages the solution which has to be realized could be fixed. The morphological box below shows each principle and the possible solutions. The blue highlighted box shows the chosen solution.

Active Principle	Solutions			
Inquiry to purchase order	SQL-Query	Draft to order(builtin)	Manual document numbers	Direct purchase order
Track open inquiries	Purchase as draft + manual report	Purchase Order & additional identifier	manual document numbers	
Print with inquiry on printout	Print layout configuration	External Tool	SQL-Query	
Response time from vendors	Manual report	additional field in purchase document		
Cross reference to customer's inquiry	activity with linked document	additional fields in activity&reference document		
No influence to stock management	external management	purchase draft document	additional reports to separate	
Reminder for open inquiries (vendor)	activity to business partner	manual report		
Reminder for open inquiries (customer)	activity to business partner	manual report		
Management of different purchase prices	price list assigned to business partner			
Purchase price history	price list assigned to business partner	price list assigned to item		

Table 13-23: Morphologic box

Source: Self

The specialty is the purchase price history which has two highlighted solutions. Each of them will be realized anyways regardless of the chosen solution.

The detailed implementation is described in the appendix.

13.5.5 Workflow for realized solution

Out of the implemented solutions results the following workflow in SAP.

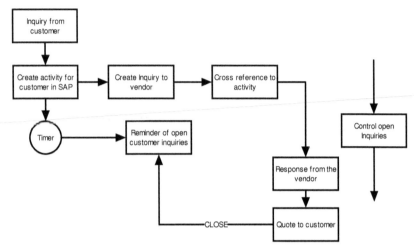

Figure 13-5: Purchase Process in SAP

Source: Self

As soon as a customer inquiry is received by Alfing Corporation a new activity is created within the system. This starts a timer which acts a reminder for the open inquires. This reminder will be closed as soon as the customer is quoted. After creation of the vendor inquiry by Alfing Corporation this vendor inquiry is cross linked to the activity which makes it possible to keep the connection between them. After the vendors responded a quote to the customers will be created. Additionally allow some reporting functions to control open inquiries manually.

Additional reminders for vendor inquiries would have been possible too, but manual reporting was preferred.

13.6 Summary and conclusion

The basic functionality of the purchasing department could be realized with most of the forms provided by Small Business One. The logical request to have an inquiry management system made it necessary to develop a solution that could be implemented and fulfilled the requested requirements. Advanced development could have been done with a Software Development Kit which was too expensive for single purpose.

Because of the multi users access many tasks can be performed faster and by different departments, too.

Additional features that where implemented are that every document in SAP has its initiation document attached as PDF. This allowed to minimize the kept paperwork and improve the accessibility of those information. Only vendor invoices have to be kept on paper due to government regulations. Integrated inventory and currency management could be realized with the implemented functionality with previously discussed advantages.

13.7 Future improvements

The main improvement which will come into existence is that different prices of vendors will be accessible in SAP. This will allow determining average prices of parts and comparisons between vendors.

Due to the implemented inquiry management in future the prices of different vendors can be managed and compared. Another possibility is to run vendor analysis and classify vendors based on several parameters.

From the management side of view, especially the accessibility of business information and running business improves.

14 Sales-Management

The sales itself covers the entire process from the initial customer request until the invoicing takes place. The intention of the sales management is to administer all sales documents related to a specific sales task. The location in the functional overview is in direct connection with the customers.

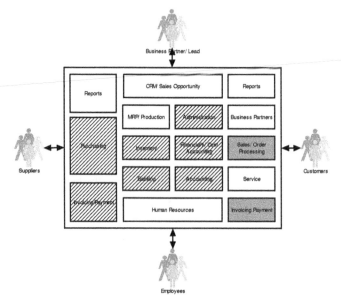

Figure 14-1: Functional overview

Source: Self

The next chapters will give a brief overview about the initial situation and review the implemented sales management requested by Alfing Corporation. Afterwards the additional information about customer and sales management will follow in the next main chapter.

14.1 Initial situation

Based on the product category, sales documents where managed by different departments within Alfing Corporation. Some of them where shared by several departments, too.

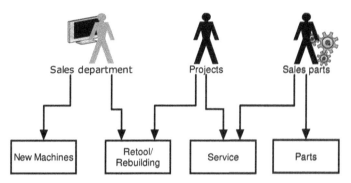

Figure 14-2: Sales Responsibilities

Source: Self

The figure above shows the sales responsibilities of each department and the corresponding sales groups. Each of the described sales area has slightly different requests which will be analyzed in the next chapters.

14.1.1 New machines

Because Alfing Corporation acts as reseller between Germany and the customer all inquiries and documents are processed through their sales department. Most of the sales documents, like quotes and contracts, are created in the German sales department. Those documents are handed over to Alfing Corporations sales people which approve the documents and make some minor adjustments before sending them to the customer. The internal process at Alfing Corporation is that the sales department processes the sale documents and hand them to the secretary who stores them into her file management system. The file management is a file server where the documents are stored. The process between the sale department and the secretary can run several times back and forth until the finished document is forwarded to the customer. This is done either by the sales department or by the secretary.

The problem of this process is that only documents handed to the secretary are stored on the file server. All other documents remain on local machines in the sales department. This lead to an incomplete sales history and nobody could be sure to access the latest document revision. Also no additional information from meetings, e-mails or other documents could be accessed. This was very unsatisfying and even dangerous due to comprehensibly reasons.

The ordering and invoicing process is easy to handle, neither mostly partial payments apply.

The next figure illustrates the described situation:

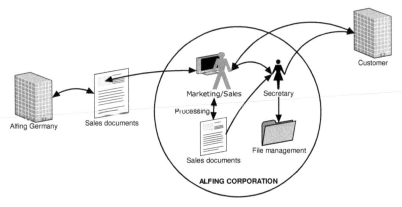

Figure 14-3: Sales processing

Source: Self

The same process applies nearly for the retool and rebuilding operations.

14.1.2 Retool/ Rebuilding

The retool quotes where processed in the same way as the quotes for new machines. The additional problem which comes into existence is that the sales and the projects department as well as several suppliers are involved. All their vendor quotes are merged into one complete quote which is sent to the customer. This increases the number of documents that has to be managed. The problem with the old file management system is, as more documents are involved and as more revisions of a document have to be managed it gets very difficult to keep the overview. In special as long as documents are saved on local computers and not moved onto the central file sever.

The differences between machine sales are illustrated in the next figure.

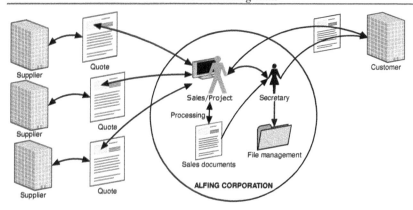

Figure 14-4: Retool sales

Source: Self

14.1.3 Service

The service is managed by the projects and by the parts department. Both of them make quotes and schedule the service technicians. Further description of service is given in chapter 16 Service Management. A special document handled in sales service is the customer blanket purchase order. This document is pack of hours which is sold to a customer, mostly for a special price. Every time the customer uses service hours the blanket order is reduced by this amount. Those blanket orders where managed in a Excel spreadsheet. Every time the customer used hours this had to be monitored in this document and reported to the accounting department, which created the invoice. This process led often to discrepancies between customers and Alfing recordings.

14.1.4 Parts

Spare parts where processed only by the parts department. This department quoted the customer, processed the order and shipped the parts. All of the shipments had to be processed also in the Excel inventory. Afterwards all documents where handed to the accounting department, which created the invoice and stored the documents. The problems resulting out of this have been discussed in the chapter 13 Purchasing. A special document, which is necessary for the shipping of parts, is the proforma invoice. This document is necessary for customs purpose to advise a taxable amount. It is basically a packing slip with additional pricing information.

14.2 Objectives

Based on the previous described situation some objectives could be determined.

Mainly the complete sales management with all its corresponding documents had to be implemented into SAP. This had to include all sales quotes and their related documents.

Likewise in the purchasing, also the sales module had to effect its transactions in the inventory. Cost accounting to the different profit centers and projects had to be integrated, too.

For the sales parts and service department different price lists had to be introduced within the system and applied to its items.

14.3 Solution

The retool/ rebuild and sales machines process could be merged together to one process. To avoid transferring all documents one by one from its external written form into SAP it was decided to create generic items. Those items are either inventory (machines, tools …) or non-inventory (engineering, documentation …) depending on their type. Those generic items represent the external document within SAP. The quotes itself will still be sent out in their external written form. By attaching them through additional created fields to the quotes in SAP, the manual file management became useless. Supplementary documents like drawings, pictures, and others can be attached there, too. A transfer of the complete document into SAP would have been a nice feature but too lavish in comparison with its benefits. In case of own production and manufacturing this would have made more sense. Due to the generic items which are integrated in SAP a complete and detailed reporting is still available.

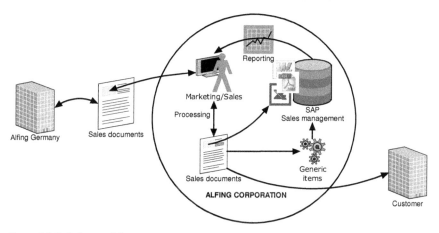

Figure 14-5: Sales workflow

Source: Self

This process allows a wide flexibility and ensures that all documents are available within SAP. Document revisions are attached to new quotes in SAP while the old quotes are closed. This guarantees a detailed history and separates them clearly from previous documents. As soon as the order state is reached the processing will follow its usual procedure complete in SAP.

The problem that turned out was that some quotes contain a range of items. For example sample manufacturing which is quoted like

- 300-500 parts, each $200

The agreement was made to enter those items as an average of 400 parts, each $ 200. This ensures that the values in SAP reflect the true values as close as possible and the reporting information comes close to reality. In case of an order the documents will be changed to the true order values and transferred to the delivery and invoicing documents, which leads to a correct history and accounting.

The service management will be done with a non-inventory item, called service. This allows to invoice it directly from SAP to the customers. Different service rates could be managed with the implemented price management system (see chapter 12 Price strategy). The blanket purchase order was realized with a special indicator field which allows separating those documents from the others. This indicator will also be used as cross reference into the service management.

14.4 Summary and conclusion

In completion the overall requests to the sales module could be covered very well. The integrated cost accounting and inventory management is the main improvement for the monitoring and reporting functionality. Getting rid of the manual file management ensures an up-to-date sales data and reduces work for the secretary. Due to the reason all of those documents are copied onto the SQL-Server the data stored on local computers will be avoid and makes the data accessible for every entitled user.

All other things work very unspectacular and improve especially the documentation and the interaction between the departments.

In conclusion to a functional sales management comes the additional customer relationship management. This will be covered in the following chapter. Many of the discussed affairs apply also to the customer relationship management due sales is part of it.

15 Sales CRM-Management

This chapter comes close with the previous chapter because a sale is part of the customer relationship management. The idea of customer relationship management (CRM) is to learn more about customers' needs and behaviors in order to develop a stronger relationship with them. It will also help to get a better understanding of the business environment of a company. This includes the customers as well as competitors and partners. Because the machining industry is more a long term oriented industry, and well working partnerships are seldom broken up, the customer relationship is one of the most important parts of the company. It is also a tool to develop new customers.

The location of the customer relationship management is directly connected to the business partners and to lead customers.

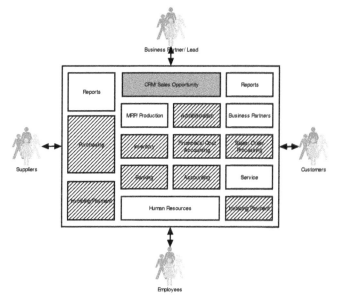

Figure 15-1: Functional overview

Source: Self

The next chapter will give an overview about the initial situation within Alfing Corporation and show what could be improved.

15.1 Initial situation

The initial situation for Alfing Corporation was that each individual made his customer relationship management on his own. Every person had his own notices, thoughts and personal folders where information about customers where managed. That information was only available for each individual and not for the complete sales department.

15.2 Objectives

The objectives of the customer relationship management in Alfing Corporation were to have a central place where all customers' related information is stored and managed.

The documents which had to be included were sales quotes, meetings, memos, e-mail, phone calls, external documents and others. It was also requested to set reminders for specific tasks.

All of this information should integrate into several reporting features which allow checking the state of a opportunity.

After completion of a sales opportunity the result had to be fixed in a won or lost state, reasons provided. All opportunities should be managed by the previous Alfing Corporation quote numbers.

15.3 Solution

For managing purpose of the sales opportunity and to have several report features the following options where specified:

- Start and Closing date
  used to report the opportunity length and start/ end dates.
- Predicted closing date
  as estimated value when the opportunity will be closed.
- Potential and closing %
  to calculate the weighted amount and report the potential of the opportunity.
- Interest area
  for specifying the area of interest, e.g. crankshafts, gearbox, housing, ….
- Level of interest
  to set priorities defined as low, medium, high.
- Stages
  to estimate the status of the opportunity, e.g. beginning-stage, connecting stage, end-stage.
- Partners/Competitor
  to have information about them.
- Won/Lost
  to have an overview about won or lost opportunities.

All of those options allow managing the sales opportunity depending on its actual state and the progress it has made. That information is always within the sales opportunity.

All additional documents are merged into one sales opportunity like illustrated below.

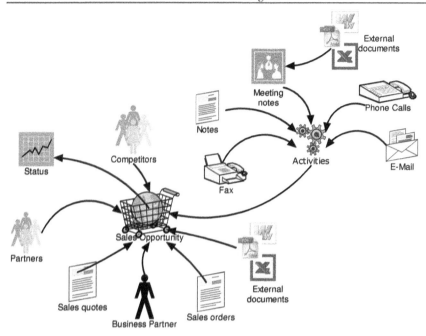

Figure 15-2: Sales opportunity

Source: Self

The initial step is to create a new sales opportunity within Small Business One. This is the collection point for all information. Each of the created sales opportunities can be categorized and judged by its priority. This sales opportunity is the basis for all related documents.

Linked to this sales opportunity are all documents, like sales quotes and orders as well as business partner information, competitors and partners. Beneath this also e-mails, phone calls, fax and other information will be attached to this negotiation. After the sales process is finished the sales opportunity is closed by setting the state to won or lost, providing reasons. The activities which are integrated into the sales opportunity have the ability to manage several different documents like fax info, phone notices, e-mails and also external documents through meeting notes. Those external documents can be linked also directly into the opportunity. Activities allow also having reminder functionality for meetings and others.

Several different reports allow monitoring the sales process and checking the actual state of each. Due to the detailed information which is linked into the sales opportunity an overview as well as a close look is always possible.

15.4 Summary and conclusion

The sales opportunities provide a complete new level of management functionality for Alfing Corporation. With all the integrated functions and the possibility to add a very detailed level of information the monitoring of the sales functionality is much better than before. One of the main advantages is that the information is now available for several persons in the office. This allows everybody to check and update an sales process.

By using all of these features Alfing Corporation will be able to improve their customer service and provide products that match the customer's criteria. Also well working partnerships can be developed and strengths of the competitors monitored and focused. For the sales department this information basis will help to improve their customer relationships and increase efficiency. The history can provide additional information about the success of shows and its resulting customers.

For the management, the data source can help to recognize and focus on the main competences of the company. It will also help to recognize business areas that need to be improved and it can be seen where partnerships can be useful to provide more suitable solutions to the customer. In the long term it can help to set up the complete management strategy in customer direction. In addition the strengths of several sales people can be found out, which allows to direct them.

The problems that can be seen is that all those features need a disciplined sales personal that reports all information to the sales opportunity module. Without this the reports will provide only wrong or blurry pictures of customer relations. This can be misleading and is not very helpful in the end.

A future improvement that can be seen after intense usage is the possibility to judge each sales opportunity by its probability to be won or lost, which could be used to trigger a manufacturing process in advance. This could decrease the delivery time and give a competitive edge for Alfing.

Another part that fits directly into the customer relationship management is the service. This is basically the main part for Alfing Corporation and will be discussed in the following chapter.

16 Service Management

The main understanding for service management is to provide the customer support for the purchased product. For Alfing Corporation the service consists out of several areas:

- Pre-order support: contains consulting and engineering
- Installation support: contains machine installation, initial training and run-off support
- After-sales support: consists of hands-on training, repairs, modifications, warranty

The area that will be covered in this chapter is mainly the after-sales support, but it will touch parts of machine installation and run-off support. The pre-order support is more part of the sales process. Staying directly in connection with the customer the service is located in the same area as sales and order processing.

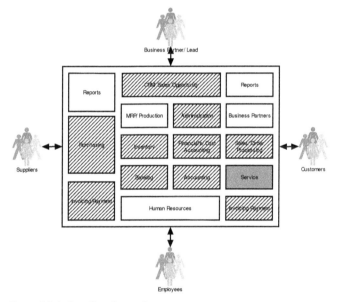

Figure 16-1: Functional overview

Source: Self

16.1 Machine installation

Every machine installation starts with building and final inspection of the machine in Germany. This inspection is already done with customer parts and under supervision of the customer. After the machine has passed this tests and the customer acknowledges the shipping the machine is disassembled into smaller assemblies and shipped to the customer. Alfing Corporation provides then the installation personal together with technicians from Germany. After the installation, a run-off ensures that the machine is able to keep the guaranteed tolerances. The last step is to run the first production shift on the machine. As soon as this shift is within the specified limitations and tolerances the machine is officially delivered and the warranty period starts.

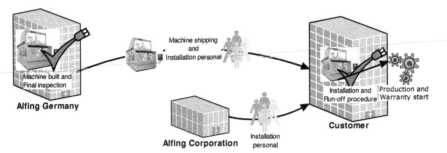

Figure 16-2: Warranty start

Source: self

All after-sales service is then provided direct by Alfing Corporation's technicians, which is also the main business of Alfing Corporation. The service itself is executed by several technicians at the customer plants. All executed service had to be invoiced either to the customer or to Alfing Germany in case of warranty. Only for special occasions the service was covered for free by Alfing Corporation. The complete service was organized and monitored by several people in the office. Those did also approve service and expense reports of the technicians before they where handed to the accounting department which had to retype them into Open Systems.

The next chapters will provide a more detailed description of the service which includes warranty management as well as the service process of the technicians.

16.2 Objectives

The main objective was to put a new organizational structure into the service management. Basically the service can be divided into two main areas:

- Executive which covers all executed tasks at the customer site and
- Management which records all executed tasks and provides information to manage the executive part.

Each of those areas has several sublevels which have to be covered.

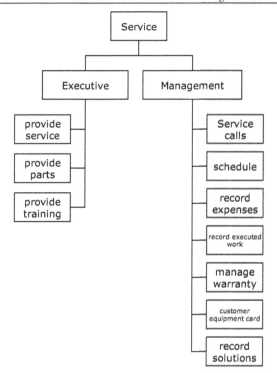

Figure 16-3: Service areas

Source: Self

The main objective was to build a system which allows transferring the management functions into SAP. The executive part itself is not part of the documentation. A detailed description of each part will follow in the next chapters.

16.3 General changes

The problem of the complete service management was that several people in the office had their hands on the service management. This lead to confusion and made it difficult to have a clear management. . This applies for Alfing Corporation itself as well as for the customers. Based on this information the decision was made to have one responsible person in the company which is the central contact for all service. This service manager is responsible for the organization and schedule of all service operations of the company.

In the same step a 24 hours, 7 days a week service phone was introduced. This phone has to be carried by the service manager all time. A push forward service allows to forward incoming service e-mails to this phone, too.

After these initial definitions had been made the service structure could be transferred into SAP.

16.4 Service calls

A service call for Alfing Corporation can be defined to every customer contact which initiates either personal or telephone support for a technical problem.

16.4.1 Initial situation

The initial situation was that every time a customer initiated service the technician was scheduled by the person who received the call. This information was sometimes documented, sometimes not. This made it very difficult to have long lasting information about service calls. The importance of this comes into existence if a customer claims other service than initially scheduled. Without documentation it is not possible for anybody in the office to have information about this.

16.4.2 Objective

The objective of the service call was to have a central location that stores the ignition of the service and all its related information. Possibly the service hours should be recorded, too.

16.4.3 Implemented solution

The service call itself will act as the collection point for all tasks and information which is related to this service call. This includes parts, technicians as well as all other management functions. Due to this integration it gets possible to track every operation related to a specific service call and built a history.

Each service call will start with its creation. During this period the service reason, the priority and a responsible technician will be assigned to it by the service manager. All activities and things that happen in connection with this service call will be recorded into this central place which makes it accessible for everyone and at every time. It is also possible to have information about the initial reason and the agreed work which has to be executed by the technician.

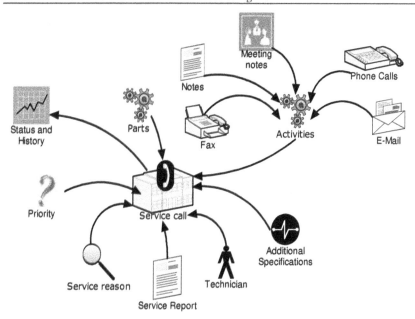

Figure 16-4: Service Call

Source: Self

After the service is finished the service call will be closed and remain as documentation within the system. This allows having a very detailed history of executed work and common problems.

16.5 Schedule

The schedule is there to keep track about each technician's time and location.

16.5.1 Initial situation

Each technicians schedule had been managed within Microsoft Outlook. Because the schedule was available in a public calendar everybody had access to it. This made it difficult because some people entered information while others didn't. The problem resulting out of this was that technicians where scheduled several times and had to be rescheduled at customers.

16.5.2 Objective

The objective was to transfer the public calendar basically into SAP.

16.5.3 Implemented solution

To avoid misleading entries and doubled schedules it was agreed that only the service manager is allowed to make entries to the calendar. Within SAP the entries are created as activities which are assigned to each technician. Those activities are linked into the service call which allows having a cross reference between the schedule and its origin. This calendar view is available for every user which allows retrieving information for everybody. An additional reminder can be used, too.

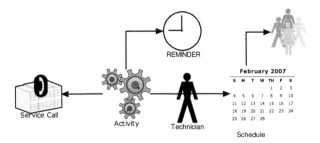

Figure 16-5: Expenses worklfow

Source: Self

16.6 Expense management

Expenses are all travel cost that applies to a technician. This includes typically the meal expenses, gas and hotel. The expenses can be granted as allowance which covers a daily money amount or repaid by bills.

16.6.1 Previous situation

Previously each technician wrote his expense reports in Excel, printed it out and attached the receipts to it. Afterwards this documents where given to the responsible project manager who approved the documents and passed them to the accounting department. The accounting department transferred the information into Open Systems and paid the technician its expenses.

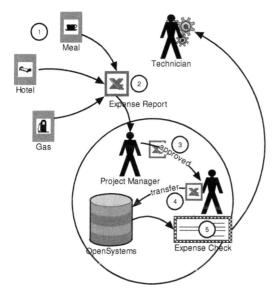

Figure 16-6: Expenses worklfow

Source: Self

16.6.2 Objectives

The objectives where to manage expenses within SAP avoiding that the technicians have to write their expense reports externally and somebody has to transfer them into accounting.

16.6.3 Implemented solution

The initial idea was that each technician will write his expenses directly as invoice into SAP. This was not possible due to several reasons. Creating invoices was denied by the accounting department and license restrictions of the CRM license do not allow creating invoices. To avoid that each expense report has to be retyped by the accounting department, technicians will enter their expenses as purchase orders into the system. The purchase order will be printed out by the technician, receipts attached and stored in the accounting for documentation purpose. The service manager will approve the purchase order and copy the purchase order into the invoice. This is also the signal for the accounting department that the expenses are approved and can be paid.

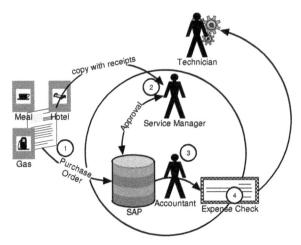

Figure 16-7: Expenses workflow

Source: Self

In a trustworthy environment this system allows to process expense reports in time. Otherwise it has to be waited until the copy with attached receipts is received by the service manager.

16.7 Record executed work

Initially each service technician wrote his service report. This report was signed by the customer and a copy of it stored within Alfing Corporation. Those reports where stored in several binders, mostly attached to its other documents like expense reports, purchase order and so on. The information written on the expense report where therefore not accessible easily, neither could they be used by other technicians for diagnosis purpose. As the reports where never accessed anymore the quality of them where very low because the technicians used only some generic idiom to explain their work

16.7.1 Objectives

The objective of this topic was to build a database that allows everybody to access service reports which could be used then for diagnosis, help and solution of actual failure reasons.

16.7.2 Implemented solution

In future every technician gets his service tasks assigned. After completion of his service operation he will report the applied solution into Small Business One and print the service report. This service report will be signed by the customer. The report within Small Business One will stay connected to the machine and serial number. Other information is the date, status and the creator.

Each of the reports will be sorted additionally into several main categories, like electrical, mechanical and hydraulics. This provides a basic structure. In advance every report gets several key words which allow advanced report features. For the detailed description each report gets a detailed area for free text.

The service report can be accessed through its category, keywords or a full text search in the details area. With this functionality the accessibility of the data is very well and flexible.

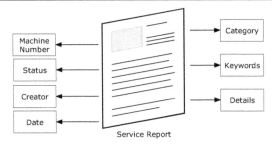

Figure 16-8: Service Report

Source: Self

By dividing the service report into those three parts it will be able to built a solutions knowledge base which is easy accessible and helpful to use.

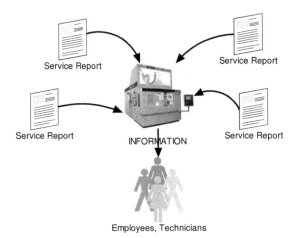

Figure 16-9: Solution knowledge base

Source: Self

Due to the reason that the technicians are very seldom within Alfing Corporation it became necessary to provide them access to the database. Because Small Business One has no web interface which would allow connecting from external locations alternate solution had to be found.

A surveillance turned out that access to the internet via HTTP is available within nearly all customer plants as well as in the hotels. Based on this information a system called "go-to-my-PC" had been introduced. This application has a server running on a local machine within the company which is accessible through the HTTP-Protocol. Due to security reasons the connections will be run through HTTPS. The client itself needs only web browser and internet connection to access the server. This server is the local machine within the company. All applications run on this machine and only the screen is transferred to the client. This allows running all applications which are installed on the server and work with them. Data that is available on the server can be print directly or transferred as file to the client machine which allows the service technicians to print their reports and having them signed by the customer. See figure below for further illustration.

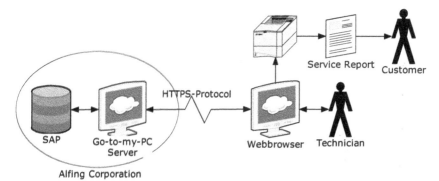

Figure 16-10: Remote access

Source: Self

In the same way can all data within SAP and other information entered and accessed. The main advantage of this system is its flexibility to work from every place with an internet connection and transferring the data back and forth.

The following chapter will provide further information about warranty management of a machine and its implementation.

16.8 Warranty management

A warranty is an obligation where the vendor guarantees the customer several conditions or facts for the specific product. For Alfing Corporation the warranty is granted for a complete machine with all of its parts. All failures and problems that take place during the warranty period have to be covered by the vendor. The warranty contract for a machine is always based on individual arrangements between Alfing and the customer. The typical warranty periods are 6, 12, 18, 24, 36 and 48 months from start of production (see also Figure 16-2: Warranty start). Those periods can be extended after negotiations.

16.8.1 Initial situation

All service executed by Alfing Corporation during the warranty period is back invoiced to the German holdings. Only in special cases, like customer operator errors, the customer had been invoiced for the service. Every service which is scheduled without warranty needs a signed purchase order from the customer.

Alfing Corporations problem was that the exact warranty periods where never recorded exactly and accessible. Whenever a customer called he claimed everything on warranty. Because of the missing documentation it was very hard to tell if this was correct or not. Therefore a lot of service was provided under warranty which was not correct. After back invoicing to Germany those documents where denied and Alfing Corporation had to cover the service on its own.

16.8.2 Objectives

The request of Alfing Corporation was to have warranty management system which manages the exact start and end date of the warranty period. An additional feature should be a reminder that provides information about an outrunning warranty period. This would allow starting a negotiation about warranty extension in time.

16.8.3 Solution

The solution for the warranty management was the creation of several different warranty templates. Depending on the arranged warranty runtime each machine (especially the serial number, see chapter 16.8.4 Serial numbers) has now an assigned warranty contract of 6,12,18, 24, 36 or 48 months. The exactly starting date for the warranty period will be created as soon as the first production parts are running on the machine. From this point the warranty will count backwards until it is run out. Every time a new service has to be scheduled a check against the warranty has to be done which allows requesting a purchase order or not. An additional timer will show up three months before the warranty runs out which allows getting into customer negotiations.

The applied workflow can be seen below:

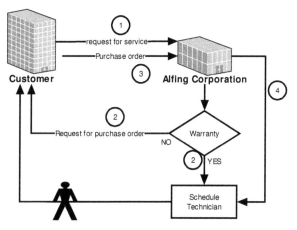

Figure 16-11: Service workflow

Source: Self

To have a unique identifier for every machine it became necessary to introduce serial numbers for the machines. Without unique numbers it could happen that several warranties could be assigned to the same machine jeopardizing the complete system. This serial number setup is described in the chapters below.

16.8.4 Serial numbers

The serial numbers where introduced due to several reasons. First of all it became necessary because of the warranty management. Additionally it became important to have a unique identifier which allows tracking a complete history of a machine.

The numbering system for the serial number was chosen with different things in mind. The numbering system should be easy to track from both sides, Alfing Corporation and the Customer. In addition it should match as close as possible the German machine number.

The following figure shows the different views of the participating parties on a machine.

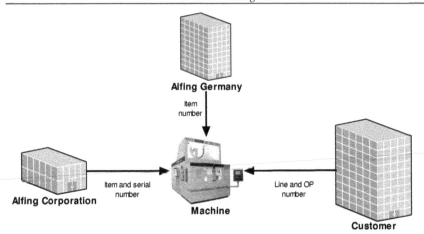

Figure 16-12: Views on a machine

Source: Self

Alfing Corporation identifies the machine by its item and from now on its serial number. Alfing Germany identifies the machine by their item number. This number matches Alfing Corporation's because all items are imported directly from the German companies.

The customer instead has its own numbering system which is based on line and operation number. This numbering system is the same for nearly all customers.

To find the machine itself easily the objective was to have a direct cross reference between the line and operation number within the system. This made it necessary to include three different numbers into the system.

- Item number
- Serial number
- Line and Operation number

Those numbers where structured in the following way:

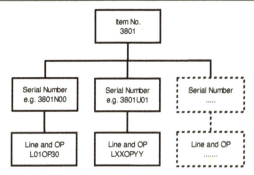

Figure 16-13: Serial numbering

Source: Self

The item number is kept within the inventory and it is a non-unique number. Below each item number is the serial number which is a unique number that identifies the individual machine. The serial number starts with the machine number, a character which indicates the status and a two digit running number. The status is N for New and U for Retool/ Rebuild. Below each serial number is the line and operation number of the customer attached.

Every time a serial number is transferred to the customer or vice versa this will be recorded in a customer equipment card which collects information about all delivered machines to one customer. The idea behind this is that every machine and machine location is recorded and allows to be tracked.

This serial number management system allows also to be extended to other components which have a manufacturer serial number. By having a unique identifier for the machines by now it got possible to build a solutions knowledge base which will act also as machine history.

16.9 Customer equipment card

The idea of the customer equipment card is to record all delivered machines as well as the executed work at those machines.

16.9.1 Initial situation

In the beginning no information about delivered machines and equipment was specifically kept. With the introduction of the serial number and addition the warranty it made sense to record specific equipment.

16.9.2 Implemented solution

The implemented solution records all equipment that has an assigned serial number automatically upon creation of a shipping document or invoice to the customer equipment card. Other parts can be recorded manually. For Alfing Corporation it was agreed only to record the machines itself and some specific equipment which has a separate warranty period, for example spindles. Recording every single item would increase work without having a specific use of the recording. Delivered items can retrieved from shipping documents and other locations which makes it useless to monitor them additionally. Also a part based warranty does not exist for machines. In case it becomes useful this feature can be added by demand.

16.10 Knowledge Base

Assigned to each machine and serial number a additional knowledge base will be built up. All service calls and service related documents will be attached to this serial number. This allows building up a machine history with all faults, service hours and replacement parts.

This will be helpful for several reasons. For the technicians it will provide helpful information in diagnosis and solutions. The office employees will be able to use this as data source for information about the executed work tasks. This will also help to document a machine lifetime and work executed by Alfing or by the customer. The information stored here can be merged into the quality assurance system within Germany. The following figure illustrates the realized solution.

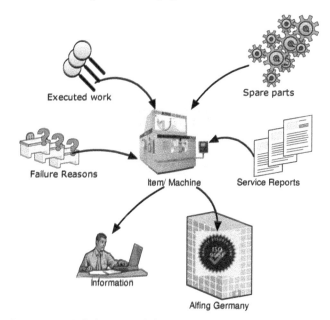

Figure 16-14: Solutions Knowledge Base

Source: Self

The solutions knowledge base and its final usage will turn out in future because it takes time until enough data is stored within there.

16.11   Summary and conclusion

Overdoing the complete service management within Alfing Corporation will help organize the service more fluent. This is mainly related to the centrally organized data structure which allows access for everybody. Due to the reason that manually kept document are now transferred into an electronic state allows to build a solutions knowledge base.

The introduced serial number management will mainly improve the tracking capabilities and ensure that an up-to-date warranty managing is possible. This will help in the end to improve the complete financial management in the company because all service hours can be either invoiced to the customer or back invoiced to Germany depending on the individual situation.

In the long term the created solutions knowledge base will help to manage built a knowledge background that is accessible for everyone in the company. Especially the technicians will improve form this because they can find previously applied solutions there. Another advantage of the solutions knowledge base is that a machine history is built up. This allows monitoring every change that is made from Alfing Corporation to a machine. Changes made by customers can be sort out and issued from warranty. In addition to this the often happening errors can be reported to the design department in Germany which improves the overall quality.

The complete service management is more a long term oriented solution which unfolds its benefits first after several months of data input.

The following chapter will provide only a short overview about the additional modules which weren't covered until now.

17 Other Modules

Looking at our functional overview there are some modules that where not covered in the previous chapters.

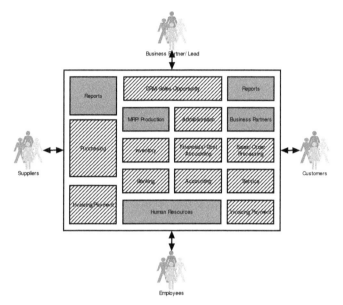

Figure 17-1: Functional overview

Source: self

The reasons that those chapters where skipped is mainly because they are not of usage within Alfing Corporation. The business partners where skipped because it was touched within several chapters and needs no special discussion. A description of each highlighted module and its usage is given in the following chapters.

17.1 Reports

The basis configuration of SAP contains about 1,500 reports. With those reports many of the common needs are covered. A description of those reports won't be given. The appendix will include several basics about SQL-Queries and the Crystal Report builder which can be used to generate individual reports based on specific needs.

17.2 MRP/Production

This module allows managing production and manufacturing of parts and machines. Because Alfing Corporation does not have any production this theme is not covered within this thesis.

17.3 Business Partners

The business partner module manages all information relevant for relationships between customers, vendors and Alfing Corporation. Typical information is address, payment terms, financial and logistic information. The business partners where touched in several chapter of this thesis. Additional description is not necessary.

17.4 Human resources

Because Alfing Corporation's human resources are managed by their certified public accountant this module was not necessary. Regardless of this the human resources module in Small Business One allows only basic functionality. This includes mainly personal information and holidays. Additional features like time management is not available.

18 Overall Summary

With introduction of Small Business One Alfing Corporation has set the basis for further growth. Because Small Business One is part of the overall business family of SAP it will allow also merging into other solutions of SAP without further problems.

Due to the reason it is the first time for Alfing Corporation to have a multi user enterprise system it will take its time until all benefits will unfold. This is due to the reason that a core data basis has to be built up before all reporting and data access features will show its capabilities. Another reason for this is that, even if the users are trained, it will take its time until they are used to the system.

Transferring the basic financial transactions worked very unspectacular and provides basically the same capabilities like Open Systems. Improvements in this area are mainly minor improvements in daily workflow without revolutionary news.

The main improvement of the system showed up in the inventory management and within the business partner relations. By merging shipments and inventory together it reduced work and made the complete process error proven. In conclusion work for the accounting department had been reduced and the auditing procedures improved.

Within the buying department the price management system and the overall documentation features allow to mange this business area much better as within Excel spreadsheets. Moving paperwork from its paper form to PDF documents and attaching them to its corresponding documents within SAP made it possible to develop better accessibility and remove manual storage procedures.

The improvements for the Sales department are basically the same as for the buying department. Additional and very important features are the customer relationship functions. They allow managing and improving customer relations. Another and especially internal enhancement is that all documents related to a specific task are now stored in a central place and accessible by everybody.

Within service the initial benefits show up in the warranty management. Another improvement applies in the better documentation of service and its resulting monitor capabilities. Forming the solutions knowledge base will show it benefits especially in future after a solid data basis has been built up. Because it will monitor and report also delivered parts feedback to the Germany quality assurance system can help to improve the overall quality.

Allover can be said that Small Business One will help to improve the interaction between the departments and helps to built an information workflow which is not dependant on key persons in the office and accessible by everybody. This is also one of the main improvements for the management. A lot of financial information provides now up to date and very exact data, which hadn't been available before or just in blurry pictures.

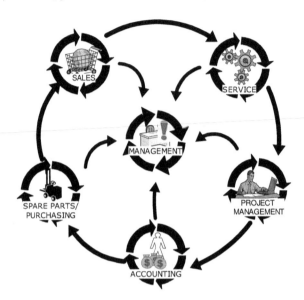

Figure 18-1: Workflow in SAP

Source: self

In comparison with the initial situation is remarkable that the management is now the center of the company and has access to all information within the company. The other departments have no much better communication which speeds the complete process up.

Looking at the software system itself it can be said that it provides a system that fulfills all needs for a midsize company. The complete business processes can be applied very well and allows managing many basic transactions. An especially missing functionality is that inquiry process within purchasing. This and many other specific need have to be implemented manually. The usability of the system for the end user is very good. It allows a smooth and easy start after several training session. It turned out to be very helpful letting users practice in a test system which provides them the ability to practice without hesitating about the results.

The administrative side of Small Business One works unspectacular. Server updates work very well and fast. Especially the client update can get tricky and there is no way to apply the update in user mode. This makes it mandatory for the administrator to process each workstation manually. This is unbearable for a company with a greater number of employees.

Looking at the roadmap provided from SAP show that the Small Business One project is very active and it is planned to implement lots of features into the system. One of them is the missing web access functionality.

19 Introduction to the Appendix

The appendix will cover the necessary setup procedures to get the Small Business System running and it provides further information about reporting and customizing.

The following pages will describe the general and detailed setup process for each module. I consider the fully detailed description leading to far. Therefore the basic setup and some customizing operations will be explained in detail. However, individual customization can be made easily based upon this description.

Separately listed follow the workflows for the main tasks within Alfing Corporation. The symbols used are the following ones:

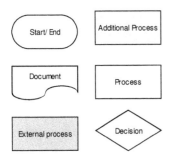

The responsible persons for each task are listed in its corresponding workflow.

Part Sale

10/31/2006

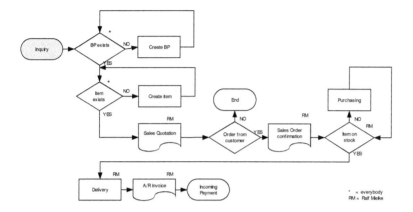

Service Call

10/31/2006

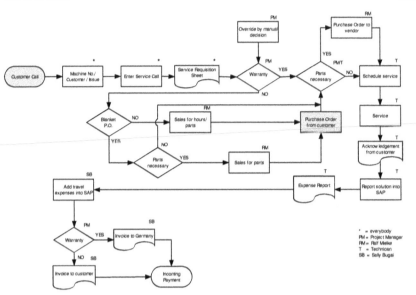

Purchasing

10/31/2006

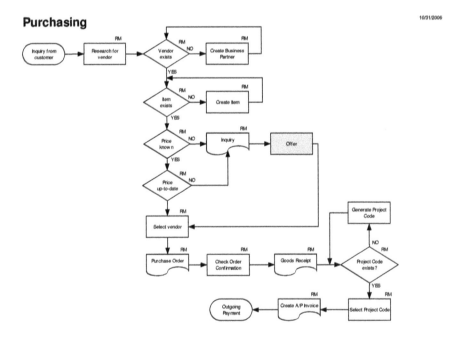

Create Business Partner

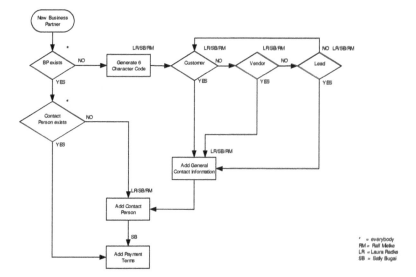

* = everybody
RM = Ralf Melke
LR = Laura Radke
SB = Sally Bugai

Create Item

10/31/2006

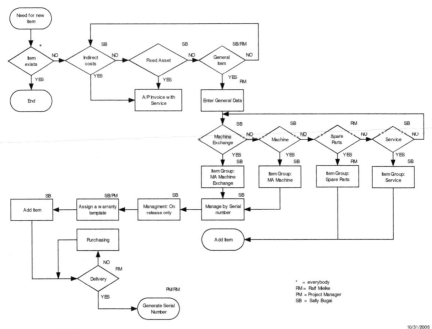

Machine Sale

10/31/2006

Incoming Payment

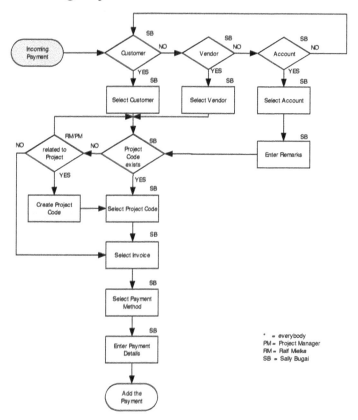

* = everybody
PM = Project Manager
RM = Ralf Mieke
SB = Sally Bugai

Outgoing Payment

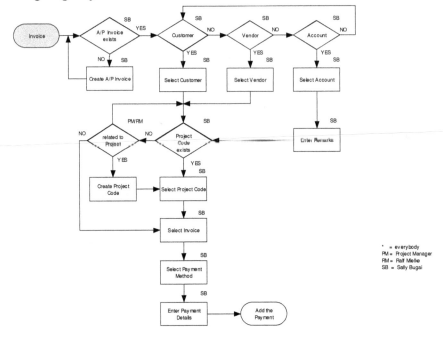

* = everybody
PM = Project Manager
RM = Ralf Mielke
SB = Sally Bugai

20 Company creation

The first thing that has to be done is to create a new company and make initial settings.

20.1 Database creation

Creation of a new database is made in ADMINISTRATION → CHOOSE COMPANY → NEW:

The system will ask for several basic parameters like

- Company name   Alfing Corporation
- Database name   do not use special characters here
- Local settings   United States of America (predefined setting)
- Chart of accounts   CUSTOMIZED or the standard US chart of accounts, depending on intention
- Base language   English
- Posting periods   specify the year and the sub-periods, e.g. 2007, 12 months

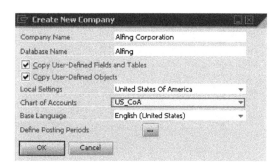

Figure 20-1: Create new company

Source: Screenshot

All those settings should be made with an accountant and system administrator to specify the correct parameters. For Alfing Corporation it is necessary to change the chart of accounts to customized.

After all information is acknowledged by clicking OK the database is created and ready for login. The initial password settings are USER: manager and PASSWORD: manager.

Due to the security risk this should be changed after the first login.

20.2 Company details

The settings made here provide some basic information about the company and apply to printed documents. It contains also the holiday settings, which are used to calculate resolution time in the service and to calculate due dates in documents.

The company details are set within ADMINISTRATION → SYSTEM INITIALIZATION → COMPANY.

Figure 20-2: Company details

Source: Screenshot

The system allows specifying this information in LOCAL and in FOREIGN language.

The holiday settings can be found in the ACCOUNTING DATA.

Based on the initial settings the American holidays are predefined. Individual company holidays can be added by clicking on the orange arrow ⇨ which opens the next window.

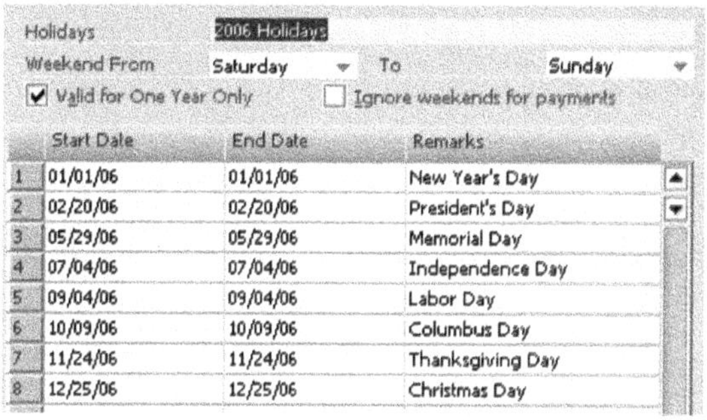

Figure 20-3: Holiday settings

Source: Screenshot

For Alfing Corporation apply no special holiday why we set only the public holidays. The other settings can be kept by their defaults.

The following chapter covers the license setup necessary for the user login.

21 Users and Licenses

This chapter describes how to setup users and assign licenses to them.

21.1 User setup

Before license distribution all users have to be setup in the system. This is done with the predefined manager account.

Go to ADMINISTRATION → SETUP → GENERAL → USERS which will open the following window.

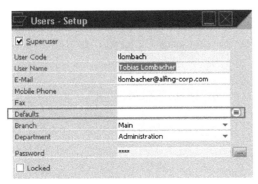

Figure 21-1: User setup

Source: Screenshot

It is necessary to specify the basic information which is used also for some of the printed forms.

The password that is assigned here is has to be changed by the user the first time he logs into the system. The system will ask automatically for this.

A superuser has access to all modules can assign licenses and log other user out of the system. The locked button is very helpful to create users and prevent them from using the system. For example if the certified public accountant should have temporarily access to the system.

To create or assign user defaults use the ⊜ button. The defaults can be used to apply some special settings to members of a group.

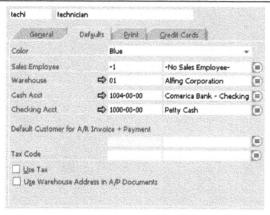

Figure 21-2: User Defaults

Source: Screenshot

The user default setup should be made together with an accountant to meet the correct account specifications. The next step is to assign licenses to all created users. In a environment with only a few users this setting can be skipped. The special reason for this is to apply some print settings and other user special things for groups of users.

21.2 License distribution

The licenses are distributed from the license server. The default port is 30000, but can be different from local installations. The licenses are assigned in ADMINISTRATION → LICENSE → LICENSE ADMINISTRATION.

To assign a licenses select the user and check the corresponding licenses in the right window. It is necessary to assign the Professional or CRM license and the SAP Add-ons license.

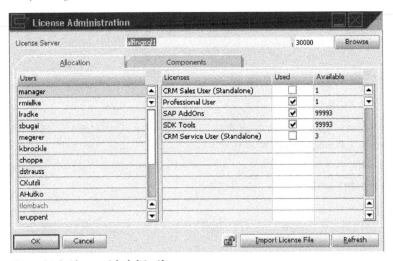

Figure 21-3: License Administration

Source: Screenshot

An overview about the total number of licenses can be retrieved from the COMPONENTS tab. This will show assigned and free licenses and helps to get an overview.

After the license is assigned the user can log into the system. By default he has all rights that the license grants him. This should be restricted by the as soon as the system is used for real work.

The next chapter will describe the basic administration of a new system.

22 Financial

All basic settings for a functional system are made here.

22.1 Setup Posting Periods

The posting periods specify the information when the Month-End-Closing or Year-End-Closing periods take time. The actual period is always determined from the system date.

This setup is made in ADMINISTRATION → SYSTEM INITIALIZATION → GENERAL SETTINGS → POSTING PERIODS

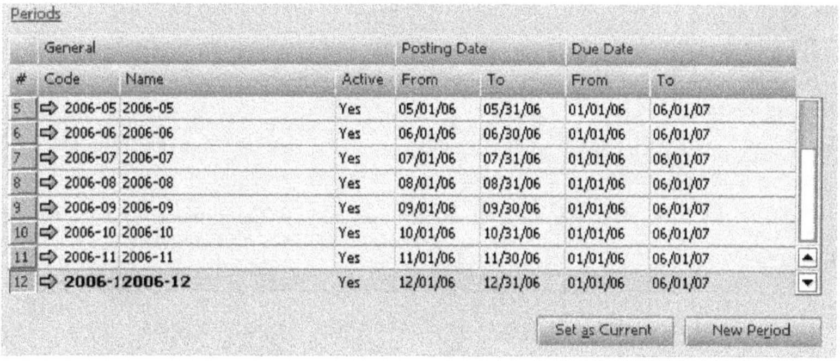

#	Code	Name	Active	Posting Date From	To	Due Date From	To
5	2006-05	2006-05	Yes	05/01/06	05/31/06	01/01/06	06/01/07
6	2006-06	2006-06	Yes	06/01/06	06/30/06	01/01/06	06/01/07
7	2006-07	2006-07	Yes	07/01/06	07/31/06	01/01/06	06/01/07
8	2006-08	2006-08	Yes	08/01/06	08/31/06	01/01/06	06/01/07
9	2006-09	2006-09	Yes	09/01/06	09/30/06	01/01/06	06/01/07
10	2006-10	2006-10	Yes	10/01/06	10/31/06	01/01/06	06/01/07
11	2006-11	2006-11	Yes	11/01/06	11/30/06	01/01/06	06/01/07
12	2006-12	2006-12	Yes	12/01/06	12/31/06	01/01/06	06/01/07

Set as Current   New Period

Figure 22-1: Posting periods

Source: Screenshot

A new period is created with the NEW PERIOD button. This opens the following window where a period code and name has to be specified.

The SET AS CURRENT button can be used to switch between the periods. This setting applies only for the current user and on the local workstation. It will also be lost after the user logs himself out.

Based on the actual date, the system switches automatically between the periods.

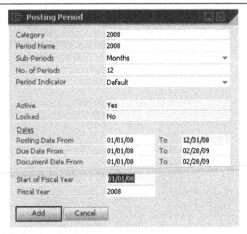

Figure 22-2: Posting Period

Source: Screenshot

It is necessary to specify the basic information of the period and add it. The category and the period name can be chosen freely.

In our case the year 2008 and 12 months as sub periods. The creation is done with ADD.

It is very recommended to extend the doc due date and document date for about 30-60 days. This allows entering documents received after closing the period.

After this step the posting periods are within the system and ready to use. It is recommended to create only the posting periods which are actual needed. New periods should be created as necessary. The reason for this is that the legal changes can make it necessary to change the period settings and after creating a period it is not easily to change.

22.2 Document numbering

Setting a document numbering system is not mandatory an can be skipped, neither it has advantages to make a setup here. Within Alfing Corporation we used this setting to separate the different documents from each other by their numbering. It can also be used to separate different department or business areas.

The setup of the document numbering system is made in ADMINISTRATION → SYSTEM INITIALIZATION → DOCUMENT NUMBERING. This will open the screen where all the available document types are listed and the numbering ranges can be specified.

Document	Default Series	First No.	Next No.	Last No.
A/R Invoices	Primary	100000	100000	199999
A/R Credit Memos	Primary	200000	200000	299999
Deliveries	Primary	300000	300000	399999
Returns	Primary	400000	400000	499999
Sales Orders	Primary	500000	500000	599999
A/P Invoice	Primary	600000	600000	699999
A/P Credit Memo	Primary	700000	700000	799999
Goods Receipt PO	Primary	800000	800000	899999
Goods Return	Primary	900000	900000	999999
Purchase Order	Primary	1000000	1000000	1099999
Sales Quotations	Primary	1100000	1100000	1199999
Incoming Payments	Primary	1200000	1200000	1299999
Deposits	Primary	1300000	1300000	1399999
Journal Entries	Primary	1400000	1400000	1499999
Outgoing Payments	Primary	1500000	1500000	1599999
Goods Receipts	Primary	1600000	1600000	1699999
Goods Issue	Primary	1700000	1700000	1799999
Inventory Transfers	Primary	1800000	1800000	1899999
Landed Costs	Primary	1900000	1900000	1999999
Inventory Revaluation	Primary	2000000	2000000	2099999
Production Order	Primary	1	1	

Figure 22-3: Document numbering ranges

Source: Screenshot

The numbering system is set by a double click on the document type. This opens a new screen where the numbering range can be set.

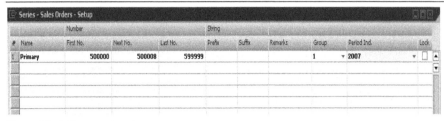

Figure 22-4: Document series

Source: Screenshot

It is essential to link the numbering to the current period indicator. Otherwise it won't be possible to create new documents.

The next step is to set on of the series as default which is done by clicking on SET AS DEFAULT. To link the numbering methods only to several person or departments select the corresponding option and specify the details. This is also the step where separation in different departments can be applied.

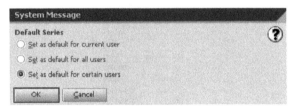

Figure 22-5: Default series

Source: Screenshot

For Alfing Corporation it is enough to set the series as default for all users.

Depending on the selected option a new screen opens up and the selected persons have to be assigned.

Figure 22-6: Select Users

Source: Screenshot

Additional possibilities are to link several document numbering systems to one period which allows a separation by departments, areas or other needs.

After locking a period no further documents in this period can be created. This should be done after legal reporting is done which ensures that no further documents can be applied.

The next step is absolutely essential as soon as user rights are applied.

Working with user authorizations makes it essential to grant users access to create new numbers. Otherwise they won't be able to create new documents. This is done in ADMINISTRATION → AUTHORIZATIONS → GENERAL AUTHORIZATIONS.

Authorizations		
AHutko	Exchange Rates and Indexes	Full Authorization
choppe	▽ System Initialization	Full Authorization
CKutzli	▷ Company Details	Full Authorization
dstrauss	▷ General Settings	Full Authorization
eruppent	Document Numbering	Full Authorization
fvolk	▷ Document Settings	Full Authorization
jthornsb	Print Preferences	Full Authorization
kblust	▷ Opening Balances	Full Authorization
kbrockle	▽ Series	Full Authorization
kschmid	Series Lock	Full Authorization
lradke	Series - Group No. 1	Full Authorization
manager	Series - Group No. 2	Full Authorization
megerer	Series - Group No. 3	Full Authorization
ppietrus	Series - Group No. 4	Full Authorization
rmielke	Series - Group No. 5	Full Authorization
sbugai	Series - Group No. 6	Full Authorization
slanger	Series - Group No. 7	Full Authorization
tlombach	Series - Group No. 8	Full Authorization
ustrobel	Series - Group No. 9	Full Authorization
	Series - Group No. 10	Full Authorization
	▷ Setup	Full Authorization
	▷ Data Import/Export	Full Authorization
	▷ Utilities	Full Authorization

Figure 22-7: Document series authorization

Source: Screenshot

It is necessary to let users create series in each of the groups as soon as no special group management is applied within. The series lock should be available only for the head of accounting so that nobody but him is able to reopen a period and add documents.

22.3 Setting currencies

The first step is to set the document currencies. Choose ADMINISTRATION → SETUP → FINANCIALS → CURRENCIES

Figure 22-8: Document currencies

Source: Screenshot

Setting US-Dollar, Canadian Dollar and EURO is enough for Alfing Corporation. It is also possible to specify the descriptions and hundredth names and other additional settings which are not seen there. The descriptions which are in the Hundredths Name apply especially for the checks.

The next step is to set the system's default for the currencies. The currency settings can be found in ADMINISTRATION→SYSTEM INITIALIZATION → COMPANY DETAILS → INITIALIZATION.

The specified currencies are the local and system currency. Both of them have to be set to US-Dollar. The default account currency has to be set to multi currency.

The setting applied here is necessary for the internal system. It specifies the settings how the system handles the currencies internally. The setting of the local currency must be set to the currency which is reporting currency for the local authorities. This setting cannot be altered as soon as the first transactions took place in the system. The available currencies are the one's which were defined in the previous step.

The system currency is an additional currency which allows managing all reports and documents in local and system currency. This setting applies mainly for companies which are a local subsidiary located in a different country than the mother company.

The default account currency allows managing accounts either only in one or in multi currencies. This is necessary if business partner should be managed in their local currency.

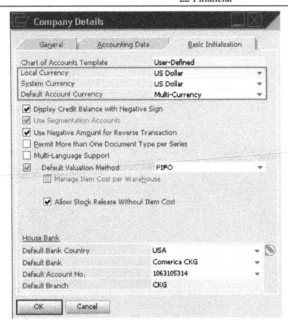

Figure 22-9: Currency setup

Source: Screenshot

After this setting is applied the next step is to set the taxes which are available within the system.

22.4 Tax setup

For the United States applies a three level structure for taxes. The first step is to generate the jurisdictions in the system. The tax setup is made in ADMINSITRATION → SETUP → FINANCIALS → SALES TAX JURISDIRICTIONS TYPES. Alfing Corporation needs State, County and City taxes.

Figure 22-10: Jurisdictions types

Source: Screenshot

The next step is to set all taxes and their corresponding accounts. This is made in ADMINSITRATION → SETUP → FINANCIALS → SALES TAX JURISDIRICTIONS. This opens a window where it is necessary to select the corresponding tax level which should be set.

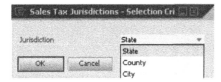

Figure 22-11: Tax setup

Source: Screenshot

After selection of the corresponding tax level a window where the taxes can be defined.

#	Code	Name	Rate	A/R Tax Account	A/P Tax Account	Use Tax Account
44	RI	Rhode Island	7			
45	SC	South Carolina	5			
46	SD	South Dakota	4			
47	TN	Tennessee	7			
48	TX	Texas	6.25			
49	UT	Utah	4.75			
50	VA	Virginia	3.5			
51	VI	Virgin Islands				
52	VT	Vermont	6			
53	WA	Washington	6.5			
54	WI	Wisconsin	5			
55	WV	West Virginia	6			
56	WY	Wyoming	4			
57	ZO	Zero Tax		⇨ 2125-00-00	⇨ 2126-00-00	

Figure 22-12: State taxes

Source: Screenshot

The A/R and A/P Tax account should be set to the corresponding tax accounts in the tax setup. The use tax account is the tax account which is used for other documents which are not invoices.

It is necessary to set the tax accounts from the chart of accounts. Afterwards the tax code that will be used on document level can be created.

This is done in ADMINSITRATION → SETUP → FINANCIALS → SALES TAX CODES

Code	Name				Rate			
MI	Michigan State Tax				6.000			

☐ Freight

#	Type	Code	Name	Tax on Tax	Rate	Effective Rate	A/R Tax Account	A/P Tax Account	Use Tax Ac...
1	Stat ▼	MI	Michiga	▼	6.000	6.000			
2	Stat ▼			▼	0.000	0.000			

Figure 22-13: Tax setup

Source: Screenshot

The Code is a shortcut for calling this tax information in the system. The name is a general description, while the Rate is the percentage amount of tax. Further lines can be used to apply Tax on Tax. The A/R Tax Account, A/P Tax Account and Use Tax Account information is populated from the corresponding field in the previous setup and not adjustable.

The next step specifies the default tax which will be used for all documents. This setting is made in ADMINISTRATION → SYSTEM INITIALIZATION → COMPANY DETAILS → ACCOUNTING.

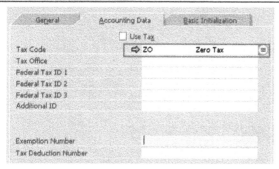

Figure 22-14: Company tax setup

Source: Screenshot

The tax code that is specified here is the default for all documents, neither it is possible to overwrite it on document level. All other settings here have informational character and have to be specified based on its local specifications. The USE TAX setup is a specialty of the US-market.

22.5 Chart of accounts

The next step which has to be done is to create the chart of accounts which need some preliminary settings. As soon as the predefined chart of accounts is not used it gets necessary to set the chart of accounts to user-defined which is done in ADMINISTRATION → SYSTEM INITIALISATION → COMPANY DETAILS → BASIC INITIALISATION.

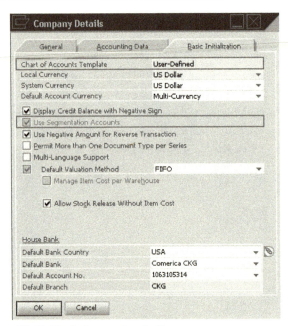

Figure 22-15: Chart of accounts selection

Source: Screenshot

This tells the system that we want to customize the accounting part. The USE SEGMENTATION OF ACCOUNTS setting is a specialty of the American accounting system. It allows make a picture of the hierarchical structure of the companies departments in the accounting. This setting cannot be changed after the first transactions took place. Alfing does not use this setting but can be used in future why it was set. The next step is to create the accounts itself.

To do so, open ADMINISTRATION → SETUP → FINANCIALS → EDIT CHART OF AC-
COUNTS.

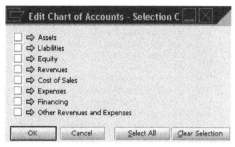

Figure 22-16: Create accounts

Source: Screenshot

Select the group you like to create and proceed. This will open the next window where the accounts are
created.

The numbering system follows this guideline:

1	1510-00-00	=	account number, 4 digits or more
2	1510-00-00	=	account segmentation
3	1510-00-00	=	category as additional divider

These settings are fixed as soon as the first transactions take place. To provide the ability for further
grow it is necessary to calculate enough characters to extend those settings.

It is possible to select the previous created currencies for the accounts and set some properties.

- Account Type: other, sales or expenditure depending on use
- Control Account: this account can be used for reconciliation within the business partner
  master data.
- Cash Account: check this box to define it as monetary account. (Bank, Cash, ...)
- Reval. (Currency): allow to generate conversion differences

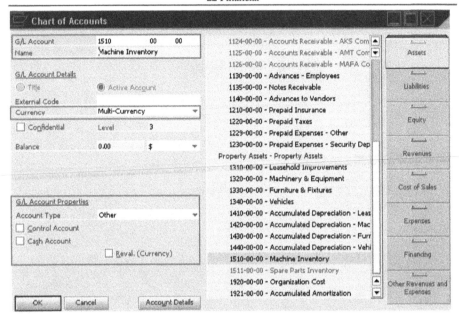

Figure 22-17: Create accounts

Source: Screenshot

A new account is created with in the Toolbar.

The EXTERNAL CODE can be used for additional search functionality in user defined queries. The currency setting should be set to MULTI CURRENCY as soon as it is necessary to work with different currencies. This applies also if a company likes to manage their overbroad business in another currency, for example a special sales account only for overbroad business. The CONFIDENTIAL setting has to be made if the accounts should not be viewable for several users. This needs an additional setup afterwards. The LEVEL specifies the level where the account is sort in. The ACCOUNT TYPE specifies the account as a expense, revenue account or other account. The CONTROL ACCOUNT has to be set if this account should be used to reconcile the business partners with this account. This applies especially for the SALES and COST OF SALES accounts. The CASH ACCOUNT is available in the first three drawers and to define them as a monetary account, for example all the bank accounts must have this setting. The REVAL (CURRENCY) setting is only necessary if the company works with different accounting currencies to generate an automatic conversion difference report. Account details can be specified by clicking on ACCOUNT DETAILS.

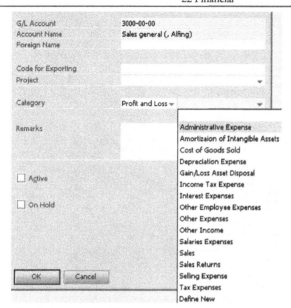

Figure 22-18: Account details

Source: Screenshot

After creation of all general ledger accounts it is necessary to set the defaults for account determination.

In the following step it is necessary to specify the account details.

22.6 G/L Account Determination

Within this part standard accounts for different transactions are specified. Those settings should be made very careful; neither most of them can be changed in the running system. The determination settings can be found in ADMINISTRATION → SETUP → FINANCIALS → G/L ACCOUNT DETERMINATION.

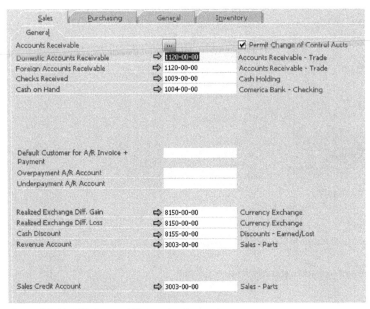

Figure 22-19: G/L Account Determination, sales

Source: Screenshot

The DOMESTIC ACCOUNTS RECEIVABLE and FOREIGN ACCOUNTS RECEIVABLE specify the accounts which are used to collect all customer sales to these accounts. This information is used reflect the totals in the system. The CHECKS RECEIVED and CASH ON HAND accounts are used for all received check and cash payments. The DEFAULT CUSTOMER A/R account can be used for one time sales like storage cleaning to account all this to a specific account. It is not necessary for Alfing Corporation. The OVER and UNDERPAYMENT accounts are the accounts which are necessary if automatic differences should be applied automatic to these accounts. The EXCHANGE DIFFERENCE accounts are the ones were exchange differences are applied automatically. CASH DISCOUNT is the account to collect all gain and loss out of discounts. The REVENUE ACCOUNT is the default where the revenues are posted, for example an A/R Invoice. The SALES CREDIT account applies for a credit memo.

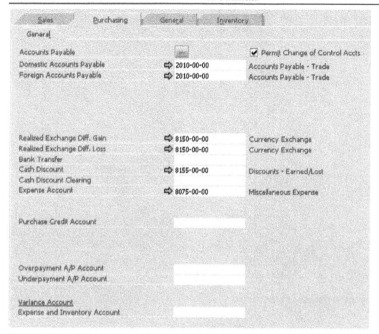

Figure 22-20: Account determination, purchasing

Source: Screenshot

Switching to the PURCHASING tab shows the different setting for the purchasing side of the company. Some of the accounts are the same as described above but there exist also some others. The BANK TRANSFER account specifies the default account which is used for outgoing payments. The only additional specialty is the VARIANCE ACCOUNT which applies for goods returns. All other settings are the opposite ones of the sales side.

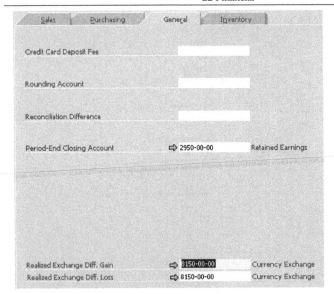

Figure 22-21: Account determination, general

Source: Screenshot

The GENERAL tab specifies some general account like the CREDIT CARD DEPOSIT FEES account which is used to apply credit card fees. The ROUNDING ACCOUNT is the account which applies if rounding differences must be applied due rounding is set in the currencies. RECONICLIATION DIFFERENCE is the account which is used for automatic balance transactions. The PERIOD END CLOSING ACCOUNT is the account where the closing procedure applies to.

Type of Account	Account Code	Account Name	
Inventory Account	⇨ 1511-00-00	Spare Parts Inventory	▲
Cost of Goods Sold Account	⇨ 4013-00-00	Cost of Sales - Parts	▼
Allocation Account	⇨ 2020-00-00	Accrued Payables	
Variance Account			
Price Difference Account	⇨ 4013-00-00	Cost of Sales - Parts	
Negative Inventory Adjustment Acct	⇨ 4013-00-00	Cost of Sales - Parts	
Inventory Offset - Decrease Account	⇨ 4013-00-00	Cost of Sales - Parts	
Inventory Offset - Increase Account	⇨ 4013-00-00	Cost of Sales - Parts	
Sales Returns Account	⇨ 1511-00-00	Spare Parts Inventory	
Exchange Rate Difference Account	⇨ 8150-00-00	Currency Exchange	
Goods Clearing Account	⇨ 2020-00-00	Accrued Payables	
G/L Decrease Account	⇨ 4013-00-00	Cost of Sales - Parts	
G/L Increase Account	⇨ 4013-00-00	Cost of Sales - Parts	
WIP Inventory Account			
WIP Inventory Variance Account			
Expense Clearing Account			

Figure 22-22: Account determination, inventory

Source: Screenshot

In the INVENTORY tab the accounts used for the inventory transactions are set. In detail this is IN-VENTORY ACCOUNT which is the final value of all inventory. The COSTS OF GOODS SOLD is used for the sales of goods. An ALLOCATION ACCOUNT specifies the clearing account which is used as an offsetting account for all goods receipts and credit memos. The VARIANCE ACCOUNT is used only if the valuation method is set to standard which cause the system to apply differences automatically to this account. The NEGATIVE INVETORY ADJUSTMENT ACCOUNT is used when the inventory is negative and the document price differs from the inventory price. INVENTORY OFFSET accounts are used as balancing accounts when the stock value is increased or decreased due to production. The SALES RETURN ACCOUNT is used for goods return while the PURCHASE ACCOUNT is used for goods receipt or A/P invoice. The PURCHASE RETURN ACCOUNT applies for goods return or credit memos. The PURCHASE OFFSET ACCOUNT is used for balancing customer documents. The GOODS CLEARING ACCOUNT is used when purchase documents are closed. The G/L INCREASE and DECREASE accounts are the ones used for increasing or decreasing the stock.

Those settings should be made together with the accounting department. Based on the chart of accounts those settings may vary.

After this step the basic accounting system is set up.

There are some additional settings which have to be determined by personal preferences.

22.7 Accounting with negative signs

This setting determines if balances are show either with or without negative sign. This setting can be found in ADMINSITRATION → SYSTEM INITIALIZATION → COMPANY DETAILS → BASIC INITIALIZATION

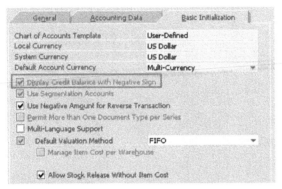

Figure 22-23: Negative sign

Source: Screenshot

Check DISPLAY CREDIT BALANCE WITH NEGATIVE SIGN to show negative amounts with a minus sign.

The setting USE NEGATIVE AMOUNT FOR REVERSE TRANSACTION uses a minus sign in journal entries which are reversed. Otherwise the debit and credit are switched. This depends on company preferences and can be changed every time.

The next step is to set the different cost accounting methods.

23 Cost accounting

This will cover the cost accounting settings for Small Business One. The cost accounting is used to determine the cost of revenues of separated business areas which are distributed over several general ledger accounts. The specific setup for Alfing Corporation determines the technicians as profit centers and the machines as projects. The idea is to have a more transparent cost accounting method which allows separating costs and revenues by their responsible party.

23.1 Setup profit centers

The first step is to declare each profit center in SAP. This is done in FINANCIALS → COST AC-COUNTING → PROFIT CENTERS

Figure 23-1: Defining a profit center

Source: Screenshot

Set a profit center code, name and a sort code.

The profit center code is the one which is called within document level. The sort code can be used for advanced reporting features. It is possible to collect all technicians to one sort code which enables automatic sorting into these categories. The name is a additional identifier which increases the usability and has no further purpose.

Afterwards the distribution rules can be created. This setting can be found in FINANCIALS → COST ACCOUNTING → DISTRIBUTION RUELS

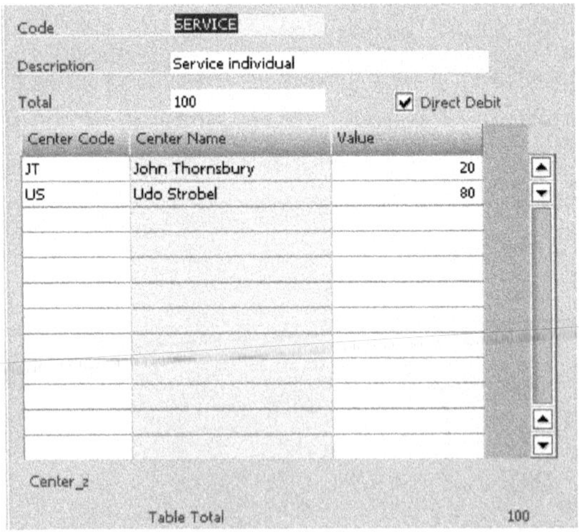

Figure 23-2: Distribution Rules

Source: Screenshot

The distribution rules allow distributing the costs of a profit center to several centers. The code is the name under which this distribution rule appears on document level and is accessible from there. The description is an identifier. The important part is the total which can be set to individual values and represents the reference for the distribution values. For example if we like to distribute an amount into three equal parts it can be set to 90 and each of the values to 30. The table total on the bottom of the page shows always the total which was entered in the total above. If the values don't sum to this total the difference is accounted to center_z which is a generic profit center. The amount accounted to this center can be distributed afterwards to individual centers.

The above given rule distributes the cost that are accounted to service 80/20 between Udo Strobel and John Thornsburry.

23.2 Specification in documents

This information applies basically to incoming and outgoing invoices. Additional specification can be made in the banking module or in journal entries.

During creation of the new document the profit center can be specified.

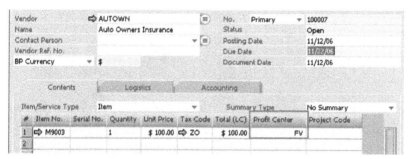

Figure 23-3: A/P Invoice

Source: Screenshot

All line totals with specified profit centers are distributed according to their distribution rule. At this level can the profit centers and the distribution rules accessed. A profit center itself will reflect 100% of the item total while a distribution rule will split the total into its corresponding parts and distribute them onto its included profit centers.

The following chapter provides some information about information retrieval in profit center reports.

23.3 Profit Center report

After distribution of all the amounts to its corresponding profit centers it is possible to access the values from different locations in the system. These locations provide either direct access with SAP's integrated reports or they allow generating additional reports which can be customized into different directions.

The retrieval of profit and loss statements for profit centers can be done in FINANCIALS → COST ACCOUNTING → PROFIT CENTER REPORT.

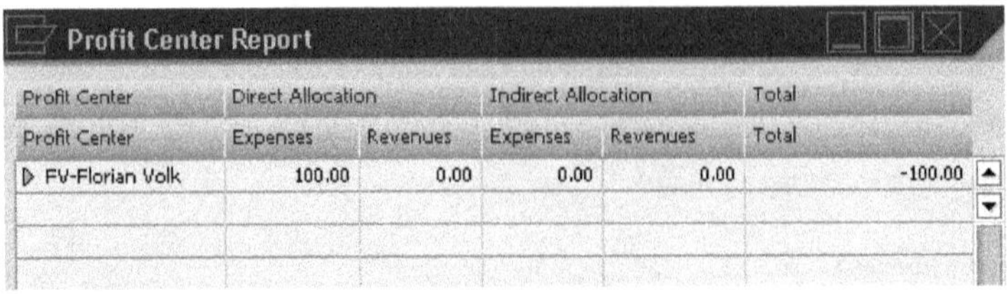

Figure 23-4: Profit Center Report

Source: Screenshot

This report shows the expenses and revenues for each profit center. The total column will show if the profit center made profit or loss. In our case it is a total of -$100.

Another place the information is stored is FINANCIAL → FINANCIAL REPORTS → ACCOUNTING → TRANSACTION JOURNAL REPORT. This shows each individual journal entry and the applied distribution rule. This is more interesting for individual reporting. It is also possible to make adjustments here.

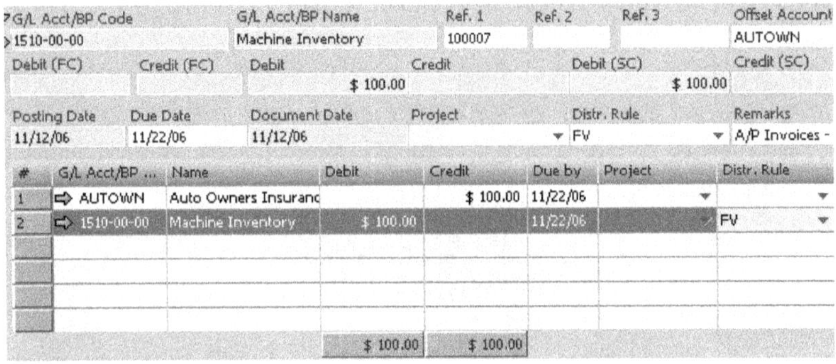

Figure 23-5: Journal entry

Source: Screenshot

The following chapter will show the projects setup.

23.4 Projects

The projects setup is made in ADMINISTRATION → DEFINITIONS → FINANICALS → DEFINE PROJECTS. The screen offers the ability to enter a project and an additional description. We used the customer's line and operation (OP) number for the details.

#	Machine No.	Machine Line and OP
6	21.30084	L01MAFA-21.30066
7	21.30092	MAFA-21.30092
8	21.30104	L01MAFA-21.30104
9	21.30112	21.30112
10	21.30113	L01MAFA-21.30113
11	21.30140	MAFA-21.30140
12	21.30141	MAFA-21.30141
13	2523N00	L01OP30-2523N00
14	2974N00	L01OP20W-2974N00
15	2975N00	L02OP20O-2975N00
16	2976N00	L01OP30W-2976N00
17	2977N00	L02OP30O-2977N00

Figure 23-6: Machine projects

Source: Screenshot

#	Machine No.	Machine Line and OP
132	GMROMU	GM,Romolus
133	GMTONA	GM,Tonawanda
134	MACMEX	Macimex,Saltillo
135	MACTRU	MackTruck,Hagerstown
136	MAHMEX	Mahle,Saltillo
137	METFRE	Metaldyne,Freemont
138	METMEX	Metaldyne,Saltillo
139	METMID	Metaldyne,Middleville
140	METNV	Metaldyne,North Vernon
141	METRID	Metaldyne,Ridgeway
142	THYDAN	Thyssen,Danville
143	THYFOS	Thyssen,Fostoria
144	THYMET	Thyssen,Puebla
145	VW	VW,Puebla

Figure 23-7: Lead projects

Source: Screenshot

The upper figure shows the machine number. The screen beneath shows the lead projects.

After this step the projects are available to be accessed from different locations in Small Business One. The next chapter will show how to assign a project code to a document and how to retrieve the report about a project.

23.5 Projects in documents

This is basis of the daily work for everybody who works with the system. The information that is provided here is the basis for all reports that show the expenses and revenues of a project. The information can be provided on line or on document level. The line level allows using several project codes in one document.

On line level the project code has to be entered into the highlighted field. To enter the code on document level it has to be specified in the accounting tab. This is shown in the figure below.

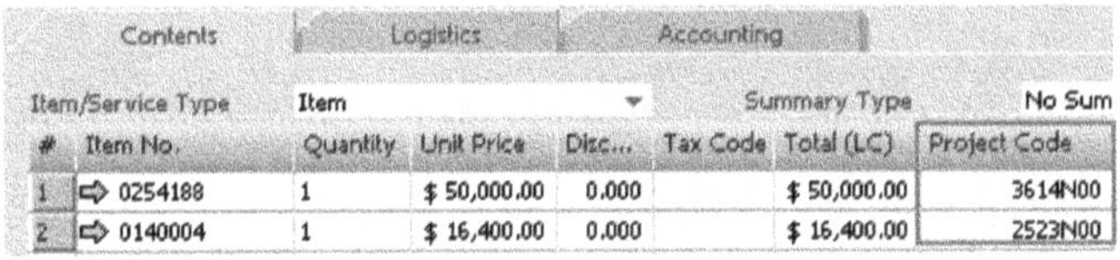

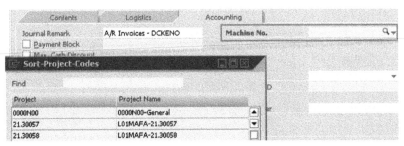

Figure 23-8: Project Code in line item

Source: Screenshot

Figure 23-9: Machine No. in accounting tab

Source: Screenshot

It turned out that the great number of projects made it very difficult to find a specific project. Therefore a small SQL-Query was developed to open new window and find project codes. The query is shown below.

SELECT T0.PrjCode, T0.PrjName FROM OPRJ T0 ORDER BY T0.PrjCode   **Sort 23-1**

Every time a document is added the specified project code has an effect on the accounting. The records will be updated and the reports will reflect this information.

23.6 Project reports

This is the area of main interest due it is the place where the recordings reflect the projects success. A summary of each project can be accessed from FINANCIALS → FINACIAL REPORTS → ACCOUNTING → TRANSACTION REPORT BY PROJECTS.

Trans. No	Project Code	Account Number	Posting Date	Debit	Credit	Total
	▽ 9999N99			$ 0.00	$ 59,792.00	$ -59,792.00
	▷	2010-00-00		$ 0.00	$ 35.00	$ -35.00
	▷	1120-00-00		$ 2,292.00	$ 0.00	$ 2,292.00
	▽	3003-00-00		$ 0.00	$ 51,207.00	$ -51,207.00
⇨ 3		3003-00-00	11/02/06	$ 0.00	$ 1,207.00	$ -1,207.00
⇨ 8		3003-00-00	11/02/06	$ 0.00	$ 50,000.00	$ -50,000.00
	▷	3005-00-00		$ 0.00	$ 85.00	$ -85.00
	▷	3007-00-00		$ 0.00	$ 5,000.00	$ -5,000.00
	▷	8175-00-00		$ 0.00	$ 3,500.00	$ -3,500.00

Figure 23-10: Project Report

Source: Screenshot

This report shows the detailed financial report for the selected project. It is possible to retrieve more detailed information for each project by opening it with the ▷ in front of each line. This allows drilling down up to document level. Another important place where the project information is stored is the journal entries. They can be viewed through FINANCIAL → FINANCIAL REPORTS → ACCOUNTING → TRANSACTION JOURNAL REPORT.

▽ G/L Acct/BP Code		G/L Acct/BP Name		Ref. 1		Ref. 2	Ref. 3	
▷ MAFAL		MAFA-SEE MAFAC		2		Charge Bac	1	
Debit (FC)	Credit (FC)	Debit		Credit		Debit (SC)		
			$ 1,207.00				$ 1,207.00	
Posting Date	Due Date	Document Date		Project		Distr. Rule		
11/02/06	12/04/06	11/02/06		9999N99	▼		▼	

#	G/L Acct/BP ...	Name	Debit	Credit	Due by	Project	
1	⇨ MAFAL	MAFA-SEE MAFAC	$ 1,207.00		12/04/06	9999N99	
2	⇨ 3003-00-00	Sales – Parts		$ 1,207.00	12/04/06	9999N99	▼
			$ 1,207.00	$ 1,207.00			

Figure 23-11: Journal Entry

Source: Screenshot

It is possible to make changes to the project code here at any time.

The creation of customized reports is described in chapters 32 Creating the print layout, 34 SQL, 35 Crystal Reports and 36 XL-Reporter.

After performing those steps the basic cost accounting methods are set and available in the system. The following steps will cover the banking setup and its definitions.

24 Banking

This chapter will cover the banking settings which apply to all incoming and outgoing payments. The topics covered within here will also apply for the sales and purchasing due to its strong connection.

24.1 Payment terms and Installments

The payment terms include the default values for which can be applied on documents and on business partners.

The definition is made in ADMINISTRATION → SETUP → BUSINESS PARTNERS → PAYMENT TERMS

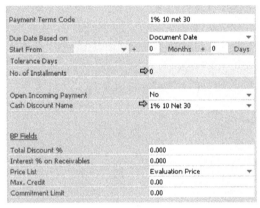

Figure 24-1: Payment Terms

Source: Screenshot

It becomes necessary to define a payment code which will be displayed on the printed document and within the sales and purchasing documents for selection.

It is possible to calculate the due date based either on document or posting date. There exist several other option which allow to manage the behavior of the document management. With the START FROM option it is possible to set new calculation basis, for example to start the calculation always based on the start, end or middle of a month. See examples below for some possibilities that will need these options:

Invoice date	Term	Payment due date	Start	+Months	+Days
May 15	At the end of current month	May 30	Month End	0	0
May 15	At the end of next month	June 30	Month End	1	0
May 15	On 15th on month after next month	July 15	Month Start	1	14
May 15	30 days net	June 15		0	30

Table 24-1: Payment definitions

Source: SAP Online Help

The tolerance days allow setting a range of date in which the documents are included in the payment run.

Creation of the payment terms with discount is done by clicking on CASH DISOCUNT NAME → DEFINE NEW which opens a new window.

Figure 24-2: Payment code

Source: Screenshot

In this case a discount of 1% applies if the invoice is paid within 10 days. It includes the deduction of sales tax, too. Freight won't be deducted.

After confirmation the window will be closed and return to the main screen.

The definition of installments is applied in the same way. Opening ADMINISTRATION → SETUP → BUSINESS PARTNERS → PAYMENT TERMS opens the screen above. Clicking on the arrow ⇨ in front of NO. OF INSTALLMENTS opens a new window.

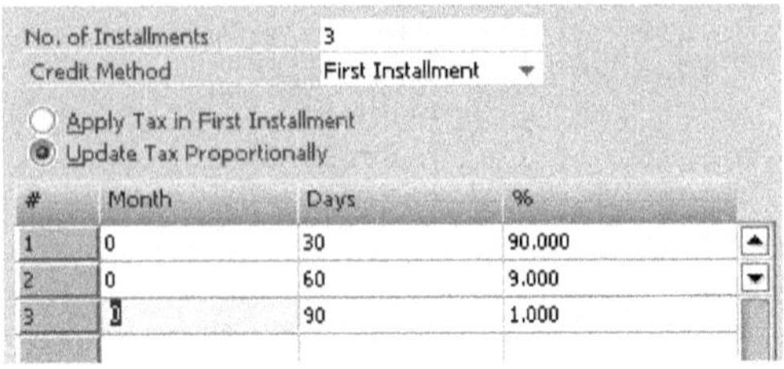

Figure 24-3: Installments

Source: Screenshot

The number of installments provides the staggering of the installments. The example shows a installment where 90% is due after 30 day, another 9% after 60 days and the remaining 1% after 90 days of the invoice date.

Payment terms can be revised any time but removed only if they are not in use by business partners or documents.

24.1.1 Setting default terms

The previously defined payment terms can be used as defaults. This is done in ADMINISTRATION → SYSTEM INITIALIZATION → GENERAL SETTINGS → BUSINESS PARTNER. This allows specifying the default payment terms for customer and vendors.

To set the payment terms as default for one business partner go to BUSINESS PARTNERS → BUSINESS PARTNER MASTER DATA → PAYMENT TERMS. The default applied here is applied for all documents which are created for this business partner.

24.2 Dunning Terms

The dunning terms are the conditions that apply after a customer does not pay his invoices in time. The setup is made in ADMINISTRATION → SETUP → BUSINESS PARTNERS → DUNNING TERMS

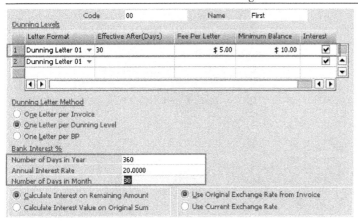

Figure 24-4: Dunning terms

Source: Screenshot

The effective days specify the days after the letter applies. It is possible to define a fee which applies per letter and a minimum balance. All invoices below this amount won't be triggered. As soon as a interest percentage should be applied it is necessary to check the corresponding box and enter the interest rate. The additional setting which has to be applied are the dunning levels which is located in ADMINI-STRATION → SETUP → BUSINESS PARTNERS → DUNNING LEVELS

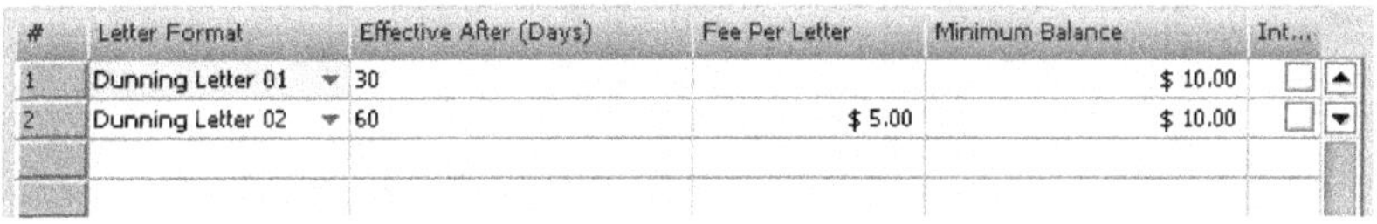

#	Letter Format		Effective After (Days)	Fee Per Letter	Minimum Balance	Int...	
1	Dunning Letter 01	▼	30		$ 10.00	☐	▲
2	Dunning Letter 02	▼	60	$ 5.00	$ 10.00	☐	▼

Figure 24-5: Dunning levels

Source: Screenshot

Here the first letter is without fee, and the second has an applied fee of $5 per each letter. The first applies after 30, the second after 60 days.

The layout of the dunning letter itself is accessible by highlighting each and chose the 📝 icon.

The following chapter covers the setup of payment methods.

24.3 Payment methods

The payment methods specify the different ways a payment can be executed by the company. The methods that are set up here are available within the payment wizard for automatic payments.

The setup can be found in ADMINISTRATION → SETUP → BANKING → PAYMENT METHODS

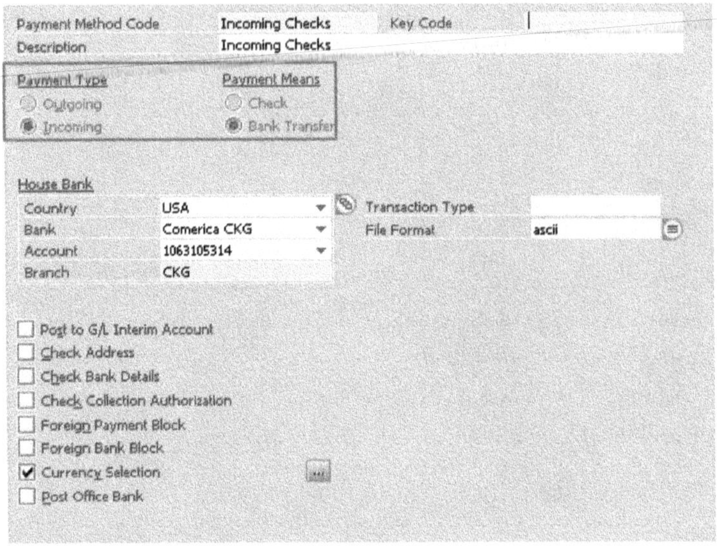

Figure 24-6: Payment methods

Source: Screenshot

The payment methods have to set up for both types' incoming and outgoing payments and for the different payment means, like check or bank transfer.

It is possible to specify the house bank for this payment method and the currencies. For electronic funds transfer the system offers different file formats which has to be adjusted with the bank.

All other settings are additional and can be skipped.

24.4 Payment Run

The payment run setup is necessary to be able to make automatic payments based on their due date. This setting is found in BANKING → PAYMENT SYSTEM → PAYMENT RUN DEFAULTS. To include and exclude specific payments from a default payment run, open the details by clicking ▦ and uncheck the methods. This is used by Alfing Corporation to set payments on hold.

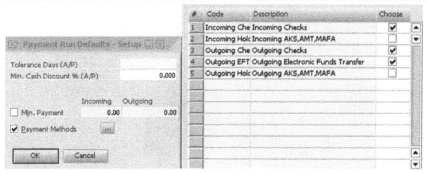

Figure 24-7: Payment run defaults

Source: Screenshot

The tolerance days specified in the defaults set the days which are added to the actual date in comparison with the due date included in the payment run. The minimum cash discount specifies the minimum discount included in the invoices. The minimum incoming and outgoing allows excluding amount from the payment run. For example all invoices below $5 or over $100,000.

24.5 Bank accounts

The bank accounts specified here are the accounts which are used by Alfing Corporation. Go to AD-MINISTRATION → SETUP → BANKING → BANKS which opens a new window.

#	Country Code	Bank Code	Bank Name	SWIFT No.	Post Office	Account No.	Branch	Next Check No.
1	USA	Comerica	Comerica CKG	072000096	☐		CKG	1
2	USA	Comerica MM	Comerica MM	072000096	☐			
3	Germany	LBBW-EUR	LBBW-EUR	SOLA DE St	☐			
4	Germany	LBBW-USD	LBBW-USD	SOLA DE ST	☐			
5	USA ▼				☐			

Figure 24-8: Bank accounts

Source: Screenshot

The banks which are setup here are Alfing Corporation's banks as well as the customer and vendor banks. The information provided in this screen specifies only the general banking information and not the account details.

The next step is to create the banks which are used by Alfing Corporation for their payments. Go to ADMINISTRATION → SETUP → BANKING → HOUSE BANK ACCOUNTS.

#	Bank Code	Country	Branch	Account No.	Next Check No.	G/L Account	G/L Interim Account	Street
1	Comerica	US	CKG		1	⇨ 1004-00-00		▲
2	Comerica MM	US	MM		1	⇨ 1005-00-00		▼
3	LBBW-EUR	DE	Euro		1	⇨ 1007-00-00		
4	LBBW-USD	DE	USD		1	⇨ 1006-00-00		
5								

Figure 24-9: House banks

Source: Screenshot

In this screen the general ledger accounts have to be specified where all the money has to be transferred to. It allows also setting some additional information and the check template which has to be used for each of the banks. The NEXT CHECK NO. specifies the number of the next printed check. This setting should be set only once. Skipping numbers has to be done within the payment system itself by voiding the check. The setting of the G/L INTERIM ACCOUNT is necessary to post the transactions which are executed through the payment run to those temporary accounts. Alfing does not need this setup but it can be used for some special purpose.

The customer and vendor bank accounts are set in the business partner master data. It is possible to set as many accounts as necessary here by clicking on the ▣ button which opens the business partner bank accounts setup.

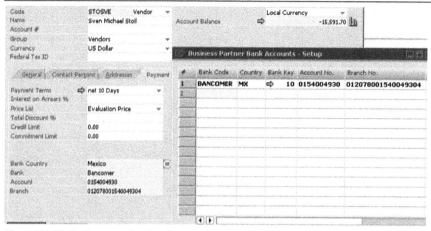

Figure 24-10: Business partner bank accounts

Source: Screenshot

24.6 Credit Cards

This setup is necessary as soon as the company accepts credit cards for incoming payments. This does not apply for Alfing Corporation and can be skipped therefore.

For outgoing payments the only setup that has to be made is a business partner which represents the credit card company.

25 Business Partner setup

Depending on the level of detail it makes sense to apply some of the initial settings which are possible within the business partners. It helps also to set some predefined formats for address and other settings.

25.1 Country setup

This setup covers country specific needs and their appliance in the documents. This feature is accessible through ADMINISTRATION → SETUP → BUSINESS PARTNERS → COUNTRIES.

#	Code	Name	Code for Reports	Address Format	EU	No. of Digi...
192	SB	Solomon Islands	▼	European Standard Address	☐	▲
193	SO	Somalia	▼	European Standard Address	☐	▼
194	ZA	South Africa	▼	South Africa	☐	
195	KR	South Korea	▼	South Korea	☐	
196	ES	Spain	▼ Zip Code Before City Without Country Code	☑	
197	LK	Sri Lanka	▼	European Standard Address	☐	
198	KN	St Kitts & Nevis	▼	European Standard Address	☐	
199	SH	St. Helena	▼	European Standard Address	☐	
200	LC	St. Lucia	▼	European Standard Address	☐	
201	VC	St. Vincent	▼	European Standard Address	☐	
202	PM	St.Pier,Miquel.	▼	European Standard Address	☐	
203	SD	Sudan	▼	European Standard Address	☐	▲
204	SR	Suriname	▼	European Standard Address	☐	▼

Figure 25-1: Country setup

Source: Screenshot

It is possible to specify some codes and standards like the number of tax codes. The checkbox EU should be set as soon as the business partner is located within the European Union. This ensures that the correct address format and tax setting is applied.

The next step is to set the address behavior which can be found in ADMINISTRATION → SETUP → BUSINESS PARTNERS → ADDRESS FORMATS.

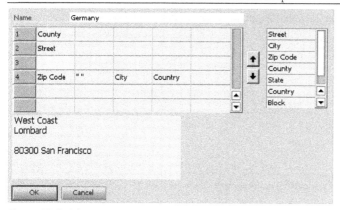

Figure 25-2: Adress Format

Source: Screenshot

Every necessary field can be moved from the right side into the address area. This address format is applied by selecting the corresponding country in BUSINESS PARTNERS → BUSINESS PARTNER MASTER DATA → ADRESSES

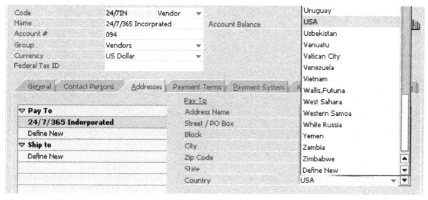

Figure 25-3: Business partner master data

Source: Screenshot

Generally splits SAP into two different addresses which are the ship-to and pay-to address. Both of them have to be specified to have a working setup, even if they are the same.

25.2 Customer/Vendor Groups

Grouping the customers and vendors in several groups allows separating them in reporting and other functions. The setup of the groups can be done in ADMINISTRATION → SETUP → BUSINESS PARTNERS → CUSTOMER GROUPS or VENDOR GROUPS

#	Group Name
1	Customers
2	Distributor
3	Automotive
4	Other
5	Aerospace
6	Heavy Truck
7	Internal
8	Vendor
9	Contacts

Figure 25-4: Group setup

Source: Screenshot

This setup can be different if it is either a customer or a vendor group.

25.3 Customer/ Vendor properties

The business partner properties allow additional separation within and/or without the group level. It can be accessed through ADMINISTRATION → SETUP → BUSINESS PARTNERS → PROPER-TIES. The settings are available from within the business partner master data.

#	Property Name
4	Product Line-Mafa
5	Product Line-AMT
6	Product Line-AKS
7	Product Line-Other
8	Equipment-MC
9	Equipment-Transfer/Rotary
10	Equipment-Automation
11	Equipment-Assembly
12	Equipment-Heat Treat
13	Part Type-Rod

Figure 25-5: Properties setup

Source: Screenshot

Those properties are available in the business partners which allow setting their interest levels in different products.

26 Inventory

This chapter covers the inventory setups which are necessary to have a working inventory and additional settings which simplify the management of items.

26.1 Set the stock valuation method

The stock valuation method is set in AMDINISTRATION → SYSTEM INITIZALIZATION → GENERAL SETTINGS → BASIC INITIALIZATION.

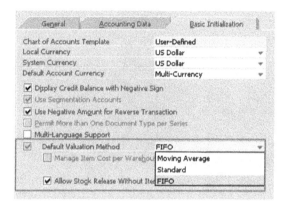

Figure 26-1: Default valuation method

Source: Screenshot

For Alfing Corporation it had to be set to FIFO which means the first part that comes in is the first on that goes out. This is especially related to the monetary side. It is not specifically fixed to the physical part itself.

When using the FIFO method for valuation allowing stock release without item cost is mandatory. As it could happen in some cases that a item is delivered without cost we set the option to allow this. Otherwise no delivery or A/R invoice could be made.

26.2 Release of items

Small Business One has several options to allow a negative inventory. Usually this should only happen intentionally in some special cases. For example in a production environment where the shipping department ships the parts directly out of the manufacturing and accounts them afterwards.

The setup could be made in different ways:

- Without warning: Only if no perpetual inventory is used. It's also impossible to keep track of the minimum quantity level.

- Warning only: Warning when the quantity drops below minimum level. It is possible to override the warning.

- Block release: It is not possible to release items when the minimum quantity drops below minimum level.

- Block negative inventory: Negative inventory is prevented.

For Alfing Corporation warning only was the right decision because it could happen in some special cases that a item is delivered directly from the vendor to the customer without going through inventory.

This setting is made in ADMINISTRATION → SYSTEM INITIALIZATION → DOCUMENT SETTINGS → GENERAL

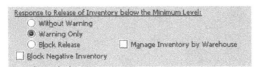

Figure 26-2: Release method

Source: Screenshot

26.3 Warehouses

SAP makes no difference between standard and consignment warehouses. They are both setup in ADMINISTRATION → SETUP → INVENTORY → WAREHOUSES.

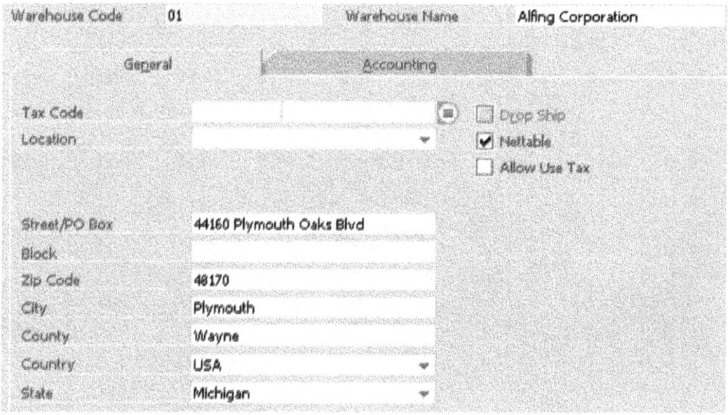

Figure 26-3: Warehouse setup

Source: Screenshot

NETTABLE includes the warehouse settings into the production module of SAP which has direct influence to the production planning and forecast functions. The ALLOW USE TAX button is necessary if the warehouse has to apply to taxes.

For Alfing Corporation a setup of three warehouses became necessary:

- Alfing Corporation
- Metaldyne, North Vernon
- Mahle, Mexico

Each of the warehouses represents a different storage location. The possibility to assign different tax options allow to work with warehouses overbroad and within the country.

The general applies some basic settings for the warehouse. The next step is to define the accounts on the accounting tab.

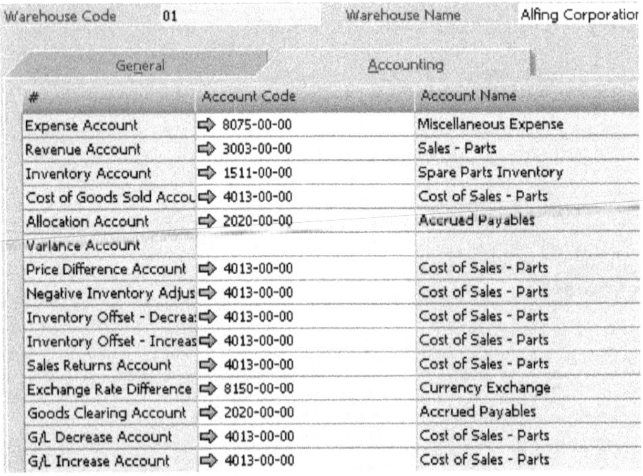

Warehouse Code 01 | Warehouse Name Alfing Corporatio

General | Accounting

#	Account Code	Account Name
Expense Account	8075-00-00	Miscellaneous Expense
Revenue Account	3003-00-00	Sales - Parts
Inventory Account	1511-00-00	Spare Parts Inventory
Cost of Goods Sold Accou	4013-00-00	Cost of Sales - Parts
Allocation Account	2020-00-00	Accrued Payables
Variance Account		
Price Difference Account	4013-00-00	Cost of Sales - Parts
Negative Inventory Adjus	4013-00-00	Cost of Sales - Parts
Inventory Offset - Decrea	4013-00-00	Cost of Sales - Parts
Inventory Offset - Increas	4013-00-00	Cost of Sales - Parts
Sales Returns Account	4013-00-00	Cost of Sales - Parts
Exchange Rate Difference	8150-00-00	Currency Exchange
Goods Clearing Account	2020-00-00	Accrued Payables
G/L Decrease Account	4013-00-00	Cost of Sales - Parts
G/L Increase Account	4013-00-00	Cost of Sales - Parts

Figure 26-4: Warehouse setup, accounting

Source: Screenshot

26.3.1 Account explanation

The next list explains the used accounts and when they are affected.

- Expense Account   expense account for purchasing documents used in non-continuous or non inventory items. It is a profit & loss account.
- Revenue Account   default revenue account for sales documents. It is a profit & loss account.
- Stock account   is the balance sheet account for posting the revaluation method. The selection of the stock revaluation method has a direct influence to the amount calculated.
- Cost of Goods Sold   is the default for recording the costs of goods sold.
- Allocation Account   used to accrue the cost of a purchase when the goods receipt is posted. This account is cleared when the corresponding purchase invoice is receipt.
- Variance Account   account used to record price differences when the standard pricing system is used.
- Price difference account   price difference account used in purchasing documents
- Stock Offset – Decrease   used in stock transactions when the stock is decreased through a goods issue
- Stock Offset – Increase   used in stock transactions when stock is increased through goods receipt.
- Sales Returns   is an alternative stock account for valuing returned stock in a continuous stock system.

The account settings should be made by an experienced accountant or a certified public accountant. Corrections are possible, but if a lot of transactions took place this can be very hard.

The next chapter will go down one level and show the group definitions with the corresponding setup.

26.4 Item group

The item group contains of a large number of items that have matching inventory accounts in the general ledger. The settings for the item groups are done in ADMINISTRATION → SETUP → INVENTORY → ITEM GROUPS. This will open a new window that shows a general and accounting tab.

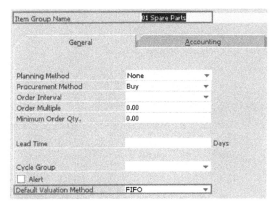

Figure 26-5: Item group general

Source: Screenshot

It is important to provide a new group name. We used a number in front of each name which sorts the group name in the inventory. It is also possible to change the default valuation method to one of the discussed methods. See.

#	Account Code	Account Name
Expense Account	⇨ 8075-00-00	Miscellaneous Expense
Revenue Account	⇨ 3003-00-00	Sales - Parts
Inventory Account	⇨ 1511-00-00	Spare Parts Inventory
Cost of Goods Sold Accou	⇨ 4013-00-00	Cost of Sales - Parts
Allocation Account	⇨ 2020-00-00	Accrued Payables
Variance Account		
Price Difference Account	⇨ 4013-00-00	Cost of Sales - Parts
Negative Inventory Adjus	⇨ 4013-00-00	Cost of Sales - Parts
Inventory Offset - Decrea	⇨ 4013-00-00	Cost of Sales - Parts
Inventory Offset - Increas	⇨ 4013-00-00	Cost of Sales - Parts
Sales Returns Account	⇨ 4013-00-00	Cost of Sales - Parts
Exchange Rate Difference	⇨ 8150-00-00	Currency Exchange
Goods Clearing Account	⇨ 2020-00-00	Accrued Payables
G/L Decrease Account	⇨ 4013-00-00	Cost of Sales - Parts
G/L Increase Account	⇨ 4013-00-00	Cost of Sales - Parts

Figure 26-6: Item group accounting

Source: Screenshot

This is the most important tab of the group setup. All accounts that have to reflect transactions of this group have to have setup here. See 26.3.1 Account for explanations. This setup can be changed every time, regardless of past transactions.

26.5 Item level

With all of the previous settings the definitions and general ledger accounts for a warehouse and/or item group is defined.

All those setting can be changed on item level which is done in INVENTORY → ITEM MASTER DATA → INVENTORY DATA

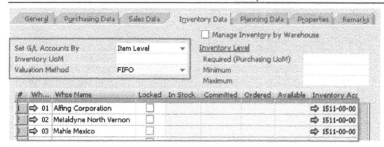

Figure 26-7: Item level

Source:

This configuration method allows changing the stock value management method and/or the inventory accounts for single items. This allows keeping items that effect different general ledger accounts in the same group. This can be helpful for exceptions or if the group levels don't match into the general ledger accounts.

26.6 Item properties

26.6.1 Measuring Units

The measuring units are defined in ADMINISTRATION → SETUP → INVENTORY → LENGTH AND WIDTH.

#	Code	Unit Name	Volume Code	Length (mm)
1	'	Foot	cf	304.8
2	"	Inch	ci	25.4
3	cm	Centimeter	cc	10
4	dm	Decimeter	cdm	100
5	m	Meter	cm	1,000
6	mm	Millimeter	cmm	1

Figure 26-8: Length and width

Source: Screenshot

The units defined here are only for measuring the width and specify their dimensions and relations.

The weight units are set in ADMINISTRATION → SETUP → INVENTORY → WEIGTH

#	Code	Unit Name	Weight (mg)
1	g	Gram	1,000
2	kg	Kilogram	1,000,000
3	Lb	Pound	453,592.4
4	mg	Milligram	1
5	Oz	Ounce	28,300

Figure 26-9: Weight

Source: Screenshot

The default values for weight and length units can be defined within ADMINISTRATION → SYS-TEM INITIALIZATION → GENERAL SETTINGS → DISPLAY

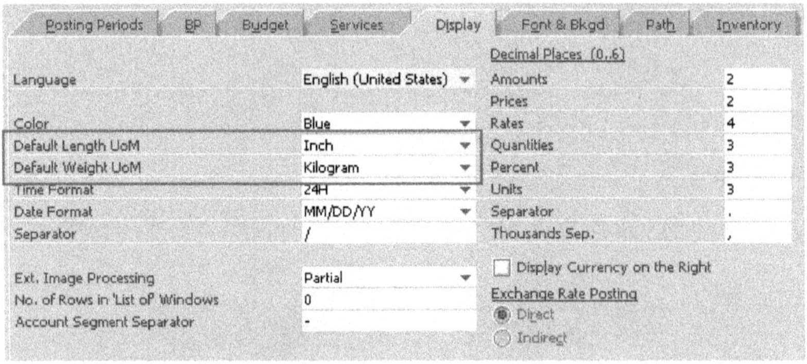

Figure 26-10: Default measuring

Source: Screenshot

26.6.2 Setup manufacturers

To setup different manufacturers got to Administration → Setup → Manufactures and define the different manufactures. All of them are available in the item master data and can be assigned to specific parts. It is also possible to assign the manufacturers or the vendor's part number for easier reference.

Figure 26-11: Manufacturers setup

Source: Screenshot

Alfing Corporation set only some basis manufacturer.

26.6.3 Setup shipping types

This setting defines the shipping types that are available to use in shipping definitions in the documents. The shipping types have mainly informational character and can be printed to help the shipping department to choose the correct shipping method for a customer. It can also be used to be printed on purchasing documents as a preferred shipment type for deliveries.

Go to SETUP → INVENTORY → SHIPPING TYPES to define the different shipping types.

Figure 26-12: Shipping Types

Source: Screenshot

The websites are for tracking packages as soon as they are delivered to the shipper.

26.6.4 Defining packing types

This defines the packing types that are available to ship goods. Go to ADMINISTRATION → SETUP → INVENTORY → PACKAGE TYPES.

Figure 26-13: Package types

Source: Screenshot

Those are the package types that are available to during the pack process in the shipping form. Depending on the kind of business the shipping types can very important to calculate several things like the weight of the shipment and others. For Alfing Corporation it is only as an informational source.

26.6.5 Define shipping types

The definition of shipping types can be used to set preferred shipping types for specific items. Those settings apply to the shipping documents which are printed in the shipping department.

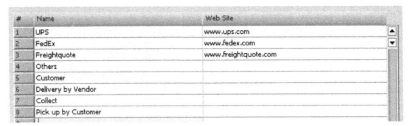

Figure 26-14: Shipping types

Source: Screenshot

The package types are for the shipping department. As soon as the documents are printed out there the shipping can be applied in the specified way.

26.7 Serial numbers

The serial number management consists out of several different setups. The first setting which has to be made is to tell the system that serial numbers are used and which management method should apply to the serial number management.

The initial setting which has to be made is located in ADMINISTRATION → SYSTEM INITIALIZATION → GENERAL SETTINGS → INVENTORY.

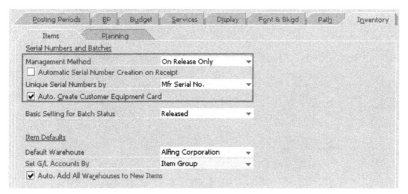

Figure 26-15: Serial number

Source: Screenshot

For the described serial number management within Alfing Corporation it is necessary to set the above keys.

Unique serial numbers specify that each serial number can be applied only once. Duplicates are not allowed. The setting ON RELEASE ONLY specifies that the serial number has to be assigned only on release and not during transactions within the company, like from one warehouse to another. AUTO CREATE CUSTOMER EQUIPMENT CARD applies each shipped item automatically to the customer equipment card.

Whenever a new item is created which should be managed by serial number it needs to have some special settings which can be seen below. A new item is created in INVENTORY → ITEM MASTER DATA → CTRL+A

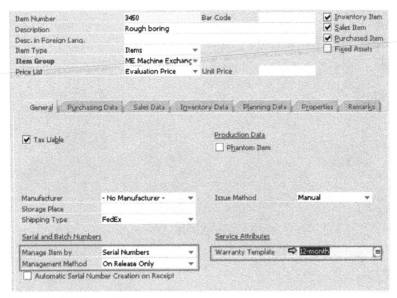

Figure 26-16: Item creation

Source: Screenshot

It is also possible to assign the warranty template which will result into automatic creation of a warranty period as soon as the item is shipped.

To generate a new serial number the item must be in the inventory. This is a result of any goods receipt procedure. To generate a new serial number go to INVENTORY → ITEM MANAGEMENT → SERIAL NUMBER MANAGEMENT

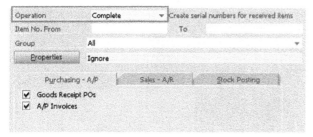

Figure 26-17: Serial number generation

Source: Screenshot

It is important to select COMPLETE for the initial generation. For all other possibilities the operation UPDATE is the correct one. Running the report lists all items which need a serial number. New numbers are generated by clicking ⟨ Automatic Creation... ⟩ and specify the details.

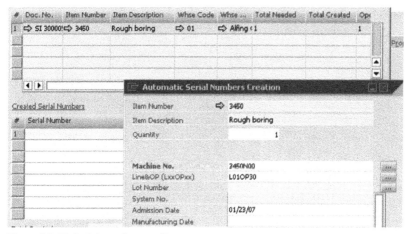

Figure 26-18: Serial number creation

Source: Screenshot

The automatic creation allows also defining rules if many serial numbers have to be created.

Every time a new part is shipped it must have an assigned serial number.

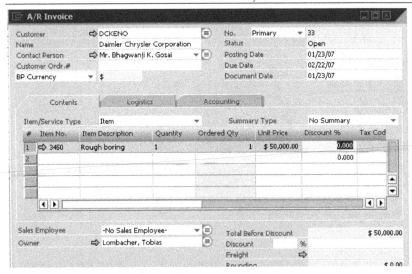

Figure 26-19: Serial number item in documents

Source: Screenshot

The created serial number is assigned with a RIGHT MOUSE CLICK and SERIAL NUMBERS.

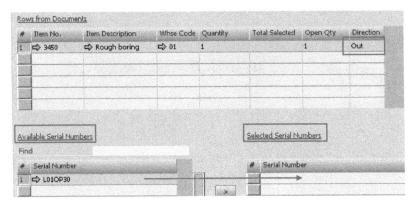

Figure 26-20: Assign serial number

Source: Screenshot

The number has to be moved from available to select which moves the serial number.

After the document is added the serial number is moved to the customer and a customer equipment card created. As soon as the item has an assigned warranty template the warranty is transferred period is also started.

26.8 Warranty templates

Creating the warranty templates is necessary to start warranty periods and having them assigned to serial number items.

The creation of warranty templates is done in ADMINISTRATION → SETUP → INVENTORY → CONTRACT TEMPLATES. This opens the following screen where it is important to set the contract type related to the serial number and the renewal period to three months. This sets a reminder which shows up three months before the warranty is expired.

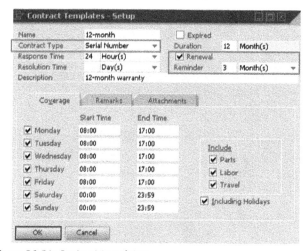

Figure 26-21: Contract templates

Source: Screenshot

The coverage setting is necessary for calculation of response and resolution time.

26.9 Defining inventory cycles

The inventory cycles define how often the inventory has to be physically counted. This setting has to be made if a permanent inventory counting should be applied.

The first thing is to set the inventory counting cycle up. This is done in ADMINSITRATION → SETUP → INVENTORY → INVENTORY CYCLES

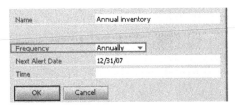

Figure 26-22: Inventory cycles

Source: Screenshot

This specifies the inventory cycle itself. The next step is to assign the cycle to specific item groups which is done in ADMINSITRATION → SETUP → INVENTORY → ITEM GROUPS

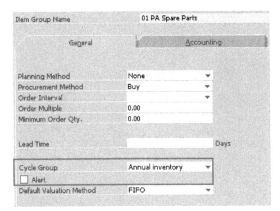

Figure 26-23: Assign cycle count

Source: Screenshot

The alert has to be set if the system should show a reminder. This is especially helpful if the inventory periods are very short ranged.

26.10   Importing the item master data

The item master data with its corresponding numbering systems had to be imported into the system. The information source was data provided by the German mother companies and it was imported into SAP by using the Data Transfer Workbench.

The data provided by the German companies contained all detailed information about the complete assembly and subassembly structure. This made it first necessary to clean up this information and import the cleaned up data. The import itself is a more complicated procedure why a more detailed description is provided below.

26.10.1 Preparation of the Excel data

To avoid a manual data input for each item we requested the data from our German holding companies. Alfing Kessler Sondermaschinen uses PENTA as their part management software. They could export the into an EXCEL format. Due to the reason the list included the complete assembly and sub-assemblies many parts where several times listed in this data source. Because it was not requested to have this information in the database it had to be cleaned up. The reason that drove this decision was that no need of a complete assembly structure can be seen for Alfing Corporation. The other reason was to keep the database as small as possible due to performance reasons.

	A	B	C	D	E	F	G	H	I
1	Material number	Machine Number	Base Unit of Measure		Description Foreign Language	Manufacturer	Item Name	Machine Number	Material number
2	0672677	0016Y00	PC	F	SCHNEIDPLATTE CCGT060204	CERAMTEC	CUTTIN PLATE CCGT060204 -SD-SC7015 SPK.NO 46.58	0016Y00	0672677
3	0674892	0016Y00	PC	F	SCHNEIDPLATTE CCMT 060204-FJ	CERAMTEC	CUTTING PLATE CCMT 060204-FJ SC40 SPK-NO 46.58.5	0016Y00	0674892
4	0675257	0016Y00	PC	F	SCHNEIDPLATTE SCMT 09T308-FJ	CERAMTEC	CUTTING PLATE SCMT09T308-FJ -SC40 SPK.NO 461551	0016Y00	0675257
5	0620375	0016Y00	PC	F	GEWINDEBOHRER M8X1-6HX110	BASS	TAP	0016Y00	0620375
6	0621544	0016Y00	PC	F	STIRNSENKER 22/16X75	GUEHRING	SPOT FACER	0016Y00	0621544
7	0621549	0016Y00	PC	F	SCHEIBENFRAESER		SIDE MILLING CUTTER	0016Y00	0621549
8	0621550	0016Y00	PC	F	SCHEIBENFRAESER		SIDE MILLING CUTTER		SIDE MILLING CUTTER
9	0621552	0016Y00	PC	F	STUFENBOHRER 9,3/12/14X88 I.K.	G.WIRTH	STEP DRILL		STEP DRILL
10	0621556	0016Y00	PC	F	SPIRALBOHRER 8/12X110 I.K.	G.WIRTH	TWIST DRILL		TWIST DRILL
11	0624127	0016Y00	PC	F	SCHNEIDPLATTE SCMT 09T308-FJ	CERAMTEC	CUTTING PLATE SCMT 09T308-FJ -SC7015 MAKE CERAMTEC		CUTTING PLATE SCMT 09T308-FJ -SC7015 MAKE
12	0624371	0016Y00	PC	F	SCHNEIDPLATTE TNMM 160408-PR-	SANDVIK	CUTTING PLATE		CUTTING PLATE
13	0624372	0016Y00	PC	F	SCHNEIDPLATTE TCMT 090208-UF-	SANDVIK	CUTTING PLATE		CUTTING PLATE
14	0082786	0812N00	PC	F	ZYLINDERSTIFT ISO 8736		PARALLEL PIN DIN 7979-D 8X32-ST		PARALLEL PIN DIN 7979-D 8X32-ST
15	0082790	0812N00	PC	F	ZYLINDERSTIFT ISO 8736		PARALLEL PIN DIN 7979-D 8X50-ST		PARALLEL PIN DIN 7979-D 8X50-ST
16	0156095	0812N00	PC	F	DRUCKSTUECK FEDERND	NORELEM	THRUST PIECE	03040-10	THRUST PIECE

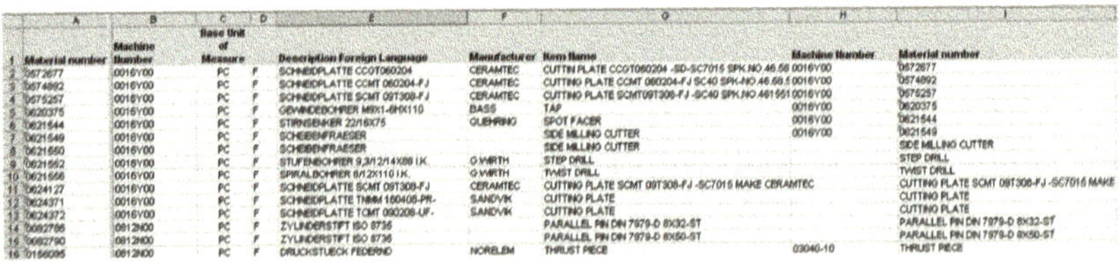

Figure 26-24: Source data columns A-I

Source: Screenshot

	A	H	I	J	K	L	M	N
1	Material number	Machine Number	Material number	Base Unit of Measure		Description Foreign Language	Manufacturer	Item Name
2	0672677	0016Y00	0672677	PC	F	SCHNEIDPLAT'	CERAMTEC	CUTTIN PLATE CCGT060204 -SD-SC7015 SPK.NO 46.58.004.01.9 MAKE CE
3	0674892	0016Y00	0674892	PC	F	SCHNEIDPLAT'	CERAMTEC	CUTTING PLATE CCMT 060204-FJ SC40 SPK-NO 46.58.546.01 4 MAKE CER
4	0675257	0016Y00	0675257	PC	F	SCHNEIDPLAT'	CERAMTEC	CUTTING PLATE SCMT09T308-FJ -SC40 SPK.NO 4615518.014 MAKE CERA
5	0620375	0016Y00	0620375	PC	F	GEWINDEBOHF	BASS	TAP
6	0621544	0016Y00	0621544	PC	F	STIRNSENKER	GUEHRING	SPOT FACER
7	0621549	0016Y00	0621549	PC	F	SCHEIBENFRAESER		SIDE MILLING CUTTER
8	0621550		SIDE MILLING CUTTER	SCHEIBENFRAESER	DURCHM.26/10X3,805		AKS	
9	0621552		STEP DRILL	STUFENBOHRER 9,3/12/14X8	ZNG.NR.1-2005-3		AKS	
10	0621556		TWIST DRILL	SPIRALBOHRER 8/12X110 I.K	ZNG.NR.1-2004-3		AKS	
11	0624127	MTEC	CUTTING PLATE SCMT 09T308-FJ -SC7015 MAKE	SCHNEIDPLATTE SCMT 09T308-FJ			AKS	
12	0624371		CUTTING PLATE	SCHNEIDPLATTE TNMM 1604(	GC4025		AKS	
13	0624372		CUTTING PLATE	SCHNEIDPLATTE TCMT 09020	GC4025		AKS	
14	0082786		PARALLEL PIN DIN 7979-D 8X32-ST	ZYLINDERSTIFT ISO 8736	8X32-A-ST		AKS	
15	0082790		PARALLEL PIN DIN 7979-D 8X50-ST	ZYLINDERSTIFT ISO 8736	8X50-A-ST		AKS	
16	0156095	03040-10	THRUST PIECE	DRUCKSTUECK FEDERND	BEST.NR.03040-10		AKS	

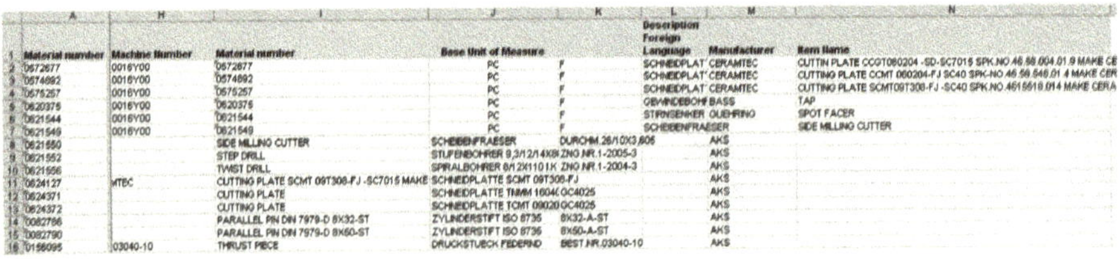

Figure 26-25: Source data columns H-N

Source: Screenshot

Some of the data had been exported into false columns as it is shown below.

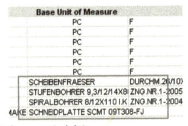

	Base Unit of Measure	
	PC	F
	PC	F
	PC	F
	PC	F
	PC	F
	PC	F
	SCHEIBENFRAESER	DURCHM.26/10
	STUFENBOHRER 9,3/12/14X8	ZNG.NR.1-2005
	SPIRALBOHRER 8/12X110 I.K	ZNG.NR.1-2004
AKE	SCHNEIDPLATTE SCMT 09T308-FJ	

Figure 26-26: False exported data

Source: Screenshot

Those false data had to be cleaned up manually before the import process could be continued. There was no way to automate the procedure; neither could the German companies export the data into another way.

26.10.2 Elimination of special characters

Another handicap that was discovered was the system its inability to handle special characters. –This made it necessary to replace all of them with their corresponding replacement characters.

Original character	Replacement character
Ö, ö	Oe, oe
Ü, ü	Ue, ue
Ä, ä	Ae, ae
ß	ss

Table 26-1: Replacement characters

Source: Self

Also all commas had to be replaced by a replacement character. This is because the export will be done as a Comma Separated Value file. We used the dash (-) as a separator. Alternatively the file could be exported with a semicolon as separator. Then no comma has to be replaced. This depends on personal preferences and the companies preferences in the imported data.

26.10.3 Removal of duplicates

As told the spare parts where provided in an assembly and subassembly structure. To avoid duplicates within the database the data had to be cleaned. To do this manually would have taken to much time and failure sensitive. Therefore an EXCEL-macro was written to do this job.

To use this macro first all item numbers had to be converted from character into number format. Afterwards all the items where sorted ascending by their item number. In the next step each item number was compared with the item number in the next line. If the number was the same the line was removed.

```
Sub Cleanup()
        ActiveCell.SpecialCells(xlLastCell).Select
        Range("I65535").Select
        ActiveCell.FormulaR1C1 = "1"
        Range("B2:B64460").Select
        ActiveWorkbook.Names.Add Name:="AREA", RefersToR1C1:= _
        "=ArtikelAC!R2C2:R64460C2"
        ActiveCell.SpecialCells(xlLastCell).Select
        Range("I65535").Select
        Selection.Copy
        Application.Goto Reference:="AREA"
        Selection.PasteSpecial Paste:=xlPasteAll, Operation:=xlMultiply, _
        SkipBlanks:=False, Transpose:=False
        Application.CutCopyMode = False
        Selection.NumberFormat = "0000000"
        ActiveCell.SpecialCells(xlLastCell).Select
        Range("I65535").Select
        Selection.ClearContents
        Cells.Select
        Selection.Sort Key1:=Range("B2"), Order1:=xlAscending,
        Header:=xlYes, _
        OrderCustom:=1, MatchCase:=False, Orientation:=xlTopToBottom, _
        DataOption1:=xlSortNormal
        'remove duplicates
        Range("B1").Select
        Do Until ActiveCell.Value = ""
        If ActiveCell.Value = ActiveCell.Offset(1, 0).Value Then
        ActiveCell.EntireRow.Delete
        Else
        ActiveCell.Offset(1, 0).Select
        End If
        Loop

End Sub
```

Figure 26-27: Macro for item cleanup

Source: Self

26.10.4 Unite the remarks

The remarks within Small Business One can only be stored in one single remarks field. The exported data from AKS offers different remarks fields. This information had to be united into one cell to import it into Small Business One. The way to do this was the next formula:

=F1&" "&G1&" "&H1   **Unite Formula 26-1**

The space between the quotation marks ensures that the contents of each cell are separated by a space between them.

26.10.5 Data Transfer Workbench

To import the data into Small Business One it had to be provided in a special format. This format has about 190 different columns that could provide information to the SQL Database. The problem was that the data had to have those 190 columns even if most of them are left blank and won't be imported.

Without those columns the import tool was not able to deal with the information. The problem is know by SAP and will be revised in further versions.

The column headers that where specified before it worked are shown below.

No.	Field name	No.	Field name
1	RecordKey	41	ManageBatchNumbers
2	ItemCode	42	ManageSerialNumbers
3	ApTaxCode	43	ManageSerialNumbersOnReleaseOnly
4	ArTaxCode	44	ManageStockByWarehouse
5	AssetItem	45	Manufacturer
6	BarCode	46	MaxInventory
7	BaseUnitName	47	MinInventory
8	CommissionGroup	48	MinOrderQuantity
9	CommissionPercent	49	MovingAveragePrice
10	CommissionSum	50	OrderIntervals
11	CostAccountingMethod	51	OrderMultiple
12	CustomsGroupCode	52	Picture
13	DataExportCode	53	PlanningSystem
14	DefaultWarehouse	54	ProcurementMethod
15	DesiredInventory	55	Properties1
16	ECExpensesAccount	56	Properties10
17	ECRevenuesAccount	57	Properties11
18	ExemptIncomeAccount	58	Properties12
19	ExpanseAccount	59	Properties13
20	ForceSelectionOfSerialNumber	60	Properties14
21	ForeignExpensesAccount	61	Properties15
22	ForeignName	62	Properties16
23	ForeignRevenuesAccount	63	Properties17
24	Frozen	64	Properties18
25	FrozenFrom	65	Properties19
26	FrozenRemarks	66	Properties2
27	FrozenTo	67	Properties20
28	GLMethod	68	Properties21
29	IncomeAccount	69	Properties22
30	IndirectTax	70	Properties23
31	InventoryItem	71	Properties24
32	InventoryUOM	72	Properties25
33	IsPhantom	73	Properties26
34	IssueMethod	74	Properties27
35	ItemCountryOrg	75	Properties28
36	ItemName	76	Properties29
37	ItemType	77	Properties3
38	ItemsGroupCode	78	Properties30
39	LeadTime	79	Properties31
40	Mainsupplier	80	Properties32

Figure 26-28: DTW Specification part 1

Source: SAP Data Transfer Workbench

No.	Field name	No.	Field name
81	Properties33	121	PurchaseFactor3
82	Properties34	122	PurchaseFactor4
83	Properties35	123	PurchaseHeightUnit
84	Properties36	124	PurchaseHeightUnit1
85	Properties37	125	PurchaseItem
86	Properties38	126	PurchaseItemsPerUnit
87	Properties39	127	PurchaseLengthUnit
88	Properties4	128	PurchaseLengthUnit1
89	Properties40	129	PurchasePackagingUnit
90	Properties41	130	PurchaseQtyPerPackUnit
91	Properties42	131	PurchaseUnit
92	Properties43	132	PurchaseUnitHeight
93	Properties44	133	PurchaseUnitHeight1
94	Properties45	134	PurchaseUnitLength
95	Properties46	135	PurchaseUnitLength1
96	Properties47	136	PurchaseUnitVolume
97	Properties48	137	PurchaseUnitWeight
98	Properties49	138	PurchaseUnitWeight1
99	Properties5	139	PurchaseUnitWidth
100	Properties50	140	PurchaseUnitWidth1
101	Properties51	141	PurchaseVATGroup
102	Properties52	142	PurchaseVolumeUnit
103	Properties53	143	PurchaseWeightUnit
104	Properties54	144	PurchaseWeightUnit1
105	Properties55	145	PurchaseWidthUnit
106	Properties56	146	PurchaseWidthUnit1
107	Properties57	147	ReorderPoint
108	Properties58	148	SRIAndBatchManageMethod
109	Properties59	149	SWW
110	Properties6	150	SalesFactor1
111	Properties60	151	SalesFactor2
112	Properties61	152	SalesFactor3
113	Properties62	153	SalesFactor4
114	Properties63	154	SalesHeightUnit
115	Properties64	155	SalesHeightUnit1
116	Properties7	156	SalesItem
117	Properties8	157	SalesItemsPerUnit
118	Properties9	158	SalesLengthUnit
119	PurchaseFactor1	159	SalesLengthUnit1
120	PurchaseFactor2	160	SalesPackagingUnit

Figure 26-29: DTW Specification part 2

Source: SAP Data Transfer Workbench

No.	Field name
161	SalesQtyPerPackUnit
162	SalesUnit
163	SalesUnitHeight
164	SalesUnitHeight1
165	SalesUnitLength
166	SalesUnitLength1
167	SalesUnitVolume
168	SalesUnitWeight
169	SalesUnitWeight1
170	SalesUnitWidth
171	SalesUnitWidth1
172	SalesVATGroup
173	SalesVolumeUnit
174	SalesWeightUnit
175	SalesWeightUnit1
176	SalesWidthUnit
177	SalesWidthUnit1
178	SerialNum
179	ShipType
180	SupplierCatalogNo
181	TaxType
182	User_Text
183	Valid
184	ValidFrom
185	ValidRemarks
186	ValidTo
187	VatLiable
188	WTLiable
189	WarrantyTemplate
190	User_Text

Figure 26-30: DTW Specification part 3

Source: SAP Data Transfer Workbench

The orange fields are the ones that are complementary to the original fields from the Excel spreadsheet. The green ones are the ones where additional information had to be specified. All fields not highlighted are those where the default values from the system where the right ones and those had not to be imported.

The next table show all imported fields and gives a short description of their content.

1	RecordKey	running number
2	ItemCode	item number within Alfing Corpration
5	AssetItem	item is only buyable, no sales
22	ForeignName	german description
36	ItemName	english description
37	ItemType	item
38	ItemsGroupCode	assigned Group (SpareParts=102)
45	Manufacturer	AKS=2, AMT=3, MAFA=4, OTHERS=5
53	PlanningSystem	bop_MRP=Material requirements
54	ProcurementMethod	bom_Buy=Item is to buy, not to manufacture
131	PurchaseUnit	PC=Piece
162	SalesUnit	PC=Piece
190	User_Text	remarks

Figure 26-31: Specification descrpition

Source: Self

Before the import of the data two rows with the description of the code had to be provided.

	A	B	C	D	E	F	G	H	I	J
1	RecordKey	ItemCode	ApTaxCode	ArTaxCode	AssetItem	BarCode	BaseUnitName	CommissionGroup	CommissionPercent	CommissionSum
2	RecordKey	ItemCode	ApTaxCode	ArTaxCode	AssetItem	BarCode	BaseUnitName	CommissionGroup	CommissionPercent	CommissionSum
3	1	0003185			N					
4	2	0003186			N					
5	3	0004535			N					
6	4	0005488			N					
7	5	0005489			N					
8	6	0006778			N					
9	7	0006793			N					
10	8	0006932			N					
11	9	0010515			N					
12	10	0010518			N					
13	11	0011255			N					
14	12	0011409			N					
15	13	0011478			N					
16	14	0011479			N					
17	15	0011771			N					
18	16	0011847			N					
19	17	0011957			N					

Figure 26-32: Spreadsheet for DTW

Source: Screenshot

It is essential to use the doubled header, though; the Data Transfer Workbench was not able to handle the format. The Data Transfer Workbench allows certainly providing the source and the target of each column but it didn't work without those double headers.

To import the data go to DATA TRANSFER WORKBENCH in the START menu. Start the login procedure and provide the server specific login information

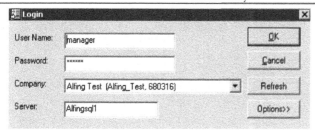

Figure 26-33: Login to SQL-Server

Source: Screenshot

It could happen that no database is displayed. If this happens the REFRESH button rereads the databases on the serve which should show the list. Afterwards it is possible to proceed with the complete procedure and move on to the IMPORT

The next step is to provide the business object which is oITEMS for the item master data.

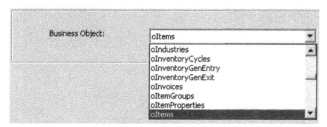

Figure 26-34: Choose business object

Source: Screenshot

Proceeding allows selecting the data source file. The file chosen here has to be the comma separate value file of the EXCEL data.

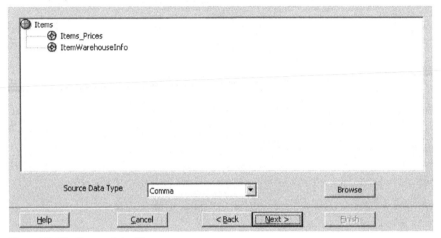

Figure 26-35: Choose data files

Source: Screenshot

The Browse button brings a new window up and allows selecting the Comma Separated Value file which has been prepared in the chapters before. It is also possible to select other source data types like Semicolon, Tab or ODBC.

The next steps allow specifying the map rules which gives the information of the source and target of the contained information. For all information from the default values or to be left blank use [LEAVE IT BLANK] as the target code.

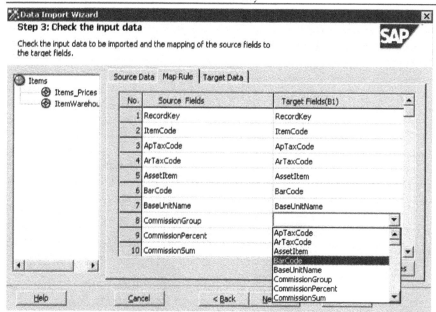

Figure 26-36: Mapping rules

Source: Screenshot

The RecordKey has always to be mapped. Without the RecordKey it is not possible to proceed because it is the unique sign in the SQL tables. To check the source and target data go to the specific tabs.

It is possible to save the mapping rules if some in case the procedure has to be repeated several times. This happens in most cases until all errors in the import file a fixed. To save the mapping rules us the MAP RULES button.

Next the import parameters could be specified.

Figure 26-37: Run parameters

Source: Screenshot

It is possible to import and update the objects. When the test run is checked all operations will be simulated without doing any changes to the data. This is the best option to find import errors.

The advanced parameters allow specifying some more detailed rollback options for the run. When the import is started with NEXT it will take some time to import the data.

After this is finished the log will show information if the run was successful.

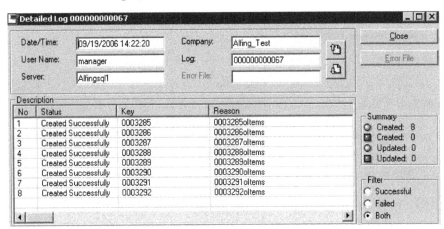

Figure 26-38: Log file from test data import

Source: Screenshot

Detailed information about the errors could be retrieved when the item is highlighted and double clicked. It takes usually several runs until the complete data import is finished and works. A checkup of the data within the system is obligatory.

27 Price list setup

The price list setup specifies the different levels which are accessible within the system.

27.1 Base price list

The price list setup is located in INVENTORY → PRICE LIST → PRICE LISTS.

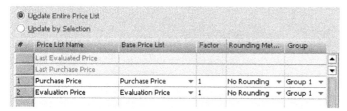

Figure 27-1: Price lists setup

Source: Screenshot

To create a new price list enter the description into the next free row and click on OK. Within Alfing Corporation we decided to add two additional price lists. One for the purchase and one for the evaluation price. It is also possible to increase this number whenever necessary. The first two line items, Last Evaluated and Last Purchase Price, are maintained by the system. It is not possible to change those price lists. The Last Purchase Price will be updated whenever a A/P Invoice, Goods receipt or a Work order is created. The same thing happens with the Last Evaluated Price when creating an A/R Invoice or a Delivery.

27.1.1 Setting prices

The prices for individual items can be set within INVENTORY → ITEM MASTER DATA by opening the item itself. It is necessary to select the price list and enter the price. Foreign currencies can be
applied through their currency indicators, like set up in the currency setup.

Last purchase and last evaluation price can't be changed manually.

Figure 27-2: Price list in item master data

Source: Screenshot

For the general setup of a new price list or to update many prices go to INVENTORY → PRICE
LIST → PRICE LISTS.

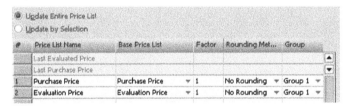

Figure 27-3: Price List management

Source: Screenshot

A double click on the line number opens the corresponding price list. It is possible to apply some filter-
ing functions and open the price list afterwards.

Find				
#	Item No.	Item Description	Base Price	Unit Price
1	⇨ 0003185	PLUG HOUSING SLEEVE/LATERAL CA		
2	⇨ 0003186	MOUNTING HOUSING 24 POLES P.O.		
3	⇨ 0003441	LEVER		
4	⇨ 0003730	LEVER		
5	⇨ 0003731	CONTROL SHAFT		
6	⇨ 0003732	SWITCH ELEMENT		
7	⇨ 0003736	SLEEVE		
8	⇨ 0003737	WASHER		
9	⇨ 0004535	PRESSURE SPRING		

Figure 27-4: Price list

Source: Screenshot

Afterwards all opening prices have to be applied. As soon as the data is available as an Excel spread-sheet the prices can be imported into the price lists.

If the prices of a complete list should be updated it can be applied through a factor which increases or decreases the prices of all items. It is very recommended to make a backup before this is applied. To update the prices got to INVENTORY → PRICE LIST → PRICE LISTS.

The system allows updating the entire price list or just a selection by highlighting the corresponding option. Additional selection criteria have to be specified if using by selection.

It is possible to specify a BASE PRICE LIST from where the base prices should be extracted and applied to the price list.

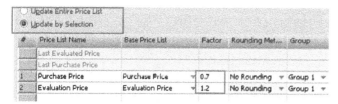

#	Price List Name	Base Price List	Factor	Rounding Met...	Group
	Last Evaluated Price				
	Last Purchase Price				
1	Purchase Price	Purchase Price ▾	0.7	No Rounding ▾	Group 1 ▾
2	Evaluation Price	Evaluation Price ▾	1.2	No Rounding ▾	Group 1 ▾

○ Update Entire Price List
◉ Update by Selection

Figure 27-5: Bulk update

Source: Screenshot

After clicking UPDATE the prices are changed. This can't be undone why it is necessary to be very careful when using this feature.

To apply authorizations within the price list management use the GROUP. If a user has not the appropriate authorizations to the group he won't be possible to change prices.

27.2 Assigning Price Lists

Small Business One allows assigning specific price lists to business partners.

Assigning a price list to a specific business partner is done in BUSINESS PARTNER → BUSINESS PARTNER MASTER DATA → PRCING TAB.

27.3 Special Prices for business partners

To assign special prices for single items to a customer or a vendor go to INVENTORY → INVENTORY → SPECIAL PRICES → SPECIAL PRICES FOR BUSINESS PARTNERS.

BP Code	BP Name	BP Type			
⇨ DCKENO	Daimler Chrysler Corporation	Customer			

Price List	Evaluation Price ▼
Discount Percentage	0.000

#	Item No.	Item Description	Price List	Disc...	Price after Disc...	Auto	
1	⇨ M9001	Service hour	Evaluation Price ▼	0.000	$ 85.00	☑	▲
2			Evaluation Price ▼	0.000		☑	▼

Figure 27-6: Special prices for business partners

Source: Screenshot

The prices can depend on a defined price list. It is possible to define a percentage discount or enter a special price directly. To avoid automatic update of the price when the master price list changes uncheck AUTO or use WITHOUT PRICE LIST in price list tab. It is possible to specify one item or a whole list of items.

In the same window the system gives the option to set validity periods for prices. To do so make a DOUBLE CLICK on the row and a new window opens up.

	Valid from	Valid Until	Price List	Disc...	Price after Dis...	Auto	
1	11/12/06		Evaluation Price ▼	0.000	$ 85.00	☑	
2			Evaluation Price ▼	0.000		☑	
							▲
							▼
OK	Cancel			Copy by Selection Criteria			

Figure 27-7: Validity periods

Source: Screenshot

The prices which have a validity period will be applied only during the specified time range.

27.4 Quantity discount

To specify a quantity based discount make a double click on the row shown in the above figure. Afterward you can specify different quantities and the discount for these prices.

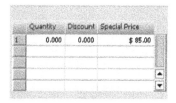

Figure 27-8: Define Hierarchies

Source: Screenshot

To delete the defined prices use the RIGHT MOUSE BUTTON → DELETE. This will remove the selected discount from the item.

Small Business One has three different colors that inform about special prices in the SPECIAL PRICES – ITEM DETAILS window. Those apply to the price and inform the user.

-            Item rows which were not changed at all.
- Black   Item rows which where changed only in SPECIAL PRICES – ITEM DETAILS window.
- Blue   Item rows with validity periods and/or quantity dependent prices.

In SALES DOCUMENTS all special prices are displayed in blue.

27.5 Discount Groups

Discount groups are given in INVENTORY → INVENTORY → SPECIAL PRICES → DISCOUNT GROUPS.

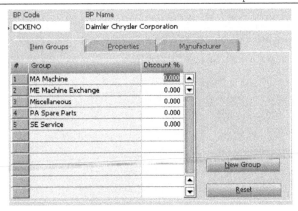

Figure 27-9: Discount Groups

Source: Screenshot

The discount groups can be based on item groups, item properties or on manufacturer. This allows a very fine distinction.

Discount groups can be applied only to one business partner at once, depending on the groups, the properties or on manufacturer. Those categories have been created within the business partner master data or during the item setup.

Within the following chapter the price history will be explained.

27.6 Price history

The previously created price lists don't provide any information about price history. The price history can be accessed through previous created documents. To retrieve a specific price history go to IN-VENTORY → INVENTORY REPORTS → LAST PRICES REPORT.

It is possible to specify different selection criteria to limit the retrieved results. It is possible to search for groups or a specific business partner. It is also possible to limit the search to specific document types and limit the number of last prices that are shown.

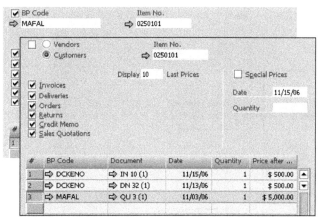

Figure 27-10: Price history

Source: Screenshot

The special prices checkbox shows the special prices that where granted. The date allows to limit it to a specific day and the quantity allows to search for a minimum quantity.

Any prices will be shown either in the local or foreign currency.

28 Approval procedures

The approval procedure has a different intention than restricting the users from document creation. The user is still able to create the document, but it needs verification from one or more persons before it is added in the system.

28.1 Approval workflow

Approval procedures allow verifying documents before they are added into the system. The most common use is that a manager or a senior member can approve the documents before they are added into the system. A document approval procedure starts when a document is created in SAP. The document can be added only as a draft until it is approved. However, for every document that is added a request for approval is send to the assigned user. The procedure ends when the user receives the final approval and adds the document.

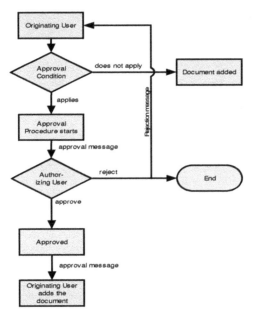

Figure 28-1: Approval stages

Source: Screenshot

Without the approval further proceeding is not possible.

28.2 Intention

SAP Small Business One has no possibility to make some field mandatory. Whenever a field has to be mandatory for a user exist two possibilities to realize that.

- Modifying the SQL-Tables of the system or
- Starting an approval procedure.

Tweaking the SQL-Tables on the server is a possibility which can cause unwanted effects. The setting which has to be applied is NOT NULL in the corresponding column within the correct table.

The second way is to set an approval procedure. This procedure can act as reminder or as a real approval procedure.

The input of the machine no./ project code was something which was requested to be mandatory for Alfing Corporation. By default this field has not to be specified by a user. Without entering this code profit loss on machine level won't be possible. It is only necessary to specify the code in documents that affect the G/L accounts and so we decided to apply this approval only to the A/R Invoice and A/P Invoice.

For Alfing Corporation we used the approval procedure instead of tweaking the SQL-tables. Tweaking the SQL-Tables worked fine in the testing environment and showed no issues, but seemed to be dangerous in a production system. Especially in view that the person introduced the feature is not working further more in the company. Updates and Patches can also be the cause for unwanted problems and it could also happen that some tables are passed without recognizing the necessary keys. Using the approval procedure avoids this problem; neither is it only a workaround.

28.3 Activate approval

First of all it is necessary to let the system know that approval has to be used. This is done in AD-MINISTRATION → SYSTEM INITIALIZATION → GENERAL SETTINGS → BP.

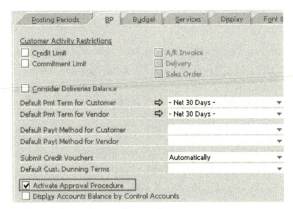

Figure 28-2: Activate approval procedure

Source: Screenshot

It is necessary to set the ACTIVATE APPROVAL PROCEDURE checkbox which activates approval procedures. Activating approval does not change anything in the system's behavior. It is first necessary to create an approval workflow for the documents which have to be approved.

28.4 Creating the approval workflow

In Alfing Corporation we use the approval stages to avoid users adding documents without certain values entered. The next steps describe therefore the setup of this approval procedure.

28.4.1 Approval stages

This step is necessary to set the approval stages a document can pass. The setup is done in ADMINISTRATION → APPROVAL PROCEDURES → DEFINE APPROVAL STAGES.

After specifying the name and description it is possible to set the users which are allowed to approve this stage. The NUMBER OF APPROVALS REQUIRED defines the number of approvals that a document has to retrieve before it can be added.

Stage Name	Project-Lookup		
Stage Description	Project Code exists or not		
No. of Approvals Required		1	

#	User	Department	
1	Ralf Mielke	Purchasing	▼ ▲
2	Sally Bugai	Administration	▼ ▼
3	Kris Brocklebank	Project Management	▼
4	Claas Hoppe	Project Management	▼
5	Carl Kutzli	Sales	▼
6	Allen Hutko	Sales	▼
7	Tobias Lombacher	Administration	▼
8	Ernie Ruppenthal	Sales	▼
9	Stefan Langer	Service	▼ ▲
10			▼ ▼

OK   Cancel

Figure 28-3: Approval stages setup

Source: Screenshot

For the project lookup it won't be necessary to have a person for approval because it is has only the intention to remind the document creator that the project is missing. The persons listed below are the one's which are allowed to approve the document. This setting can be revised anytime. The idea to set many approval persons was to allow reciprocally approval. The NO. OF APPROVALS REQUIRED says that only one of the listed persons has to approve a document until it can be added. If the setting is increased more people have to approve the document.

28.4.2 Approval templates

The next step is to set an approval template. This template defines the document the approval procedure applies to, links the stages and specifies the approval condition.

This setup is located in ADMINISTRTATION → APPROVAL PROCEDURES → DEFINE APPROVAL TEMPLATES which allows defining the following steps:

- ORIGINATING USER   the user who starts the document
- ORIGINATING DOCUMENT   the document the procedure applies to
- APPROVAL STAGES   several stages that will be launched
- TERMS   approval conditions

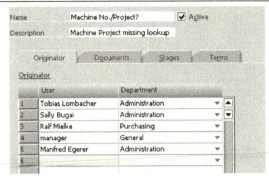

Figure 28-4: Originator

Source: Screenshot

The originating user will be the user starting a document. In our case it is necessary to add all people in the office due to the reason it applies to all documents. In case it applies only to invoices it can be set only to users with professional licenses. Depending on individual demands this can be specified individually. The ACTIVE checkbox ensures that the procedure is active.

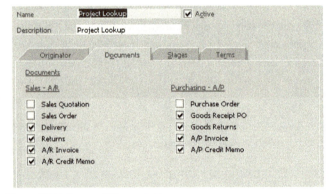

Figure 28-5: Approval Documents

Source: Screenshot

The documents which are checked within this window are the ones the approval applies to. Due to the reason the project lookup should apply to nearly all documents it is necessary to make the above selection.

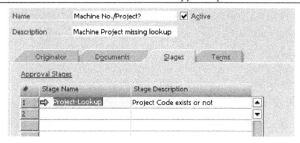

Figure 28-6: Approval stages

Source: Screenshot

In the stages setup the previously created stages can be selected. It is also possible to select several stages within this area which allows a very detailed level of approval. Whenever the first of the stages is completed the second one will be launched. The order in the window specifies the order in which the procedures are launched. In our case the project lookup is the stage which should be launched.

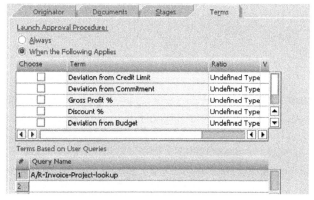

Figure 28-7: Approval terms

Source: Screenshot

In the terms window it is possible to use on of the six standard terms or to link a user defined query. The user defined queries allow more flexibility to set different approval terms. This option was used to generate a query which makes a lookup for the project code. The queries which are used for those approvals have some special terms which are described below.

28.4.3 Terms for a approval query

Whenever a user based query should be created to be used in approval terms it has to follow a specific structure.

The SQL Query has to start with SELECT 'TRUE' or SELECT DISTINCT 'TRUE'. This query structure indicates whether the defined term is fulfilled or not. It will return only true or false. This query can not be used to return names, number etc.

- SELECT 'TRUE' query is used when a single true result is returned
- SELECT DISTINCT 'TRUE' is used whenever the query returns one or more true results.

It is possible to run the query on data that is currently processed in a certain document. This data is not necessarily stored in the company database because the storage procedure starts first when the document is added/updated. In order to pick up a certainly processed field in the query exist two ways to pick this information direct from the screen.

To find the necessary field name open the VIEW in the toolbar and select SYSTEM INFORMATION. This will show the system information of the currently activated field on bottom of the screen.

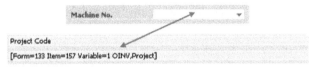

Figure 28-8: System information

Source: Screenshot

To pick this information in a query exist two ways. The first one is to use the convention $[Table.Field] ($[OINV.Project]). The second is to use the form description $[$No.Item.Variable], ($[$133.157.1])

It is only possible to use those queries in the header tables (e.g. OINV, ORDR) and not in row tables (e.g. INV1, RDR1). Whenever a user tries to add a document in the approval template and as soon as the user queries retrieve the result TRUE the approval procedure is launched.

The following query asks if there is any information in the machine no./project field and returns true when this applies.

SELECT DISTINCT 'TRUE' WHERE $[$157.1.1]="   **Approval 28-1**

This query applies whenever one of the defined users tries to add a document. He will get the approval message. The usage of $[$157.1.1.] is better than $[OINV.Project] because the first one applies to all documents (purchase order, packing slip ....) while the second one applies specifically to the OINV table which is the invoice.

For the user the approval procedure shows up the following way where he can cancel to enter the missing information or launch the approval procedure.

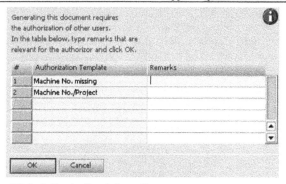

Figure 28-9: Authorization information

Source: Screenshot

Whenever the approval procedure is launched the corresponding person gets an inbox message and can either approve or reject the document.

It is also possible to renounce the internal mailing and use the report functions instead.

The approval procedures can be extended fairly well, but this makes more sense when the company has much more employees and/or is distributed in several branches spread around.

29 Service

The service module is used to manage and keep track about all things that happen to specific items. The service module itself shows its full functionality with the proper setup of the items and the serial numbers which was covered in the previous chapters.

29.1 Transfer into SAP

With the initial definitions from the item management and the warranty templates it is possible to manage the service procedure in SAP. Starting the service is done SERVICE → SERVICE CALL

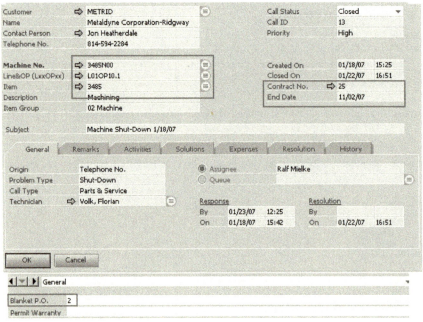

Figure 29-1: Service Call

Source: Screenshot

Based on the agreements of the numbering format of serial numbers the system allows to find the machine no. as well as the line and operation number from the customer. Each of the fields can be populated by information known and will show up the missing ones. Because all items have an assigned serial number the warranty shows up within the warranty area. The information shows the contract number if applicable the end date of the contract.

The information in the BLANKET P.O., which is a user defined field, is populated with a manual query from within the purchasing module. Like it was mentioned in the thesis each of the sales order documents has a manual indicator which marks it as an blanket p.o. or not. Based on this information which is combined with the customer code from the form the system performs a lookup to the corresponding purchase order.

Figure 29-2: Blanket p.o.

Source: Screenshot

The corresponding lookup function in the service is based on the following query:

```
SELECT T0.DocNum
FROM ORDR T0
WHERE T0.U_BLANKET_PO='Y' AND  T0.CardCode = $[OSCL.customer]
```

Blanket p.o. 29-1

This query can be assigned within the service module by selecting the user defined field a pressing the F2 key. This opens a new window where the following options have to be specified. The name of the query and that it should be AUTO-REFRESHed WHEN FIELD CHANGES. In our case we selected the Customer Code as reference. The option REFRESH REGULARY or DISPLAY SAVED VALUES can be set by personal preferences. The first one will refresh the field every time the customer code changes even in previously opened service calls. The display saved values option won't refresh the field on regular basis and will show always the purchase order which was saved in the initial creation of the p.o.

Figure 29-3: Formatted search

Source: Screenshot

The next chapter will show the implemented solution for the purchasing and inquiry process.

30 Purchasing

The main problem of the purchasing process was that the inquiry functionality is not available within SAP. The further steps will show the implemented solution and its realization. Like it was mentioned in the diploma thesis the workflow consists out of several different steps which lead to the demanded solution. The starting point is to create a new activity.

30.1 Creating the activity

To create the activity go to BUSINESS PARTNERS → ACTIVTY

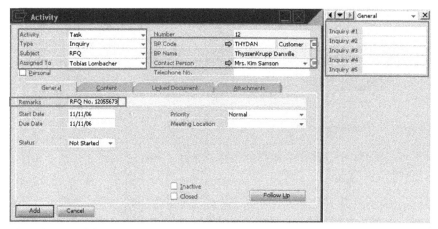

Figure 30-1: Activity

Source: Screenshot

It gets necessary to specify the basic information in those fields. Within Alfing Corporation it is essential to select the Type INQUIRY because the cross reference from the purchase orders refers to this field. The inquiry fields on the right side can be populated when the inquiries are created.

The formatted search within the INQUIRY fields are called with SHIFT + F2 consisting out of this SQL-Query

SELECT T0.DocNum, T0.CardCode, T0.CardName, T0.DocStatus, T0.DocDate,   **Activity 30-1**
T0.NumAtCard, T0.DocTotalFC, T0.U_INQ_CUSTOMER,
T0.U_REF_ACTIVITY FROM OPOR T0 WHERE
T0.U_PO_INQURIY = 'Y' AND T0.DocStatus ='O'

This SQL-Query selects all documents from the purchase order table where the PO_INQUIRY indicator is YES and the Document status is OPEN. The query shows a list of all purchase orders that match those criteria.

To proceed with creating the purchase order go to PURCHASING A/P → PURCHASE ORDER.

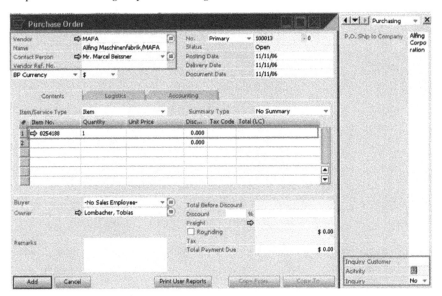

Figure 30-2: Purchase Order

Source: Screenshot

After entering the basic information like the vendor and the line items, some special fields have been added for the cross reference. The INQUIRY CUSTOMER field is just additional for the purpose to have a fast reference. It is populated through a SQL-Query. The ACTIVITY field is the cross reference to the previously created inquiry. The Inquiry field is an added dropdown field which indicates the inquiry as inquiry or purchase order. This field is important for the cross reference from the activity to the open inquiries.

The SQL-Query in INQUIRY CUSTOMER is this one,

```
SELECT
T0.CardCode, T0.CardName
FROM OCRD T0
ORDER BY T0.CardCode
```

and shows a list of all business partners for selection. This query calls the OCRD table where all business partner information is saved and shows them. Only the code and the name from the business partner are shown.

#	BP Code	BP Name
1	⇨ 24/7IN	24/7/365 Incorprated
2	⇨ ABSWAT	Absopure Water Company, Inc.
3	⇨ ADVMAC	Advanced Machine & Engineering
4	⇨ ADVSYS	Advanced Systems & Forms, Inc.
	⇨ AICEOLI	AIC Equipment & Controls, Inc.

Figure 30-3: Business partners from SQL-Query

Source: Screenshot

The next figure shows the SQL-Query in the activity field which is used for the cross reference to the activity.

```
SELECT
T0.ClgCode, T0.CardCode, T0.Details, T0.Closed
FROM OCLG T0
WHERE T0.CntctType ='1' AND  T0.Closed != 'Y'
```

This query picks the table OCLG where all activities are stored. It looks for activities with the type INQUIRY (Code=1) having no closing remark in the closed field and shows them for selection.

#	Activity Number	BP Code	Details
1	⇨ 4	⇨ THYDAN	RFQ 600001455
2	⇨ 5	⇨ THYDAN	RFQ 6000001455
3	⇨ 6	⇨ THYDAN	RFQ 6000001455 - war bei mir in der INBOX - nicht Kalender
4	⇨ 8	⇨ GMTONA	RFQ TA0058309
5	⇨ 9	⇨ AKS	test
6	⇨ 10	⇨ AKS	TEST
7	⇨ 11	⇨ THYDAN	Inquiry No.1234567
8	⇨ 12	⇨ THYDAN	RFQ No. 12055673

Figure 30-4: Activity list

Source: Screenshot

Within this procedure comes another problem into existence. The standard report functionality doesn't recognize the inquiry field which can lead to wrong conclusions within the reporting. To separate them we had to create two new reports, one with the open inquiries and one with the outstanding deliveries.

For the outstanding deliveries the following query was generated.

```
SELECT
T0.DocNum, T0.CardCode, T0.CardName, T0.DocStatus, T0.DocDate,
 T0.NumAtCard, T0.DocTotalFC, T0.U_INQ_CUSTOMER, T0.U_REF_ACTIVITY
FROM
 OPOR T0
WHERE T0.U_PO_INQURIY !='Y' AND  T0.DocStatus != 'C'
```

Deliveries 30-4

This query shows all of the main information, like business partner, document number and some other information. The selection criteria are that the INQUIRY field is not Y and the document status (Doc-Status) is open.

For the open inquiries apparently the opposite query was generated.

```
SELECT
T0.DocNum, T0.CardCode, T0.CardName, T0.DocStatus, T0.DocDate,
T0.NumAtCard, T0.DocTotalFC, T0.U_INQ_CUSTOMER, T0.U_REF_ACTIVITY
FROM
OPOR T0
WHERE T0.U_PO_INQURIY  = 'Y' AND  T0.DocStatus ='O'
```

Inquiries 30-5

It picks up the same information but the selection criteria are that the INQUIRY is Y and the document status (DocStatus) is open.

After completion of all this tasks it is now possible to mange the complete inquiry process within SAP. This functionality has still its limits due to the reason the inquiries show up in standard reports as regular purchase orders but with manual reporting a separation could be made easily.

Neither this is a complete solution which has also reminder functionality it is still remarkable that SAP overlooked such a quite necessary functionality. To have a much more complete function basis which works also better with all of the integrated report features it is absolutely necessary to create a inte-grated solution. Even if every company would have the possibility to create a new solution on its own with an additional Software Development Kit it turns out that the pricing of the kit itself and the addi-tional working hours are way to expensive to get as much benefits out of an individual developed solu-tion that it would pay the price.

31 Sales Opportunities

The sales opportunities are the collection point for all customer related activities. This module needs some general setup before it works properly.

31.1 Commission

This setting is only necessary if commissions apply either by items, customers and/or sales employees.

This setting is located in ADMINSITRATION → SYSTEM INITIALIZATION → GENERAL SETTINGS → BP.

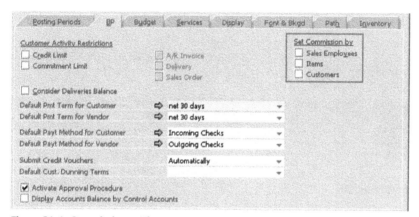

Figure 31-1: Commission setting

Source: Screenshot

Select the option how the commission should be calculated and go to ADMINSITRATION → SETUP → GENERAL → COMMISSION GROUPS to set the different commissions.

Figure 31-2: Commission group

Source: Screenshot

The commission will show up in a query and has to be posted manually afterwards.

31.2 Sales Employees

The sales employee is a mandatory setting if commissions are applied. This setting can be found in ADMINISTRATION → SETUP → GENERAL → SALES EMPLOYEES.

#	Sales Employee Name	Remarks
1	-No Sales Employee-	
2	Ralf Mielke	RM
3	Laura Radke	LR
4	Sally Bugai	SB
5	Kris Brocklebank	KB
6	Manfred Egerer	ME
7	Claas Hoppe	CH

Figure 31-3: Sales employees

Source: Screenshot

The sales employees created here are afterward available in sales and purchasing documents.

31.3 Sales Stages

The sales stages allow monitoring the progress of an opportunity. Defining sales stages is done in AD-MINISTRATION → SETUP → SALES OPPORTUNITIES → SALES STAGES.

#	Name	Stage No.	Closing Percentage	Cancelled
1	Lead	1	5	☐
2	Presentation	2	10	☐
3	Meeting	3	30	☐
4	Negotiation	4	45	☐
5	Quote	5	60	☐
6	Order	6	100	☐

Figure 31-4: Sales Stages

Source: Screenshot

Within this window it is necessary to specify the different stages and a closing percentage. This will affect the closing percentage in the sales opportunities reports. The closing percentage can be overwritten manually whenever necessary. The closing percentage will also be used to calculate the weighted amount in reports.

31.4 Partner Relationships

The partners can be set up from ADMINISTRATION → SETUP → SALES OPPORTUNITIES → RELATIONSHIPS.

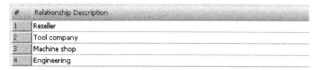

#	Relationship Description
1	Reseller
2	Tool company
3	Machine shop
4	Engineering

Figure 31-5: Relationship

Source: Screenshot

The settings here are especially for some general partner definitions. The partner or competitors itself can be created in ADMINISTRATION → SETUP → SALES OPPORTUNITY → COMPETITORS or PARTNERS

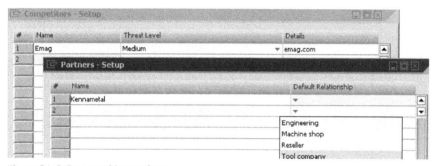

Figure 31-6: Partners/Competitors

Source: Screenshot

The settings applied here will be populated on going.

31.5 Sales Territories

The territories can be any kind of settings. It is not specifically a geographic one. The setup is located in

ADMINISTRATION → SETUP → GENERAL → TERRITORIES

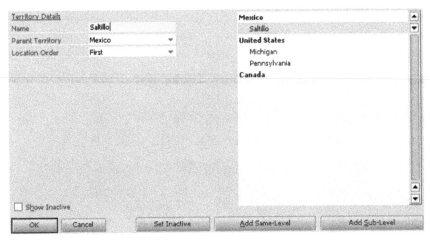

Figure 31-7: Sales territories

Source:

To add a new territory enter a NAME and specify the additional options. Clicking on UPDATE adds the territory. To add levels click on the corresponding boxes.

31.6 Sales Opportunity

To implement this process into Small Business One go to SALES OPPORTUNITIES → SALES OP-
PORTUNITIES.

This window allows specifying a new opportunity and managing its stages.

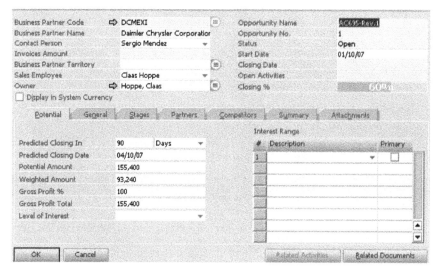

Figure 31-8: Sales opportunity

Source: Screenshot

All previous defined descriptions are available from here, neither there exist additional ones.

31.7 Sales opportunities reports

The most important part of the sales opportunities module is the report section. With proper entered
data in the input section the report help to locate and understand reasons for failure or success of the
company's sales process. The reports can be accessed through SALES OPPORTUNITIES → RE-
PORTS. Because there are about 100 built in reports it makes no sense to give a detailed list of them.
Merely it depends on each individuals preferences and the goal he likes to achieve with the report what
functionality is selected.

32 Creating the print layout

The print layouts are for all documents which are basically for external purpose. For all predefined records that need no separate SQL Queries the Print Layout Designer was used. For documents that need extensive SQL-Queries and/or are combined from a whole bunch of different tables the Crystal Report XI writer was used. Simple queries which have no advanced needs for the report functionality a internal solution of queries and the Print Layout Designer would also work.

32.1 Development of a template

In succession with the SAP a redesign of all customer related documents where made. The reason to do this was to represent a new corporate identity that is consistent through all documents. This will give a more professional impression to the customer and will also be easier to read as all forms will have the same design.

Due to the companies history decision was made to match the letterhead with AKS in Germany. Therefore the special font for the ALFING stroke was used and the additional information translated into English. Also a new footer was set up and added into the document.

In addition to generate a matching layout for each document several areas with specific content, position and height as well as fonts and alignments where defined.

The general layout was designed as an Illustrator document. This made it possible to use this template also in Word documents which should also show the new corporate design. After all the specifications where done externally this design was adapted into SAP and the Crystal Report Writer.

To keep the generated Layout for future usage and have a definition that applies to all other documents definitions where fixed to the below parameters:

- Color:
  only two colors are allowed
  ALFING in blue, RGB 67,64,137
  Lines for heading in green, RGB 90, 186, 169
  only for use in direct assignment with ALFING as part of the letterhead or the address.
  black for all other letters and designs.
- ALFING Logo
  Width: 99 pt, Height: 43 pt
  TRANSFER LINES – FLEXIBLE MANUFACTURING SYSTEMS in Arial Narrow, Size 14 pt
- Font:
  Address and ALFING name is written in Arial Narrow (exception footer, Arial), Name in capitals
  all other letters in Arial, regular
  three sizes are allowed 8, 10, 12
  to highlight it is allowed to bold the letters or
  to write in capitals and italic.
- Borders and lines
  borders for field and lines within the document are 1 pt thick and black
- Margins
  Left 30 pt, Right 30 pt, Upper 0 pt, Bottom 0 pt
  Alfing letterhead 20 pt from top of page, upper side of address footer 24 pt from bottom of page

To achieve a clean look of the document which is modern and timeless the number of colors where drastically reduced to a minimum of two. The same reason drove the decision to apply only three different font sizes for different proposals.

The positions and sizes of the fields are given in points. This compromise was made because the print layout designer in SAP can only deal with this measurement unit.

Those regulations are the guideline for all documents, reports either internal or external.

On the next page the Illustrator layout for a regular page with corresponding fields is shown. The layout contains all necessary measurements which makes it also possible to send it to an external printing company having preprinted letters created.

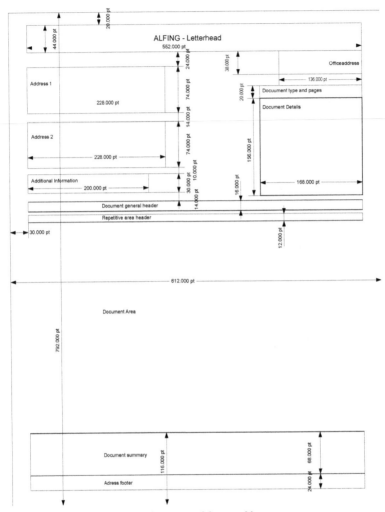

Figure 32-1: Alfing document layout, positions and boxes

Source: Self created layout

At this figure the black lines show the one which will appear within the document itself while the light ones display the areas which can be used to apply the text.

After finished implementation of the document layout the results can be seen in the next figure.

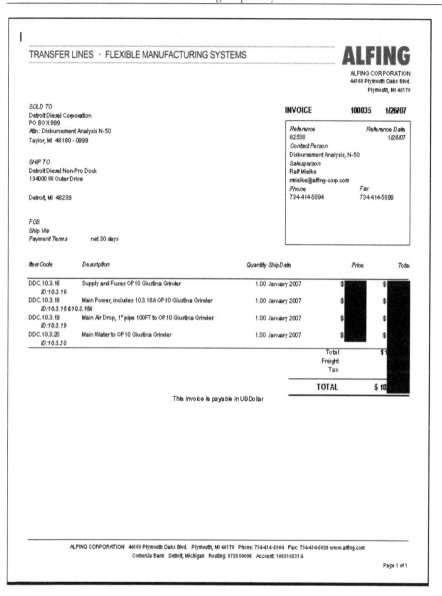

32.2 Print Layout Designer

The Print Layout Designer (PLD) is the built in tool from SAP to generate print layouts. A print layout can be opened from every document within SAP, even from self generated reports. To design a new print layout the document has to be opened.

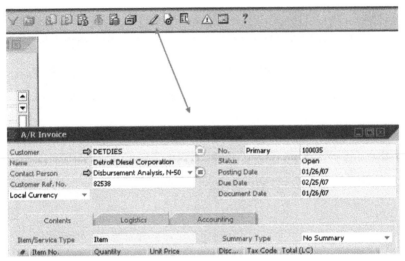

Figure 32-2: Print Layout Designer

Source: Screenshot

Afterwards the layout is accessible through TOOLS → PRINT LAYOUT DESIGNER or through the pencil button. This opens the layout designer for this specific document. A list of all previously created layouts shows up and is accessible from there on. The default document will be shown in bold letters.

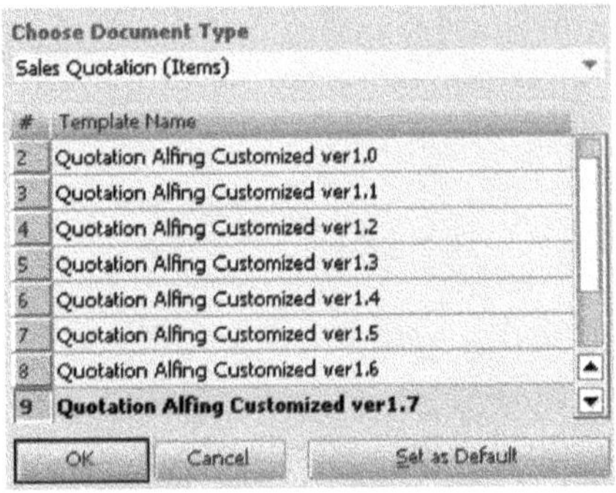

Figure 32-3: Print layout

Source: Screenshot

This shows a list of all previous created print layouts. The bold one is the actual default layout. To create a new one, click on OK. This opens some new windows with the actual print layout. From within this window it is possible to save the document as a new version or to replace the existing document.

The function can be found within PRINT LAYOUT DESGINER → SAVE AS or SAVE depending on the intention.

The print layout designer is split into several areas, which are the main window, field index and the properties. The main window shows the print layout itself while the field index shows a list of all fields within the print layout. The properties field contains additional information of each single field.

This chapter will give basically a description of the functionality and advise some of the issues and benefits of this tool. Due to the versatility it won't cover the complete description how to generate documents which is remaining in the hand of every end user.

32.3 Main area

The main area shows the document, field index and the properties.

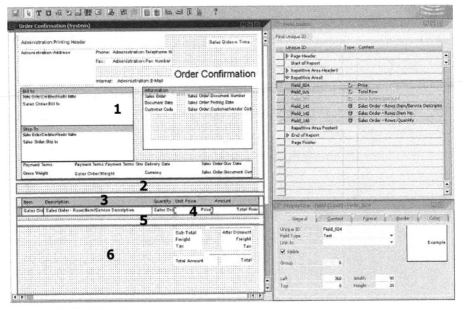

Figure 32-4: PLD Main windows

Source: Screenshot

A description of each single are within the report is given in the next chapters.

First of all it is necessary to define the page layout setup. This layout specifies the size of the paper, the margins and some other settings. This is done in PRINT LAYOUT DESIGNER → DOCUMENT PROPERTIES. The next figure shows each of the options which are accessible within this menu followed by a detailed description.

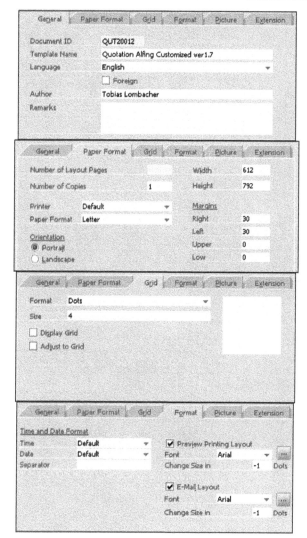

Figure 32-5: Document settings

Source: Screenshot

The next table gives a short description of each field.

Field Name	Description
General	
Document ID	Combines document type (QUT=Quotation), Item type (2) – Service type (1) and the sequence number
Template Name	Name of the print template
Language	The document language (important for Multilanguage use)
Foreign	When printing a document in foreign language it shows the currency code for this country
Author	The user who created the document
Remarks	Some additional information
Paper Format	
Number of Layout pages	Increase the number of layout pages. Needs a number indicating for each page
Printer	Specifies the default printer
Paper Format	Default paper format fort his print layout
Width, Height	Manually set a specific paper format
Orientation	Paper orientation
Margins	Margins that apply to the entire docuemnt
Grid	
Format	Specifies the grid's line style
Size	Size of the squares in the grid (measured in pixels)
Display Grid	Select to display the grid in the layout
Adjust to Grid	Select to make the fields snap to the grid
Format	
Time and Date Format	Default picks the values from the system settings
Separator	Separator between the date and time templates
Preview Printing Layout	Defines the layout of the printing preview in SAP
E-Mail Layout	Specify a different layout for the e-mail layout
Picture	
Picture Tab	It is possible to specify a background picture
Extension	
Extension Tab	Allows to specify a .dll file with a embedded picture that is integrated

Table 32-1: Document parameters

Source: SAP, Print Layout Designer

The report area itself consists of six parts as shown in figure Figure 32-4: PLD Main windows:

1. Page Header   is printed on every page of the report
2. Start of Report   is printed only on the first page of the report
3. Repetitive Area Header   is printed above the detail area on each page
4. Repetitive Area   duplicates itself according to the rows in the report
5. Repetitive Area Footer   located one time under the repetitive area
6. End of Report   is printed on the last page of the report

32.4 Field Index

The index window shows up on the right side of the screen. This window displays all fields in the template and its field type. Hidden fields are listed in light grey color. Every selected field is highlighted in yellow.

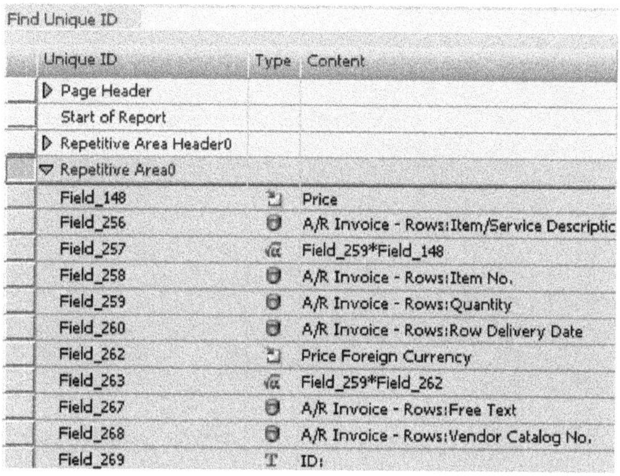

Figure 32-6: Field Index

Source: Screenshot

Field name	Description
Unique ID	Is an unique identifier which is generated upon field creation, manual override is possible
Type	Displays an icon matching field type and Source type
Content	Shows the field content or formula

Table 32-2: Field Index

Source: SAP, Print Layout Designer Help File

32.5 Field properties

This window shows details for the actual selected field or area. This is also the area where the contents of each field are specified.

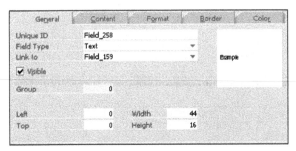

Figure 32-7: Field properties

Source: Screenshot

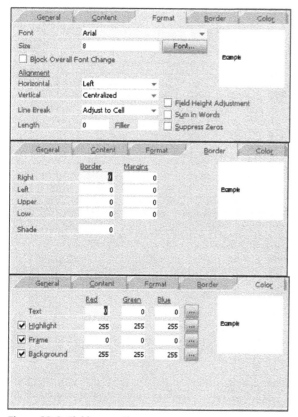

Figure 32-8: Field properties

Source: Screenshot

It is possible to modify the field or the report area from this window. When multiple areas are selected some options will be disabled and only common characteristics can be modified. A description of each field can be found in the next table.

Field name	Description
GENERAL	
Unique ID	Unique identifier
Field Type	Text, Picture, BarCode, External Data
Link to	Create links between several fields
Visible	Print/ not print this field
Group	Group to which the field is linked to, used in subtotals
Left, Top, Width, Height	Position and Size of the field measured in points
CONTENT	
Source Type	Free Text, Variable, Database, Formula
Specification	Vary depending on source type
FORMAT	
Font, Size	Selects the font style and size
Block overall font change	Keeps this font even when changed in the document properties
Horizontal	Horizontal alignment
Vertical	Vertical alignment
Line Break	Allow overflow (extend over frame border), Adjust to cell (cut text at frame border), Divide into rows (continue text in next row when reaching frame border)
Length	Fixed number of characters to be printed, e.g. 5 prints only first 5 digits
Filler	Filler symbol that fills up the remaining spaces when field contains less characters than specified in length
Field height adjustment	Automatically adjust the field height to the text
Sum in Words	Converts number into written text, e.g. for checks
Suppress Zeros	Remove decimal zeros, e.g. 233.00 → 233
BORDER	
Border: Right, Left, Upper, Low	Specifies the border thickness for each side, given in pixels
Margin: Right, Left, Upper, Low	Space between the border and the field content, given in pixels
Shade	Allows to specify field shading
COLOR	
Text	Specifies the text color, either RGB or select from
Highlight	Background color of the text
Frame	Color of the frame
Background	Background color of the field

Table 32-3: Field properties

Source: SAP, Print Layout Designer Help File

32.6 Creating new fields

It is possible to create seven different field types within the print layout. They can obtain their value from on of the seven sources. The type of the field and its source can be changed after creation. To create a new field, select the field type in the toolbar T 🗔 √α 🗐 🖳 ▥ 🗃 and use the mouse to create the field.

The field types, and a short description, can be seen within the next table.

Field	Field type	Default Source Type
T Text	Text	Free Text
▣ Database	Text	Database
va Formula	Text	Formula
▣ Variable	Text	System Variable
▣ File	Picture	File
▦ Barcode	Barcode	Free Text
▣ External Data	External Data	Procedure Name

Table 32-4: Field types

Source: SAP, Print Layout Designer Help File

A further description of each type won't follow. I will give only some more details on important functions which where used in our print layouts.

32.6.1 Text fields

The text field type (shown with blue background) was used for all headings and explanations that are printed on the document.

Figure 32-9: Text field examples

Source: Screenshot

The creation starts by clicking on the text **T** button. The field itself is created by dragging using the mouse to drag it to the necessary size. Afterwards the text has to be entered and formatting applied. All of this information can be changed every time. A description of formatting options was given before.

32.6.2 Database fields

The database field is used to print information from selected tables and columns. It is possible to create as many database fields as required. Whenever possible the database fields should be preferred instead of system variables. The reason is, that variables sometimes change when an upgrade is made and because there is no documentation available from SAP that specifies the variables. In some cases it is possible to retrieve the information through VIEW → VIEW SYSTEM INFORMATION, which will show some variables in the information area. But mostly the interesting variables, for example the TOTAL that is converted into the $, EUR or other currencies is not retrievable there. The only way to find those variables is to create a document that includes every variable number from 0 to 999 and find the relationships between them.

We used the database source type for every field in a document that varies, either because of the user who created it (e-mail, name, and phone), different contents (items, address …) or to create dependencies that are linked together.

To create a new database field, use the 🔲 button. The information in the print layout designer follow this convention: TABLE:COLUMN. The system knows two important database tables. The first one is the master table for general document data. The second one is the document row data which contains the line items for the document. For example for a invoice the master table is A/R Invoices including Name, Address, Document No. Doc. Date and so on. The row table contains the information for each single row, for example Item No., Order Quantity, Unit Price, Row Total and more. Depending on the information that should be printed it is important to select the corresponding row or general table.

Next figure gives a example of the layout in the print layout (left side) and from the final document (right side).

Figure 32-10: Database fields example

Source: Screenshot

Every database field needs the specification of the source table and the source column.

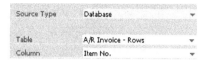

Figure 32-11: Source table and column

Source: Screenshot

32.6.3 Formula fields

The formula field allows calculation and some string operations to the content. Creating a new formula field is done with 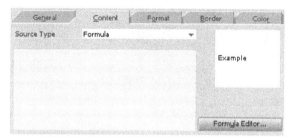. The content area shows a blank area where the formula could be defined.

Figure 32-12: Formula field

Source: Screenshot

The easiest way to create a new formula is to use the FORMULA EDITOR. Before describing its functionality I will give a short overview about the functions available.

Operation	Description
Arithmetic Operations	
%	Displays the remainder of a division, e.g. 10 %3 returns 1
*, +, -, /	Multiplication, Addition, Subtraction, Division
Abs (Number)	Displays the absolute value of a number.
Avg (, …)	Displays the average of a list of numbers.
DecimalLeft (Number)	Displays the integer part of a numeric value, e.g. 241.3 results in integer number 241
DecimalRight (Number)	Displays the decimal fraction of a numeric value, e.g. 241.3 returns the fraction .3
Pow (Base as Number, Exponent as Number)	Displays a number raised by a power.
see next page	
Round (Number, Decimals as Number)	This operation rounds a numeric value according to the number of characters selected in Field 2. For example Round(514.34, 1) will return 514,3
String Operations	
Amount (Money)	Extracts only the number out of a field containing a value and a character. Usage for example to remove a currency symbol Amount(€154) results in 154.
Concat (,…)	Concatenates strings, e.g. Concat(A,B) will result in AB
Currency(Money)	Extracts only the currency symbol in the selected field
Length(Text as String)	Displays the number of characters in this field

Sentence (Text as String, SentenceIndex as Number)	This cuts an entire sentence from the selected field. The SentenceIndex specifies the number of sentence to cut. A sentences is indicated through the ENTER mark
Substring (Text as String, SubStringLength as Number)	Cuts a selected number of characters from the right side of a selected field.
Substring (Text as String, SubStringStartIndex as Number)	Cuts a selected number of characters from the left side of a selected field
Date Operations	
Day (Date as String)	Returns the day part of a date.
Month (Date as String)	Returns the month part of a date.
MonthName (Month as Number)	Returns the name of the month.
Year (Date as String)	Returns the year part of a date.
Condition Operations	
	The condition must be IF, and must consist of 2 fields. Further description below
Cast Operations	
ToNumber (String)	Explicit cast from string to number
ToString (Number)	Explicit cast from number to string
Others	
ColAvg(UniqueID as String)	A calculation of the average value of numbers in a selected column.
ColSum(UniqueID as String)	A calculation of the total values in a selected column.
CopyNumber()	Enables the user to manage the number of printed copies.
CurrentPage()	The number of the page in the document printout.
Date()	The printing date.
GroupLineNum()	The row number in the group for which a sub-sort or subtotal is calculated.
LineNum()	The successive number of the row in the repetitive area.
PageAvg(UniqueID as String)	A calculation of the average value of numbers in a selected column in every printed page.
PageSum(UniqueID as String)	A calculation of the total pages in the document.
ReportAvg(UniqueID as String)	A calculation of the average value of numbers in a selected column for the entire report.
ReportSum(UniqueID as String)	A summary of the values in a selected column for the entire report.
SortFieldName(SortNumber as Number)	The name of the sort field selected in the template, for example, Item Group.
SortValue()	The content of the sort field selected in the template. for example, the item group name.
SystemString(B1Notice)	Prints *Printed by SAP Business One*
Time()	The printing time
TotalPages()	The total number of printed pages

Table 32-5: Formula functions

Source: SAP, Print Layout Designer Help file and self

32.6.3.1 Formula Editor

The formula editor allows creating formulas through drag and dropping instead of typing them in. It is a nice feature neither it allows only some basic operations. For more complex or string operations the manual programming works much better.

A click on Formula Editor... opens a new window.

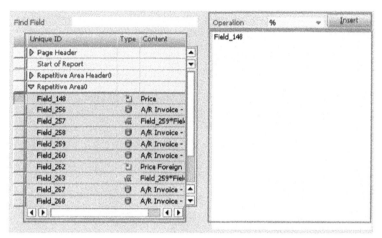

Figure 32-13: Formula Editor

The left area shows all report fields. A double click selects the field and imports it into the, right aligned, formula area. A click on the ⁻ in the top area opens the list with all operational functions. It is necessary to select the required one. The INSERT button imports it into the formula area. Leaving this field goes back into the FIELD PROPERTIES. The formula is now imported and applied to the field. It is possible to use the formula editor or to manipulate the formula directly.

32.6.3.2 If comparison

The following description will provide further description how to use the if clause within the formulas. The reason is that the function applies in a very unusual way and has some difficulties that apply.

The easiest way to explain the functionality is to give an example. The realized function should be the following one:

Whenever an invoice has EUR, instead of $, as currency indicator the foreign price should be picked from the database and shown in the invoice. Without this option the system prints only the $ amount on the invoice.

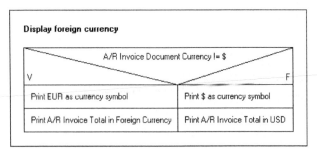

Figure 32-14: IF clause for foreign currency

Source: Self

To transfer this into the print layout designer it is necessary to create several fields.

- The document currency from the database
- $ as comparison from a text field
- A field for the TRUE clause comparison as formula field
- A field for the FALSE clause comparison as formula field
- The corresponding database field for the currency symbols and the totals. Text and/or database origin.

The steps to use the conditions are the next ones:

- Create the database field that picks the document currency from the database (A/R Invoice:DocumentCurrency) (in example = Field_242)

- Create a text field that contains $ (in example = Field_252)

- Create a formula field that compares the first and second field with "is not equal" This will return a 1 if the condition is met, otherwise NULL.

- Create a formula field that compares the first and second field with "is equal". This will also return a 1 if the condition is met and otherwise NULL.

All of these fields are created as hidden fields which can be seen in the next figure.

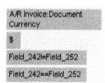

Figure 32-15: Condition fields

Source: Screenshot

These fields will now provide the possible information to show or hide the currency symbol and the price in the document itself.

The next step is to create fields for displaying the currency symbols and the total and link them to them to the conditions. This is illustrated in the following figure.

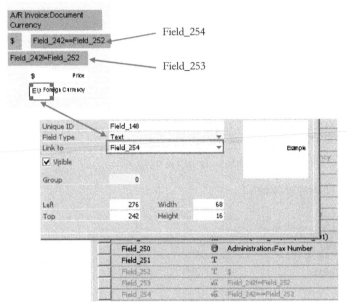

Figure 32-16: Print fields and link to

Source: Screenshot

The LINK TO option indicates if the field is shown or not. The field is shown whenever the indicator returns 1 instead of NULL. For the above example this means when Field_254 returns a 1 the EU is displayed. As the $ amount fields have the opposite condition they won't be shown on the printed document. See below figure for the results.

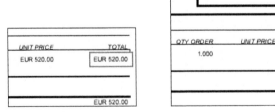

Figure 32-17: Results

Source: Screenshot

Another option we realized with this option was the proforma invoice. Due to the reason the system has no built in option for a proforma invoice first of all a user defined field had to be added. This field has two options YES/NO to decide if a proforma invoice is necessary or not. The function for this is the following one:

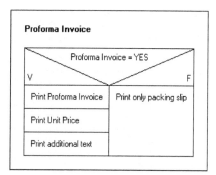

Figure 32-18: Proforma Invoice

Source: Self

The figure below shows the field in the sales document, the packing slip and the proforma invoice.

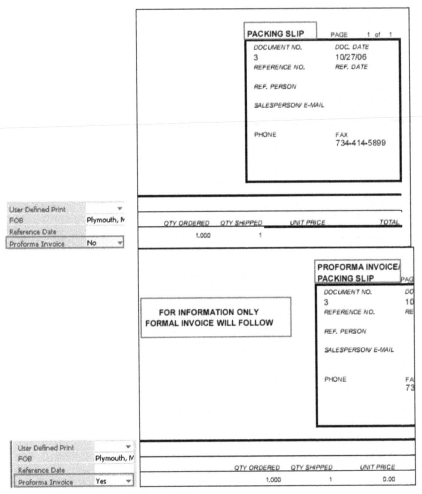

Figure 32-19: Proforma Invoice

Source: Screenshot

33 User defined fields and tables

Small Business One has many built in fields ready to use but for special purpose it can become necessary to add additional field into the standard forms. Therefore we used the user defined fields and tables.

The user defined field goes along close with the user formatted search. This allows creating valuable calculations, cross references and formulas. Those user defined fields can also be used in reports and print layouts. Especially when up to date information from several SAP tables has to be retrieved a combination of both tools can get very helpful. Beneath the user defined fields exists the user defined tables used for storage of valid values for a user defined field. Additional use of the formatted search allows using this data in fields, calculations and printing templates.

33.1 Creation of user defined fields

The creation of user defined fields is done from TOOLS → USER DEFINED FIELDS → MANAGE USER FIELDS.

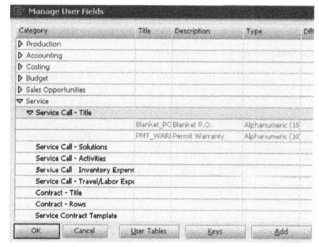

Figure 33-1: User defined fields

Source: Screenshot

There is a difference between the header and row area. The header area applies to a document in general. The row area applies to each single row. The categories are combined into main document categories like it can be seen above. Whenever a new field is created it shows up in all corresponding documents. It is not possible to restrict user defined fields to specific forms or users. This has its advantages because it reduces the administrative work but it has also its limitations in customizing documents.

Creating a new field is done with the ADD button on the bottom. This opens a new window where the field options have to be specified.

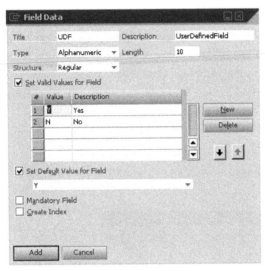

Figure 33-2: Field data

Source: Screenshot

The necessary information which has to be applied is

- Title   is a unique identifier and could not be change in future
- Description   contains a description of the field, can be changed every time
- Type   give the field type (Alphanumeric, Numeric, Date/Time, Units and Totals, General)

The following step is the most important because it specifies the field type. The types have the succeed-
ing distinctions:

Type	Description/ Activity
Alphanumeric	Regular text Regular – Allows up to 254 characters in the field Address – Allows to connect to the Web Phone – Allows to dial a phone Text – Text up to 2 GB/ 255 KB in Header/ Rows
Numeric	Usage for integer number only. Maximal size is 11 characters
Date/Time	Restricts to legal hours/dates only. Formatting as specified in system settings
Units and Totals	Allows entering fractions as well as integer numbers. Field type is floating Rate/ Amount/ Price/ Quantity/ Percents/ Measure structures are displayed as given in initialization settings.
General	This field allows to link external information into the document Link – can be a web address, a file from loacl or network drive Image – allows to link a picture into this field. The picture will be displayed within SAP

Table 33-1: Field types

Source: SAP, Small Business One Help File

The other options are:

Option	Description
Setting valid values for fields	Is optional and allows reducing the number of values that are available for selection.
Set default value for a field	Allows defining a default value for the field.
Mandatory field	Allows making a field mandatory. Either a value has to be entered or the default value for this field is chosen from the list
Create Index	This option creates a index on the SQL-Server. Usage for extensive lists to improve search speed.

Table 33-2: Field options

Source: SAP, Small Business One Help File

After those options are specified click on ADD which adds the field into its corresponding tables.

The common field which where used within Alfing Corporation where GENERAL-LINK and AL-
PHANUMERIC for linking external documents and adding user defined fields.

The system check if any users are connected and shows them.

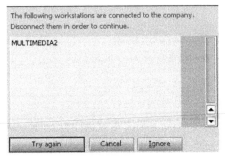

Figure 33-3: Connected workstations

Source: Screenshot

The user shown here should be the one who adds the field. If other users are listed they have to log out before performing this action. Otherwise the database could get corrupted and data lost. Whenever the SQL-Server appears in the list it could be the mailer or backup daemon running on the server. It is recommended to shut them down and try again.

After confirming with IGNORE the system will ask again if the update procedure should be performed.

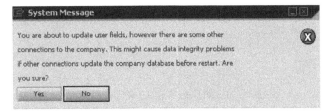

Figure 33-4: Security question

Source: Screenshot

Choose YES to perform the modification finally. This will change the user tables and the user defined field will appear in the list. The tables modified are the UFD1 (User Field Valid Values) and CUFD (User Field Definition).

The same procedure applies if the user defined field is updated or deleted.

33.2 Display the user defined field

After the user defined field is created it is possible to show it in the corresponding document type. The option can be found in VIEW → USER DEFINED FIELDS which shows the fields in the relevant window.

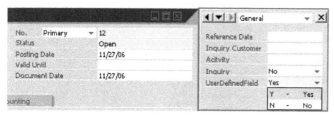

Figure 33-5: User defined fields

Source: Screenshot

All user defined field appear in the separate area that opens up. The window can be moved to several positions around the main form by clicking on the ◄▼► icons within the window.

Closing is done with the ☒ cross. This will close only the user defined fields' window but not the document.

33.3 User defined field options

The separate window offers some options which can be applied to the fields within there.

Choosing TOOLS → USER DEFINED FIELDS → FIRST FIELD allows selecting the field which should be activated first in the user defined area.

It is also possible to order and categorize the field which is done in TOOLS → USER DEFINED FIELDS → SETTINGS. This opens the following window.

Figure 33-6: Settings – User defined fields

Source: Screenshot

The options that apply here are described in the next table

Column	Description
Field	Contains the name of the field
Visible	Checked means the window is shown, unchecked the window is hidden
Active	When selected, the user is able to enter data or to clear the field
Order	Establishes the display order of the fields in the additional window
Category	Organizes the user defined fields in different categories.

Table 33-3: Settings - User defined fields

Source: Screenshot

All options that are specified here apply only for the selected form and for the actual user.

To define a new category the dropdown option has to be used. Selecting DEFINE NEW makes it possible to create new categories.

Figure 33-7: Define categories

Source: Screenshot

Selecting one of the categories order the user defined field into its corresponding category. After closing the window the changes apply immediately. According to Figure 33-6: Settings – User defined fields the changes will show up the following way.

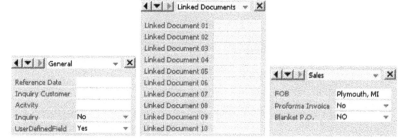

Figure 33-8: Example categories

Source: Screenshot

For user defined fields created within a row table exists another option to make them visible and active.

To display the user defined field in the document it is oblige to open the corresponding input form and to click on the FORM SETTINGS in the toolbar. This opens a new window. The Table Format tab allows setting necessary fields either visible and active or only visible.

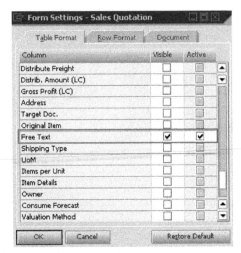

Figure 33-9: Form settings – row format

Source: Screenshot

After performing this operation the field will appear within the document form.

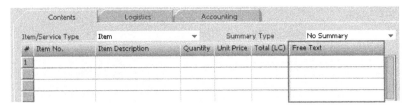

Figure 33-10: User defined field – row level

Source: Screenshot

Entering data is done in the same way as in all other fields. Whenever a picture is linked the system makes a copy to the SQL-Server directory specified in ADMINISTRATION → SYSTEM INITIALI-ZATION → GENERAL SETTINGS → PATH is made and stored there.

33.4 Creating User Tables

It is nearly the same procedure like creating a user defined field. Go to TOOLS → USER DEFINED FIELDS → MANAGE USER FIELDS and click on USER TABLES.

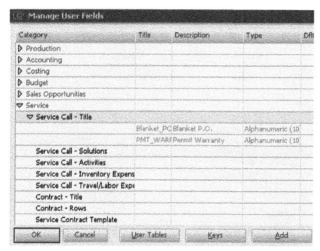

Figure 33-11: Creating user tables

Source: Screenshot

This opens the user tables window with the possibility to add, modify and remove user defined tables

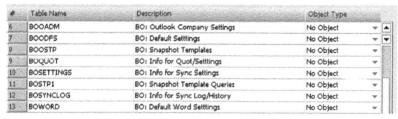

Figure 33-12: User defined tables

Source: Screenshot

To create a new table select the last row and enter the following data:

Field	Description
Table name	Name for the user table
Description	A corresponding description for the table
Object type	Relevant for working with User defined object from third party.

Table 33-4: User tables

Source: Self

Entering Values in User Tables

After creating user tables the values can be added in TOOLS → USER TABLES.

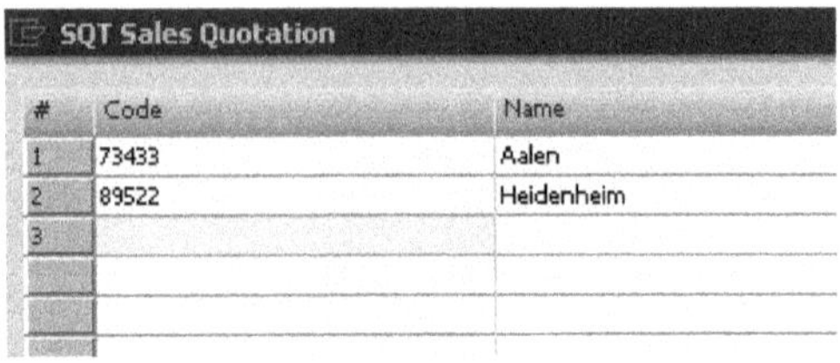

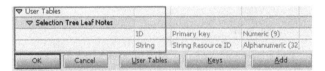

Figure 33-13: Table values

Source: Screenshot

The code is a unique identifier for the row item. The name is a relevant description for the values.

It is possible to create additional columns in User tables. This is done in TOOLS → USER DEFINED FIELDS → MANAGE USER FIELDS. After selecting the user table ADD allows to add new columns.

Figure 33-14: Add table columns

Source: Screenshot

When those steps are completed it is possible to link this table to a new or existing user defined field. This is done in TOOLS → USER DEFINED FIELDS → MANAGE USER FIELDS → ADD/ UPDATE

Figure 33-15: Link user defined tables

Source: Screenshot

Whenever this user defined field is opened the table will show up and the information can be selected from within the predefined table.

34 SQL

In this chapter a description of the common and used SQL-Functions will follow. No description of the database structure itself or of the database design is included here. This is something done by the Software designers and already finished when this part starts.

34.1 Short History

SQL originates to one of the IBM's research laboratories. In the early 1970s IBM researchers developed the DataBase Management Systems (DBMS). To operate those systems they developed a data sublanguage called Structured English QUEry Language. When the product was released the name was shortened to SQL. Since the other companies released several different languages once an ANSI standard was created. This process was continued and transferred to the last version called SQL:2003 (ISO/IEC 90755-X:2003). A detailed description of this standard can be bought from www.webstore.ansi.org.

34.2 SQL Basics

SQL is a flexible language that can be used in different ways to communicate with relational databases. It is important to understand that SQL isn't a programming language like C++ or Java. Those languages are procedure based. This means that one task after the other is performed until the operation is complete. The SQL language is nonprocedural. When starting a SQL request it is not necessary to tell the system how it should retrieve the information from the database, but to tell what information you want from the database. The database management system (DBMS) decides the best way how to retrieve this information. It is like asking the database a question. For example to get a list of all employees who are older than 40 or earn more than $60.000 the following query performs this job.

```
SELECT *
FROM employee
WHERE age > 40 OR salary > 60.000
```
SQL-Example 34-1

This query retrieves the specified data from the employee table and it looks in the age or the salary column for the specified data.

Basically exist two ways to extract the information from the database.

- Creating a new query from a computer console by typing the query into the input screen. This is the way used for the FORMATTED SEARCH in SAP. Also some ad-hoc queries to retrieve information in an unformatted way are made in this way.

- Execute a program that collect this information from the database and reports this information, either on the screen or in a printed report. This is what is done through the Print Layout Designer or CrystalOne.

34.3 SQL Commands

The SQL command language consists of a very limited number of core commands. Those core commands are fixed in the SQL:2003 standard. Mostly those commands are important to create and alter database structures. Therefore no detailed description of all following commands will follow.

ALTER DOMAIN	DECLARE CURSOR	FREE LOCATOR
ALTER TABLE	DECLARE TABLE	GET DIAGNOSTICS
CALL	DELETE	GRANT
CLOSE	DISCONNECT	HOLD LOCATOR
COMMIT	DROP ASSERTION	INSERT
CONNECT	DROP CHARACTER SET	OPEN
CREATE ASSERTION	DROP COLLATION	RELEASE SAVEPOINT
CREATE CHARACTER SET	DROP DOMAIN	RETURN
CREATE COLLATION	DROP ORDERING	REVOEK
CREATE DOMAIN	DROP ROLE	ROLLBACK
CREATE FUNCTION	DROP SCHEMA	SAVEPOINT
CREATE METHOD	DROP SPECIFIC FUNCTION	SELECT
CREATE ORDERING	DROP SPECIFIC PROCEDURE	SET CONNECTION
CREATE PROCEDURE	DROP SPECIFIC ROUTINE	SET CONSTRAINTS
CREATE ROLE	DROP TABLE	SET ROLE
CREATE SCHEMA	DROP TRANSFORM	SET SESSION AUTHORIZATION
CREATE TABLE	DROP TRANSLATION	SET SESSION CHARACTERICSTICS
CREATE TRANSFORM	DROP TRIGGER	SET TIME ZONE
CREATE TRANSLATION	DROP TYPE	SET TRANSACTION
CREATE TRIGGER	DROP VIEW	STRAT TRANSACTION
CREATE TYPE	FETCH	UPDATE
CREATE VIEW		

Table 34-1: SQL core commands

Source: Microsoft SQL Help File

34.4 Reserved Words

In addition to the core commands SQL has several reserved words used to retrieve data from the database. There exist about 200 reserved words in the SQL specification. Due to the reason that this will lead much too far into details only the important ones will be introduced on going.

34.5 Data Types

The SQL:2003 data specification recognizes five predefined data types

- Numeric's: INTEGER, SMALLINT, BIGINT, NUMERIC, DECIMAL
- Strings: CHARACTER, VARCHAR, CLOB
- Booleans.   TRUE/FALSE
- Date times: DATE, TIME, TIMESTAMP, all with/without TIMEZONE
- Intervals: INTERVAL DAY

Within each of these general types may exist several subtypes, which allow storing more or less detailed data.

A special thing that needs to be talked about is NULL VALUE. In a numeric field, a NULL VALUE is not the same as the value of ZERO. Also in a character field a NULL VALUE is not BLANK. A NULL VALUE indicates that the field's value is not known. This is important to know because this can produce surprising results when running a report. Beneath making a table column a primary key the option NOT NULL doesn't accept a blank field. This can be very helpful to prevent users to leave some fields blank.

34.6 Basic database concepts

Whenever a database is created each of the tables has a unique column with the primary key. This ensures that each table has a unique identifier. Through those unique identifiers different tables can be linked together.

For example in SAP the main data of an invoice is stored within the OINV table while the detailed information about each line item is stored in the INV1 table. The OINV table includes the customer, the summed totals of tax and other information that applies in general to this document. The INV1 table includes the details of each line item, like delivery date, quantity, item description and other things.

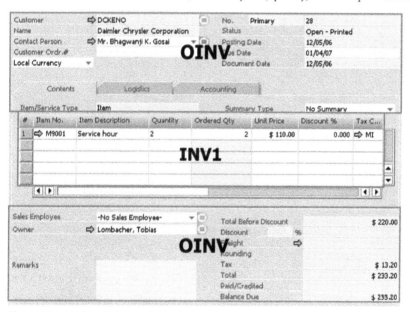

Figure 34-1: Main-detail-area in the form screen

Source: Screenshot

When looking in the query structure it can be seen that the tables are connected through their primary keys.

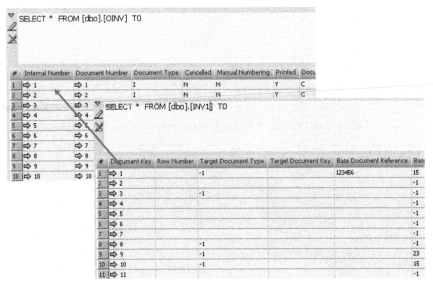

Figure 34-2: OINV-INV1 linked through primary keys

Source: Screenshot

This structure can be found through the whole database and it allows going from one starting point to each connected table in the database. This is essential to understand how to retrieve information from the database.

SAP does not offer any documentation how they linked their tables together. Neither the system allows finding out about this connections. This makes it necessary to manually figure those connections out.

The possibly best way is to select VIEW → SHOW SYSTEM INFORMATION. By placing the mouse into the field of interest it shows the information on the bottom of the screen.

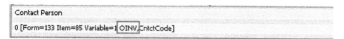

Contact Person

0 [Form=133 Item=85 Variable=1 OINV.CntctCode]

Figure 34-3: System Information

Source: Screenshot

This shows the table OINV, which is for the A/R Invoice. By placing the fields into several field of the form it is possible to retrieve the different tables. The next step is to find out how the tables are linked together. A option to gather this information is located in REPORTS → QUERY GENERATOR. This tool allows making some queries and it is the best place to find the connections between the tables.

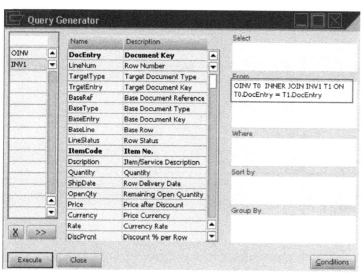

Figure 34-4: Query Generator

Source: Screenshot

After entering the OINV and INV1 table into the query generator the system makes automatically an inner join of those tables. If the system is not able to connect the tables together they will be listed only in the order they are added. Another way to find connections to other tables is to drag the bold written key into the left area. This will link the table into the query.

The system will make always an inner join between the tables regardless if this is correct or not. The functionality of several joins will be described in the next chapters. It is important to gather those connections for reporting with CrystalOne.

34.7 Wildcards and Strings

Before we start to retrieve records from the database a short description of the wildcard conventions will follow.

Pattern	Equivalent
? or _	Single character
* or %	One or several characters
#	Single number
[character list]	Characters included in pattern, can include numbers also
!	Negation

Table 34-2: Wildcards

Source: Self

Equivalent	Pattern	Returns TRUE	Returns FALSE
Several characters	a*a	aa, aBa, aBBBa, a124435a	aBC, a3453b
	ab	abc, AABB, Xab, 5aa6	aZb, bac, 45a45b
	ab*	abc, abdefeg, abc, abdghe345	Acb, aab, a4b
Special characters	a[*]a	a*a	Aaa
Single character	a?a	aaa,a3a, aBa	aBBBa, a45a
Single number	a#a	a0a, a1a, a2a, a3a	Aaa, a10a
Character range	[a-z]	f,p, j	2, &, $
Out of character range	[!a-z]	9, &, %	a, c, e
No number	[!0-9]	A, a, &, ~	0, 1, 9
Combination	A[!b-m]#	An9, az0, a99	Abc, aj0

Table 34-3: String pattern

Source: Self

Those strings work in each of the below described functions. Depending on the database the pattern could have a slightly different meaning.

34.8 Retrieve Records

After knowing how to retrieve the correct tables the different query commands can be introduced.

The first and most important command is the SELECT command. Using the special character "*" allows us to retrieve all columns of the table.

SELECT * FROM dbo.OINV   **SELECT-Function 34-2**

This returns all columns of the OINV table. Selecting only a specific column of the table is done by specifying the column name.

SELECT DocNum FROM dbo.OINV **SELECT-Column34-3**

This will show only the column DocNum from the table. In this case the DocNum is enough information, but as soon as more than one table is selected the complete information consisting out of table.column has to be specified.

SELECT dbo.OINV.DocNum FROM dbo.OINV, dbo.INV1 **SELECT-Column detailed34-4**

In most cases only some specific information from the database should be extracted. This is something which can be done with the WHERE clause.

SELECT DocNum FROM dbo.OINV WHERE DocNum = 10 **WHERE-Function 34-5**

With this clause it is possible to select only the document with number 10. There are also some other comparison operators as:

- =, != or <>   equal, not equal
- <, >   smaller than, bigger than
- <=, >=   smaller or equal than, bigger or equal than

In most cases a closer description of the clause is demanded which brings the AND/OR operators.

Searching only the records that have a document number bigger than 20 and a total which is greater then $10.000 the following query would apply.

SELECT DocNum FROM dbo.OINV
WHERE DocNum > 10 AND Total >= 10,000 **AND/OR-Function 34-6**

If either the one or the other condition should be fulfilled the AND can be replaced with an OR and the query will select those records. This query will search also the Total field, but it won't display this information. The result will show only the document number of all matching documents.

It is also possible to make a combination out of both conditions.

SELECT * FROM dbo.OINV
WHERE {DocNum > 10 OR Discount > 8 } **Combination of AND/OR 34-7**
AND Total >= 10,000

Another option is to specify a range between two conditions. This is done with the BETWEEN function.

SELECT DocNum FROM dbo.OINV
WHERE (DocNum BETWEEN (1000) AND (2500)) **BETWEEN-Function 34-8**

This will return all documents between 1,000 and 2,500. To use a date range the start and end point has to be entered as (#1/1/2004#) AND (#12/31/2005#).

To retrieve data, very specific information is know, the IN function can help.

SELECT * FROM dbo.OINV WHERE DocNum IN (1345, 1453,1556)   **IN-Function34-9**

This will return only the specified invoices.

Mostly the column names returned from the tables are very cryptic and hard to understand. Therefore the SQL language offers a functionality to rename those columns.

SELECT DocNum AS Document Number FROM dbo.OINV   **AS-Function 34-10**

This renames DocNum into Document Number. This gives the opportunity to give each user an easier way to read the queries. It is also possible to refer to the renamed columns within the query.

Whenever it gets important to merge several columns into one single column the + operator helps.

SELECT Name + 'works as a' + Position FROM dbo.OEMP   **Merge columns 34-11**

The result will show up as "Name works as a Position" in one single columns. This can be very helpful when several fields have to be merged into one single field. We used this for the shipping and billing address.

The next step shows how to use conditional logic in the SELECT statement. Conditional logic in SQL is made through CASE – WHEN – ELSE.

```
SELECT Name, Sal                                    CASE-Function34-12
FROM dbo.OEMP
CASE    WHEN Sal <= 2000 THEN 'UNDERPAID'
        WHEN Sal >= 4000 THEN 'OVWERPAID'
        ELSE 'OK'
END AS status
FROM dbo.OEMP
```

This will select all data from the dbo.OEMP table and it will check if the salary of each person is below $2000, above $4000 or between. The text 'UNDERPAID', 'OVERPAID' or 'OK' will be printed in an extra column called status.

Using the TOP condition allows to limit the number of returned rows. This is mostly important for very large tables to save system resources and improve the speed.

SELECT TOP 5 * FROM dbo.OEMP   **TOP-Function 34-13**

As this lists strictly the first five rows it can be of interest to use a random function to show five ran-domized rows. The option to do so is called ORDER BY NEWID.

SELECT TOP 5 * FROM dbo.OEMP ORDER BY NEWID()   **Random-Function 34-14**

This will return five randomized row out of the specified table. We will come back to the ORDER BY functionality later and learn how it will allow us to sort things.

When talking about allowed values we found that a special value is IS NULL. To find rows that contain this particular value a special search function is necessary. The next search will return all rows where the position field was left blank.

SELECT * FROM dbo.OEMP WHERE Position IS NULL   **IS-NULL-search 34-15**

The reason for having this special function is that NULL is never equal/ not equal to anything, not even itself. Therefore it is impossible to use the usual clauses =, <> for testing if a row is NULL. To find all columns those have a value instead of NULL use the IS NOT NULL command.

The next step will describe how to find row that contain a specific pattern or a substring. Finding all names in the department 10 and 20 that contain an 'I' somewhere in their name or a job title ending with 'ER' is done with the subsequent query.

SELECT * FROM dbo.OEMP
WHERE deptno in (10,20)   **Substring-Pattern 34-16**
AND (name LIKE '%I%' or jobtitle LIKE '%ER')

When using the LIKE operation, the percent ("%") operator matches any sequence of characters. An underscore ("_") matches a single character. Note the difference between finding the "I" and the "ER". In the second case the percentage operator is place only before the "ER". In the first it is placed before and beneath the "I". This affects the search criteria. In the second case only words that end with "ER" are shown, while in the other case all words that contain "I" show up, regardless what stands before or after this character. It is also possible to use the NOT LIKE operation which is the opposite of the LIKE operator.

34.9 Sort Records

To display the currently retrieved records in a special way SQL offer different sort functions.

SELECT * FROM dbo.OEMP
WHERE deptno =10   **ORDER-Function 34-17**
ORDER BY salary ASC

This will sort the results by salary in ascending order. To sort in descending order use DESC instead of ASC. It is necessary to specify the name of the column on which to sort. It is also possible to specify a number representing the column. The numbers for the columns start with 1 from the left to the right and increases in single steps.

Generally the following clauses are relevant for ascending sort order:

- Dates are sorted from the oldest to the newest
- Numbers are sorted in numerical order from the smallest to the greatest
- Characters are sorted in alphabetical order, starting with A

For the descending sort function the same clauses are relevant, but vice versa. Without any specification the ascending sort order is standard.

To sort the rows first by employee number, then by department number, both ascending, afterwards by salary descending, the following construct will help.

SELECT * FROM dbo.OEMP   **Extended ORDER-Function34-18**
ORDER BY emplno asc, deptno asc, salary desc

Due no WHERE clause is specified here it will display all table records. Generally it is allowed to specify a column which is not in the SELECT list, but the name has to be specified explicitly. However, if grouping or distinct functions are in the query the system cannot order by columns not displayed.

The next step is to sort not by the whole column, but by substrings within the column. For example ordering the results by the last two digits of the job title

SELECT * FROM dbo.OEMP   **IS-NULL-search 34-19**
ORDER BY SUBSTRING(jobtitle, len(jobtitle)-2,2)

To sort by the last two characters of a string needs to find the end of the string and subtract 2. The start position will be the second to last character in the string. Because the SQL-Server needs a third parameter to specify the numbers of characters to take the second 2 is given.

There exist several other sort options like sorting mixed numbers and characters, dealing with NULL fields and some other things. These basic functions allow handling of about 90 percent of what is needed in daily business A further description won't be given therefore.

34.10   Grouping results

Grouping allows to group the results into main headers. Creating a little example is the easiest way to illustrate the function. Looking at the A/R Invoices returns a whole bunch of invoices. The only thing that is interesting is to know how much each customer has on his account balance. Therefore the GROUP option can be very helpful. Also a mathematical operation called SUM is needed therefore. A further description will follow.

```
SELECT * SUM(Total)
FROM dbo.OINV
GROUP BY CardCode
```
IS-NULL-search 34-20

This query will sum the total field for each customer (CardCode) and display the grouped results.

34.11   Functions

To sum the content of a column into a total the sum functions delivers the necessary operation. The total of all invoices can be retrieved through

```
SELECT SUM (Total) FROM dbo.OINV
```
SUM-Function 34-21

The result will be one single value that equals the total of all single totals.

To get the average amount of the column the AVG-Function is necessary.

```
SELECT AVG (Total) FROM dbo.OINV
```
AVG-Function 34-22

The AVG Function will calculate the average amount of all invoices and return it. It is also possible to combine this with one of the above find functions.

Also functions to retrieve the maximum and minimum of a column exist

```
SELECT MAX (Total) FROM dbo.OINV
```
MAX-Function 34-23

```
SELECT MIN (Total) FROM dbo.OINV
```
MIN-Function 34-24

This will return either the minimum or the maximum total of a invoice. If this function is applied to a non-numerical field it will return either the alphabetically first or last record.

The last mathematical function we want to look is the absolute function.

```
SELECT ABS (Total) FROM dbo.OINV
```
ABS-Function 34-25

This will return the number of invoices that are in the table. Regardless of the column that is selected.

There exist several other mathematic functions in the system, but they won't be discussed here.

Beneath the mathematical functions several functions that allow manipulating strings exist.

The first function is the CHR function. This function will return the corresponding numerical value of the character.

```
SELECT Type, CHR(Type) FROM dbo.OINV
```
CHR-Function 34-26

This function returns the code of the character in the Type column and displays it. This can get important when document types are specified through alphabetical characters and you like to perform some numerical operations with it. Depending on the character base which is valid in the database the numbers can change.

When different columns should be merged to one single column the CONCAT-Function will provide this functionality.

SELECT CONCAT (Surname," ",Name) FROM dbo.OINV   **CONCAT-Function 34-27**

This will merge the surname and name into one single column. The blank "_" between the two columns ensures that a space is between both names.

With the substring command it is possible to extract some strings out of the name.

SELECT *, SUBSTR(Name,-5,2) FROM dbo.OINV   **SUBSTR-Function 34-28**

The first argument specifies the column; the second specifies the point where to start. In this case it would be the 5th character from the beginning, but as we entered a minus sign before this it will count from the end. This means that if the Name field is 15 characters long it will start from the 10th character to count. The third parameter gives the number of character to display. If the number is positive it will count from the left to right, with minus from right to the left.

Another possibility we have with this function is to format the output in a user friendly way. In the next example the social security number is reformatted into XXX-XX-XXXX.

SELECT
SUBSTR(SSN,1,3)||'-'||SUBSTR(SSN,4,2)||'-'||SUBSTR(SSN,6,4)   **SUBSTR-Function 34-29**
FROM dbo.OEMP

The result will display in the above specified number.

Another functionality is the REPLACE option.

SELECT Name, REPLACE(Name, 'OE', 'Ö') FROM dbo.OINV   **REPLACE-Function 34-30**

This gives the option to display foreign names in the correct spelling. As the American keyboard layout offers no special characters, like Ö,Ä,... this is an option to return to the correct spelling. The arguments given to the function are first the name, second the string to be replace and third the replacement string.

34.12 Connect tables

We have figured out that we have to join different database tables together to retrieve the information we want. The SQL-Language offers different options to join tables together, which are

- EQUIJOIN
- NATURAL JOIN
- INNER JOIN
- OUTER JOIN
- LEFT JOIN
- RIGHT JOIN

There exist several other joins, like SELF JOIN, THETA JOIN and so on. But neither this can get very complicated not every database management system supports this. For a further description the SQL Server 2005 Books Online, is a proper repository.

The first question that comes up when joining tables is why tables should be split into smaller parts instead of storing all information in one huge table. The main reason for splitting the information up is performance. Most of the information would be redundant when stored in one big table. For example for each invoice that is written the complete address information would have to be stored in the table. What happens by splitting the tables is to create one table for the customer data, with address and one that contains the invoice information. This reduces the amount of data that is stored and reduces maintenance. In reality this goes much further. One single invoice consists out of ten or more tables that are merged together. Without going into the details this will give an idea why information is stored into so many small tables. To keep the relationship between the tables it is necessary to have unique identifiers in the main table and the related sub tables. They are called primary keys.

To get from one big table into this divided tree structure the following decomposition algorithm is necessary. First of all recognize the functional dependencies, afterwards reformat the table by candidate keys and determinants into the Boyce-Codd-Format. This will lead to the described tree structure. The next picture shows a partial tree for the A/R Invoice.

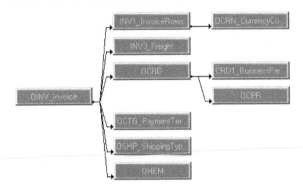

Figure 34-5: OINV Database Tree

Source: Screenshot

This shows only the connected tables without pointing out the connected keys/ columns. To get further description about database design and structure it is recommended reading further literature e.g. [13]**SAP (November 2006):** *SQL-Server 2005 Upgrade Guide.* SAP Library.

After knowing some background about basic database structure and design it is possible to look at the join functions.

34.12.1 EQUIJOIN

The equijoin is the oldest join function. It doesn't consider NULL-values. Making an equijoin is done with the following command.

SELECT * FROM table1, table 2 WHERE table1.column = table2.column   **Equijoin 34-31**

SELECT * FROM employee, subsidiary
WHERE employee.subsidiary# = subsidary.subsidiary#   **Equijoin-example 34-32**

This will result in the following construct.

Employee (table1)				Subsidiary (table2)			
Column 1	Column 2	Column 3	Column 4	Column 1	Column 2	Column 3	Column 4
Number	Name	Subsidiary#	Address	Number	Subsidiary#	City	SubName
253	Allen	A2	Plymouth	642	A2	Ann Arbor	Design
4563	Peter	A3	Ann Arbor	674	A3	Plymouth	Sales
342	Rainer	A4	Detroit	789	A4	Detroit	Buying
124	Manfred	A1	Plymouth	457	A1	Plymouth	Production

Table 34-4: EQUIJON

Source: Self

The FROM clause specifies the tables which are joined, while the WHERE marks the columns that are connected together.

The columns have to have the same data type to be connected. A typical mark of the EQUIJOIN is that the subsidiary# column shows up twice.

34.12.2 NATURAL JOIN

In the projection of the EQUIJOIN the subsidiary# appears twice and is therefore one column to much. If one of the columns would be omitted the result would be the natural exposition of the data.

SELECT * FROM table1, table 2 WHERE table1.column = table2.column   **NATURAL JOIN 34-33**

SELECT * FROM employee, subsidiary   **NATURAL JOIN-example 34-34**
WHERE employee.subsidiary# = subsidary.subsidiary#

This will result in the following joined tables.

Employee (table1)				Subsidiary (table2)		
Column 1	Column 2	Column 3	Column 4	Column 1	Column 3	Column 4
Number	Name	Subsidiary#	Address	Number	City	SubName
253	Allen	A2	Plymouth	642	Ann Arbor	Design
4563	Peter	A3	Ann Arbor	674	Plymouth	Sales
342	Rainer	A4	Detroit	789	Detroit	Buying
124	Manfred	A1	Plymouth	457	Plymouth	Production

Table 34-5: NATURAL-JOIN

Source: Self

It is remarkable that the redundant data from the subsidiary column is removed.

However, the problem with the NATURAL JOIN is that it gets very unclear when more tables are joined together. This isn't very problematic as long as only two or three tables are joined together. As soon as more tables are joined it could happen that it results in a Cartesian product of tables. This means each row of the first table is multiplied with each row of the second table. The result will be useless.

Another problem is that the WHERE clause is still used to connect the columns. To resolve this issue the INNER JOIN was introduced.

34.12.3 INNER JOIN

The INNER JOIN rule has a different syntax.

SELECT *
FROM table1 INNER JOIN table 2   **INNER-JOIN 34-35**
ON table1.column3 = table2.column2
WHERE (optional clause)

INNER-JOIN-example 34-36

```
SELECT *
FROM  employee INNER JOIN subsidiary
ON employee.subsidiary# = subsidiary.subsidiary#
```

The join is made through the FROM clause. Conditions are assigned through the WHERE clause.

The result of this join is the same as with the INNER JOIN, but additional parameters can be specified.

Employee (table1)				Subsidiary (table2)		
Column 1	Column 2	Column 3	Column 4	Column 1	Column 3	Column 4
Number	Name	Subsidiary#	Address	Number	City	SubName
253	Allen	A2	Plymouth	642	Ann Arbor	Design
4563	Peter	A3	Ann Arbor	674	Plymouth	Sales
342	Rainer	A4	Detroit	789	Detroit	Buying
124	Manfred	A1	Plymouth	457	Plymouth	Production

Table 34-6: INNER-JOIN

Source: Self

If we specify a additional parameter during the join operation the result will change.

SELECT *
FROM employee INNER JOIN subsidiary
ON employee.subsidiary# = subsidiary.subsidiary#
WHERE employee.number=253

INNER-JOIN-example 34-37

Employee (table1)				Subsidiary (table2)		
Column 1	Column 2	Column 3	Column 4	Column 1	Column 3	Column 4
Number	Name	Subsidiary#	Address	Number	City	SubName
253	Allen	A2	Plymouth	642	Ann Arbor	Design

Table 34-7: INNER JOIN with parameters

Source: Self

Due to this reason exist much more options to retrieve the results wanted.

34.12.4 OUTER JOIN

The OUTER JOIN displays all data rows of the left and right table, even when no corresponding records exist in the dedicated table. The result is that also NULL values are considered.

SELECT *
FROM table1 OUTER JOIN table 2
ON table1.column3 = table2.column2
WHERE (optional clause)

OUTER-JOIN 34-38

SELECT *
FROM employee OUTER JOIN subsidiary
ON employee.subsidiary# = subsidiary.subsidiary#

OUTER-JOIN-example 34-39

Note that the column three has a blanked out field.

Employee (table1)				Subsidiary (table2)		
Column 1	Column 2	Column 3	Column 4	Column 1	Column 3	Column 4
Number	Name	Subsidiary#	Address	Number	City	SubName
253	Allen	A2	Plymouth	642	Ann Arbor	Design
4563	Peter	A3	Ann Arbor	674	Plymouth	Sales
342	Rainer	A4	Detroit	789	Detroit	Buying
124	Manfred		Plymouth	457	Plymouth	Production

Table 34-8: OUTER-JOIN

Source: Self

The previous described joins would not display the blue highlighted row, as there no values in the join field exist. This could be even in table1 or table2. As soon as one of the references is missing the row won't display. This is the advantage of the OUTER JOIN functionality as there is no data missing.

34.12.5 LEFT JOIN

The LEFT JOIN functionality considers also NULL values. It creates a query over two tables which can include empty target cells.

In the next example we want to see for each employee if he is assigned to a specific task or not. This means we have to have the NULL results within.

SELECT *
FROM table1 LEFT JOIN table 2   **LEFT-JOIN 34-40**
ON table1.column3 = table2.column2
WHERE (optional clause)
SELECT *
FROM employee LEFT JOIN job   **LEFT-JOIN example 34-41**
ON employee.empl-no = job.empl-no

The results will display as:

Employee (table1)				Job (table2)
Column 1	Column 2	Column 3	Column 4	Column 2
Empl-no	Name	Subsidiary#	Address	Job
253	Allen	A2	Plymouth	
4563	Peter	A3	Ann Arbor	Project 36754
342	Rainer	A4	Detroit	
546	Claas	A3	Ann Arbor	Design 5346
653	Cindy	A5	Farmington	Project 47532
124	Manfred	A1	Plymouth	CEO

Table 34-9: LEFT-JOIN

Source: Self

The join was made through the empl-no which let it show up only once in the joined table, neither it has to exist in the second table. The blue highlighted cells show NULL. The reason they are displayed is that LEFT-JOIN was used which shows all data from the left table, even if no corresponding information in the right table exist.

Generally it could be assumed that a LEFT JOIN shows all data from the left table regardless of the information stored in the right table. As soon as the right table has NULL values the system will display them also.

34.12.6 RIGHT JOIN

The right join is nearly the same as the LEFT-JOIN, but vice versa. It has the right semantics but the tables that will be joined are switched.

Pretending in our previous example that we have jobs in table2 where no related employee in table1 exists we would miss some information from table2. The RIGHT JOIN will resolve this issue.

SELECT *

FROM table2 LEFT JOIN table1

ON table1.column3 = table2.column2

WHERE (optional clause)

SELECT *

FROM job LEFT JOIN employee

ON employee.empl-no = job.empl-no

Note that the RIGHT JOIN is done also with the LEFT JOIN command, but the tables are switched.

The results will display in the following way:

Employee (table1)				Job (table2)
Column 1	Column 2	Column 3	Column 4	Column 2
Empl-no	Name	Subsidiary#	Address	Job
253		A2	Plymouth	Secretary
4563	Peter	A3	Ann Arbor	Project 36754
342	Rainer	A4	Detroit	Administration
546		A3	Ann Arbor	Design 5346
653	Cindy	A5	Farmington	Project 47532
124	Manfred	A1	Plymouth	CEO

Table 34-10: FULL-JOIN

Source: Self

Usually this should not happen, but in case it does it is easy to find out.

With a RIGHT JOIN the inclusion to the right side is made. This means that all the data from the right table is displayed. Whenever the information on the left side is NULL value it will show the row also.

35 Crystal Reports

Crystal Reports is an additional report writer. It allows retrieving data directly from the database tables and displaying this information in a formatted way. Crystal is not only a tool for working with SAP, but allows also accessing other databases and collecting data from them. Even merging the data from several databases together to one report is possible. Another advantage of this tool is the extensive grouping and formula functions which allow to generate customized views and forms. Also the usability for the users to reformat and rearrange database information in the finished report is much easier. As conclusion to those possibilities we decided to use this report tool for several forms and external reports. Basically the financial reporting will be covered through the XLReporter, another reporting tool that is specialized for work with financial data.

35.1 Installation procedure

Before creating Crystal reports, the Crystal writer has to be installed. After downloading the installation files from the website they need to be unzipped into a folder on the hard disk.

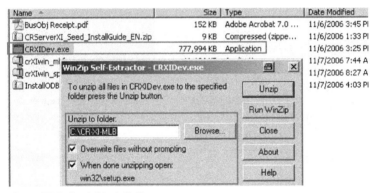

Figure 35-1: Crystal installation

Source: Screenshot

The setup file should run automatically, otherwise browse to the folder and run it manually. Afterwards follow the instructions on the screen to install the application. Enter the serial number from the confirmation sheet and follow the standard installation.

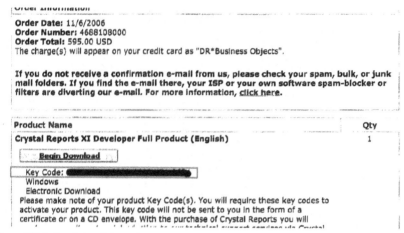

Figure 35-2: Crystal serial number

Source: Scanned document

Additional or specific settings are not necessary. This is only a single license for the report writer tool. The clients need separate licenses.

After installation the application is started through the Crystal icon.

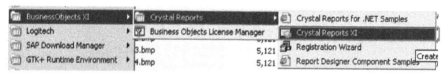

Figure 35-3: Crystal in start menu

Source: Screenshot

35.2 Connecting Crystal

After starting the application the first thing is to connect to the database server. In the described case the Crystal report writer runs on a client machine and not on the server itself. After starting Crystal the following screen will show up.

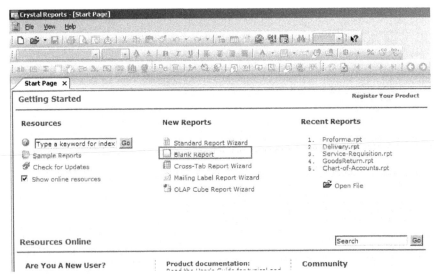

Figure 35-4: Crystal startup screen

Source: Screenshot

To establish a new connection click on Blank Report and Crystal will ask for a new connection.

When using a SQL-Server 2005 as data source location the OLE DB (ADO) is the correct option to connect. Beneath this Crystal allows connecting to many other database sources and retrieve data from them.

Another option to connect the database is to install an ODBC data source in the Windows Control Panel. Depending on the data source additional drivers could be necessary. After doing this source is available for every application which has built in database connectivity. When connecting from Crystal Reports select ODBC as data source and connect to the previous created source.

For Alfing Corporation the OLE DB connection directly to the SQL-Server is the correct connection.

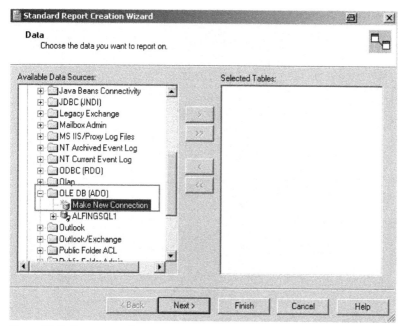

Figure 35-5: New connection

Source: Screenshot

Selecting the MAKE NEW CONNECTION opens a new window where additional information can be specified.

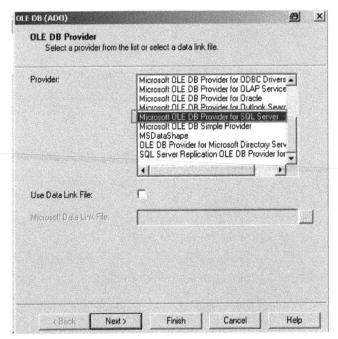

Figure 35-6: OLE DB Provider

Source: Screenshot

To connect to a SQL Server the Microsoft OLE DB Provider for SQL Server has to be chosen. Clicking on NEXT proceeds with the following steps.

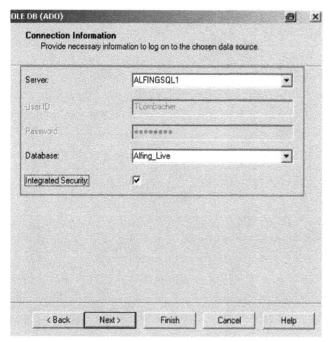

Figure 35-7: Figuresbeschriftung

Source: Screenshot

The server is the SQL-Server that provides the database. The User ID has to be a user with special rights on the database. The reason for this is that Crystal needs read and write accessibility to the data source, though, Crystal can't be used to alter data in the tables.

⚠ It is very important to enter the name and password first and then select the database. Afterwards the checkbox INTEGRATED SECURITY has to be checked. If this isn't done the users won't be able to use the report viewer in SAP.

Clicking on NEXT proceeds to the next screen and it shows some special options. Proceed until finished or click on FINISH.

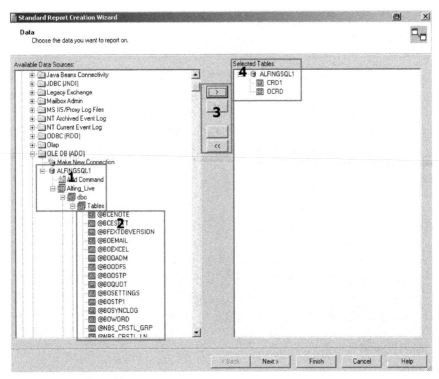

Figure 35-8: Adding tables to report

Source: Screenshot

This screen will appear again, but it has the connection established.

On the left side it shows the database server, ALFINGSQL1, the database Alfing_Live and the tables
(1). Below this it shows the single tables (2). To include a table in the report use the arrows (3) and the
table will be moved into the Selected Tables area (4).

Proceed by clicking on NEXT. This will open the window to link the tables together.

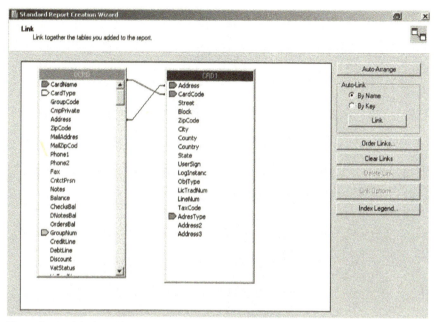

Figure 35-9: Link the tables

Source: Screenshot

This window shows the detailed information about the table columns. By default Crystal links the tables together by NAME or KEY. Crystal is not able to retrieve the correct table joins from SAP. Therefore this has to be determined manually. The correct information can be retrieved from SAP as described in chapter 34 SQL.

Establishing a new or different connection between the tables is done through dragging the column from one table to the second.

Crystal offers four different link types, like described in chapter 34 SQL. To access them click on the link connector and use the RIGHT MOUSE BUTTON. This will open the next screen and the join can be changed. By default Crystal uses the INNER JOIN.

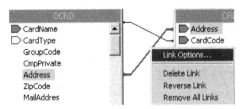

Figure 35-10: Link options

Source: Screenshot

This opens the next screen.

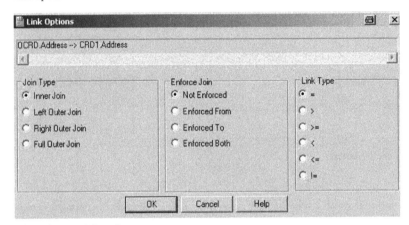

Figure 35-11: Link options

Source: Screenshot

It is possible to select between the four standard joins. Also some checkboxes to enforce the link or to add special conditions are available.

After modifying the links and establishing the correct joins leave this screen with the OK button and FINISH. This will open the report design window.

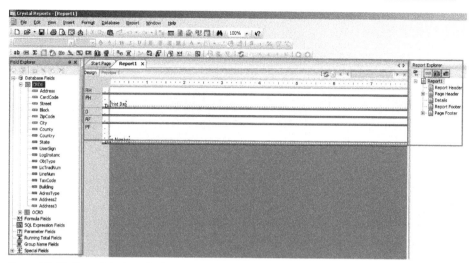

Figure 35-12: Report design window

Source: Screenshot

By default the screen has three main parts. The left side shows the database fields, groups, formulas and other data fields that can be used in the report. The middle pane shows the report itself and the right pane shows the report sections. Those sections can also be seen in the middle area.

35.3 Default Settings

Before starting a new report it is useful to set some defaults for the area fields, formulas and the display. Go to FILE → OPTIONS.

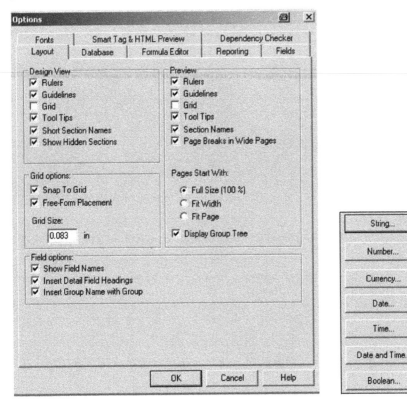

Figure 35-13: Report options

Source: Screenshot

A recommended setting is SHORT SECTION NAMES, SHOW HIDDEN SECTIONS and SNAP TO GRID. Also very helpful is to set some default formats for STRING, CURRENCY, DATE AND TIME. Those default options should be specified to personal needs and company regulations. We won't detail this out:

35.4 Generate a Report

Generally it is very helpful to generate new report with Nassi-Schneidermann charts which provides the best way to generate complex reports.

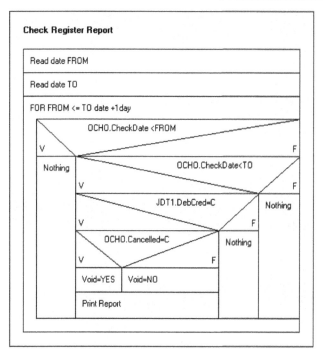

Figure 35-14: Nassi-Schneiderman

Source: Self

This chart shows the workflow for a check register report. The workflow starts from the top with reading the date range FROM and TO fro the input. Afterwards it starts a repetition from the start date to the end date increasing its value by single days. It checks each of the conditions and either the values is true V, or false F, shows the corresponding information in the report.

35.4.1 Report Areas

Crystal Reports has five standard areas:

- Report Header   is printed on the first page of the report
- Page Header   is printed on each page header
- Details   duplicates itself according to the rows in the report
- Report Footer   is printed at the end of the report
- Page Footer   is printed on the footer of each report page

Those areas show on the right side in the Report Explorer and in the Report design area as shortened description (RH, PH, D, RF, PF). It is also possible to add some more report sections into the report when necessary. Use the right mouse button in the description area.

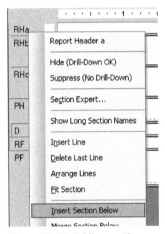 

Figure 35-15: Adding sections

Source: Screenshot

After inserting the section it shows up on the right side in the Report Explorer, too. The area will have the same behavior as its main area.

35.5 Adding fields

Generally Crystal supports some different types of report fields. They can be accessed from the toolbar on top.

ab   Text field: is a standard field to enter free text. This has no connection to the database, neither it is possible to add database fields into a text field.

⊞   Group field: allows to group fields, e.g. invoices by business partners

Σ   Sum field: allows summing the totals and subtotals. It allows also calculating the average, standard deviation or variance value in a group. Additional the minimum and maximum can be retrieved.

   Cross table: a cross tab report is a spreadsheet like report for identifying trends.

   OLAP Grid: Online Analytical Processing (OLAP) to refer to external data storage

   Subreport: for adding a subreport in the actual report. It allows passing parameters and selection criteria to this subreport. A subreport is a self-contained report that has the same report characteristics and abilities as a usual report.

   Line: allows drawing horizontal and vertical lines anywhere in the report area.

   Box: allows drawing boxes in the report area.

   Picture: this field is used to add external pictures into the report. The picture is can be scaled and modified to fit into the box.

   Chart: opens the chart expert to generate different looking charts.

   Map: calls the map expert which helps to analyze the report data and identify trends.

To add one of those fields into the report click on the symbol and take action.

To add database fields to the report pick the field from the left side and drop it in the corresponding report area. If dropped into a detail area the system adds automatically the corresponding header.

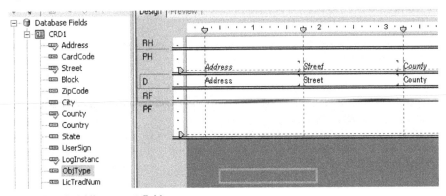

Figure 35-16: Adding report fields

Source: Screenshot

Whenever a field is used in the report it gets the green check mark 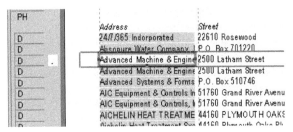 in the field explorer.

To see a preview of the report click on the ⟳ refresh and the report will be shown.

Figure 35-17: Display report

Source: Screenshot

This gives a impression about how the report looks. It is possible to move and rearrange fields in the preview. This has the same effect as moving them in the design area. To see the formatting options of each field use the RIGHT MOUSE BUTTON and select FORMAT.

We started to create one standard layout and save it as a template for generating new reports. Basically this template includes only the header and footer of the report. As Crystal does not allow saving a report without any tables in there we added OCRD which is the business partner main data.

35.5.1 Text field

The text field is generally to be used for free text that has no corresponding database field and/or does not have the need to change.

To add the field into the report use the **ab** button and create a box of the necessary size. A special ability of the text field is its allowance to drag database fields into it. This can be very helpful to have database fields within a floating text or to merge text together.

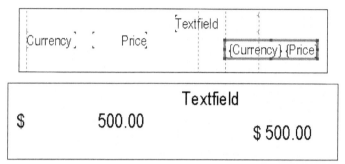

Figure 35-18: Textfield merge, design and preview

Source: Screenshot

Starting from the left we can see the CURRENCY and PRICE field. Both are fields from the database. To merge them together we created the TEXTFIELD. After dragging the CURRENCY and PRICE field into the TEXTFIELD they are merged together (right side). The curly braces show that the contents are from the database. It could be seen that the merged field looks much better in the report.

35.5.2 Group field

The group field allows to group fields by several conditions. Use the group button ⊞ to open the wizard. In the example we like to group the records by the DocDueDate.

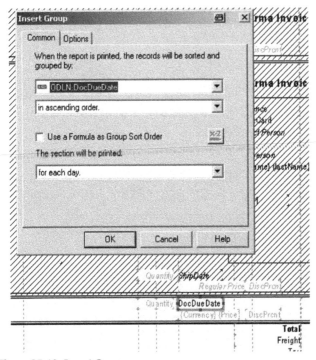

Figure 35-19: Insert Group

Source: Screenshot

There are some additional options depending on the field type. Numerical fields have different options than date or string fields. The OPTIONS tab gives the opportunity to assign formulas or replace the description. In the finished report the data will show up in the specified groups.

10/27/2006		
3493	Rough and Bolt hole machining, Drill oil hole pin end	1.00
ID:		
3494	Laser scribe, fracture split, torque twice, insert bush	1.00

Figure 35-20: Group by date

Source: Screenshot

Due to the reason a group field creates a new report section consisting out of group header and footer it is possible to hide or suppress the detail area. The difference between hide and suppress is that hiding a field makes it possible to open the detail area with a double click, while suppress doesn't allow this.

35.5.3 Sum field

The sum field allows making subtotals, totals, calculating average amounts, derivation and variance. The sum function is called through Σ. Afterwards the sum expert opens up and you can specify the options.

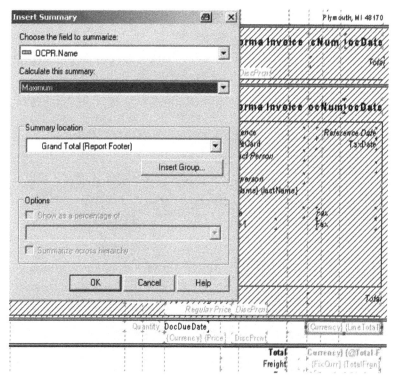

Figure 35-21: Insert Summary

Source: Screenshot

It is also possible to calculate a percentage amount of a field value.

35.5.4 Cross Table

A cross table is a special function that returns values based on specified criteria. The example given is from the Crystal Reports help file.

With a cross tab it is possible to calculate a horizontal and vertical sum of a table. The summary fields are found ate the intersection of rows and columns. The value at each intersection represents a summary that meets the row and column criteria.

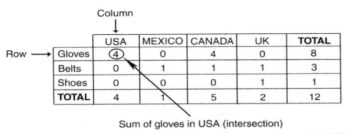

	USA	MEXICO	CANADA	UK	TOTAL
Gloves	4	0	4	0	8
Belts	0	1	1	1	3
Shoes	0	0	0	1	1
TOTAL	4	1	5	2	12

Sum of gloves in USA (intersection)

Figure 35-22: Cross section

Source: Crystal One help file

In this example it shows the total of the Gloves and USA columns, which are four.

Additional a cross tab includes several totals. At the end of each row a total of the product in the row is calculated. At the end of the column a total of the column values are calculated. At the intersection of the row and total column a grand total is summed. This could be seen in the next figure.

	USA	MEXICO	CANADA	UK	TOTAL	
Gloves	4	0	4	0	8	←— Total of products in row (gloves)
Belts	0	1	1	1	3	
Shoes	0	0	0	1	1	
TOTAL	4	1	5	2	12	←— Grand total all products (row) all countries (column)

Total of products in column (USA)

Figure 35-23: Cross section

Source: Crystal One help file

35.5.5 OLAP

The OLAP function allows connecting to additional data sources. To do so click on the OLAP button and select the type of the external data source. The data source can be an OLAP Server, a local cube or an HTTP Cube. Once the server is added the data source is available in the report.

35.5.6 Subreport

With the subreport button it is possible to add a subreport into the main report. A subreport consists basically out of the same elements as the main report. Parameters from the main report can be passed to the subreport. A subreport can be a new created report, or an already created one.

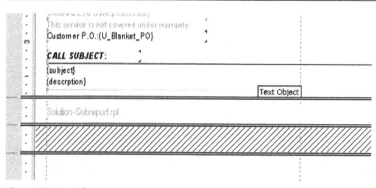

Figure 35-24: Subreport

Source: Screenshot

Whenever a new subreport is started Crystal will ask for a now or existing one.

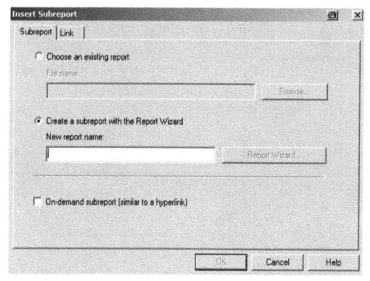

Figure 35-25: Subreport wizard

Source: Screenshot

It is possible to create the new subreport by specifying the name. The next step is to establish a connection to the datasource and select the tables and fields which are used. Some options like selecting, grouping and summing will follow. After this is finished the subreport can be edited in the same way as the main report.

Another main thing that is very important is passing parameters to the subreport. To add, change or edit subreport links select it and use the right mouse button to open the menu. Select CHANGE SUBREPORT LINKS to open the corresponding window.

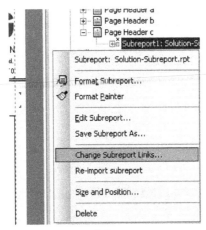

Figure 35-26: Change subreport links

Source: Screenshot

The following screen shows the parameters that can be passed to the subreport.

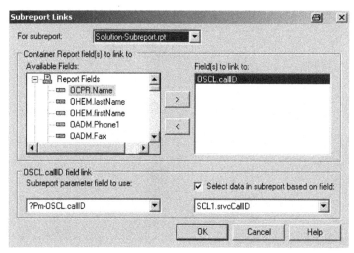

Figure 35-27: Subreport links

Source: Screenshot

The available fields list all fields that are available in the container report. The link to box lists the fields that are currently selected. The subreport parameter field is the one that is used to link the subreport and report together. The field in the right lower corner allows selecting data based on the field list.

35.5.7 Drawing

The drawing functions line and box allow drawing lines and boxes in the report. Those can be used to design the report and change the appearance. The lines can be formatted in an individual way.

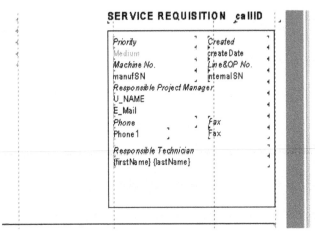

Figure 35-28: Boxes and lines

Source: Screenshot

Through placing the boxes in front or background

35.5.8 Picture

The picture function allows adding pictures into the report. The picture function allows pictures in bitmap, TIFF, JPEG and PNG format. The picture can be scaled, resized and reformatted in several ways to have appropriate appearance in the report. The pictures can be used in the several report areas and show therefore the corresponding behavior.

Figure 35-29: Picture

Source: Screenshot

35.5.9 Chart

With the chart function it is possible to create charts out of report data. To insert a chart use the chart button 📊 and draw the rectangle where the chart should be displayed. Crystal has four different types of charts.

- Advanced chart
- Group chart
- Cross-Tab chart
- OLAP chart

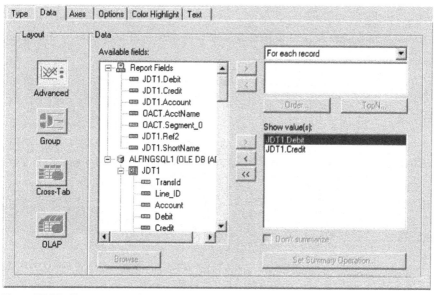

Figure 35-30: Chart Expert - datasource

Source: Screenshot

All data fields added in this screen are used for the chart. In the other tabs some options like the diagram type, the axe description and ranges or color options can be specified. Detailed can be obtained from the different screens and the online help. After finishing all the options the chart will be displayed in the report.

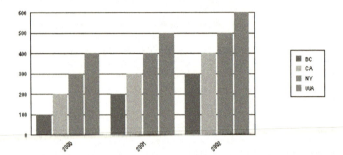

Figure 35-31: Finished chart

Source: Screenshot

The finished chart will be updated when the report data is updated. Modifying options are available through the right mouse button.

35.5.10 Map

The map button allows making some analysis with locations and places. It allows to display for example areas of interest when selling consumer goods to a large number of people and you like to gather information about areas of interest. Using the map button opens the map expert which will guide through the process of creating a map.

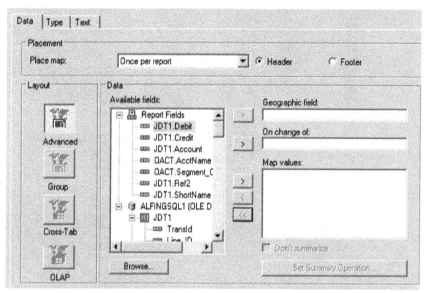

Figure 35-32: Map expert

Source: Screenshot

The map expert allows also selecting several different data sources. We hadn't any use for this feature. Therefore no further description will follow.

35.6 Formatting

Crystal offers several formatting options to change the appearance of the report data. The formatting options for each object can be accessed through a right mouse click on the related object. The formatting options change depending on the selected object. As all options are very self explaining no detailed description will follow.

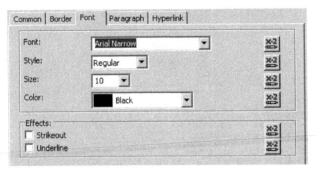

Figure 35-33: Formatting options

Source: Screenshot

Some more details can be seen in the next chapter, as we used formulas to format some objects.

35.7 Formulas

Crystal offers several formulas which go hand in hand with formatting options. The formulas allow calculating subtotals, totals and some other things. Also the option to show or hide objects is possible. This makes it possible to show/ hide objects depending on several conditions. This is very useful for different reasons. We will go through some of those possibilities. Crystal will display fields with assigned conditions grayed out.

The conditions can be applied to all types of fields, including pictures, database fields, formulas, totals, lines and boxes. It is also possible to assign conditions to whole report or subreport areas. It is not necessary that the conditional field is displayed in the report as long the field is accessible through the database.

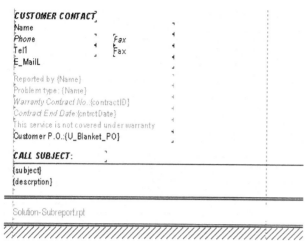

Figure 35-34: Conditioned fields

Source: Screenshot

It is possible assign several conditions to one field, referring to each other. Accessing the options shows if some special conditions are assigned by turning from blue to red.

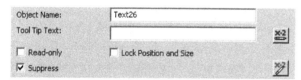

Figure 35-35: Condition assigned

Source: Screenshot

It is essential to understand that the rules apply if the conditions are true. This means the field will be suppressed if the formula that is assigned returns true. If fields should be hidden usually and displayed only for some special purposes a inverted formula has to be used.

To add/ change a condition click on the ![icon] field and the formula editor will open up.

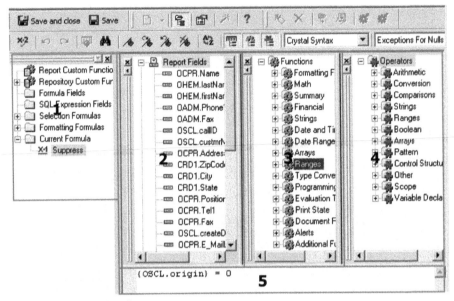

Figure 35-36: Formula editor

Source: Screenshot

The formula editor consists of five areas. The left side shows all the formulas in the whole report (1). Then the report fields (2), the functions (3) and the operators (4). Downsides the formula itself is displayed (5). In the example the field will be suppressed if OSCL.origin = 0 returns a true. We used this option for example to show warranty only in case it was applicable.

Some possible applications for the functions are:

- Change colors of boxes, lines, characters
- Highlight extraordinary ranges of numbers
- Change font sizes depending on some reasons
- Convert the report data into several ways depending on some conditions

The functions are very flexible and it is possible to realize a lot of different solutions. Therefore it depends on each individual requirement. A good source for a detailed description is the Crystal online help file. In there are several examples and some tricks how to use the provided functionality.

35.8 Integration in SAP

To integrate the reports it is necessary to install the Crystal One runtime into the SAP main application. The installation is started within SAP through selecting the .ard file which includes the registry information. The file has to be placed in the same folder like the installation file. Afterwards it is necessary to log into SAP as a manager or superuser. Within ADMINISTRATION → ADD ON S→ ADD ON ADMINISTRATION, clicking on REGISTER ADD-ON opens a new window where the .ard file can be selected.

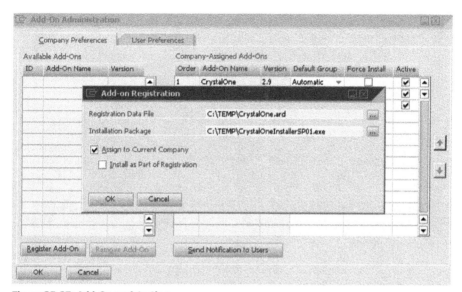

Figure 35-37: Add-On registration

Source: Screenshot

After registering the add-on logging out of SAP and logging in again starts installation. The installation procedure will start automatically. In case an error that the path of the CrystalOne Setup can't be used shows up opening the TASKMANANGER looking for the Crystal Process and ending the process allows proceeding. Afterwards continue with the installation.

To change the installation folder click Browse.

C:\Program Files\SAP\SAP Business One\AddOns\NBS\   Browse

To continue please click Next.

Cancel   Back   Install

Figure 35-38: Crystal installation

Source: Screenshot

For Crystal One some special preparations on the SQL-Server have to take place. The reason for this is that Crystal One needs read and write access to the database because it needs to initialize the databases. Therefore each SAP user has to have the read/ write access to the database. To prepare the SQL-Server Server Management Console has to be opened.

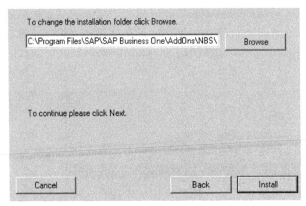

Figure 35-39: SQL-Server console

Source: Screenshot

After providing the login information the server management studio will open. Opening the SECU-RITY → LOGINS allows to continue.

Afterwards it is necessary to add all people that have to have access to the database. In a correct domain setup the easiest way is to add the domain users, as long as they match the SAP users. Otherwise a good way is to create an additional group SAP-Users and add users there.

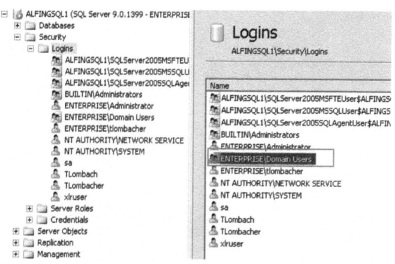

Figure 35-40: SQL-Console groups

Source: Screenshot

To add new users/groups the right mouse button opens a dropdown where New Login... has to be selected. Afterwards all users and/or groups have to be chosen.

It is necessary to grant each user/ group access to each individual database, especially read and write access. This is done in USER MAPPING by selecting each database, in our case Alfing_Live and Alfing_Test, and granting read/write access. This could be seen in the figure below.

Figure 35-41: Database access

Source: Screenshot

After all those steps are performed it is possible to log out of SAP and log in again. The installation procedure for the add-on will start and initialize the databases. Afterwards Crystal One Setup will appear as new menu point in the Tools menu. Calling the setup will open a new window which has several options.

Figure 35-42: Crystal One Setup

Source: Screenshot

It is possible to add new reports into the main menu, as well as override the standard SAP reports and forms. Also an option to sent reports by mail and fax is possible. To add new reports a report name has to be provided. Additionally the location of the report and the menu position it should appear has to be specified. The location of the report should be accessible for all users and it should be on a network drive which is not a mapped network drive as the drive letter can change under several circumstances.

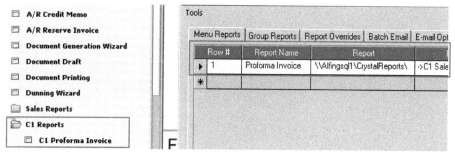

Figure 35-43: Crystal setup

Source: Screenshot

It could be seen that the corresponding menu appears in the SAP menu. From there the report can be called. To override the built in reports go to REPORT OVERRIDES and replace the built in reports with the customized reports. Whenever a report from SAP is printed out the Crystal Report will open and display the report.

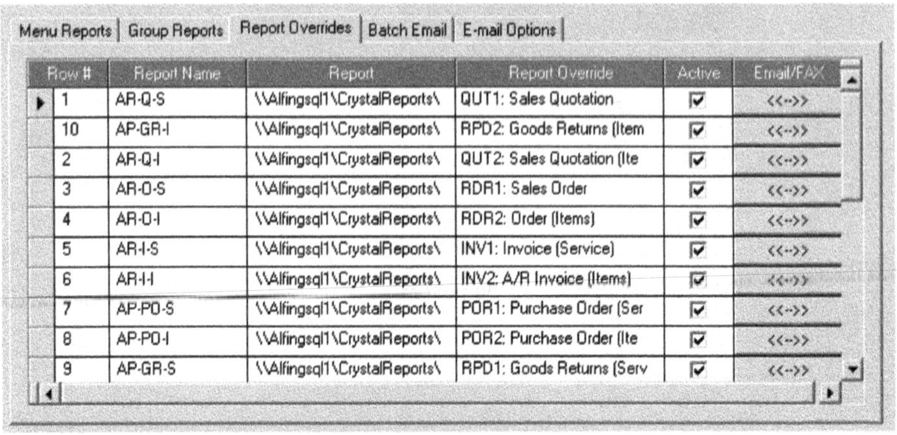

Row #	Report Name	Report	Report Override	Active	Email/FAX
1	AR-Q-S	\\Alfingsql1\CrystalReports\	QUT1: Sales Quotation	☑	<<-->>
10	AP-GR-I	\\Alfingsql1\CrystalReports\	RPD2: Goods Returns (Item	☑	<<-->>
2	AR-Q-I	\\Alfingsql1\CrystalReports\	QUT2: Sales Quotation (Ite	☑	<<-->>
3	AR-O-S	\\Alfingsql1\CrystalReports\	RDR1: Sales Order	☑	<<-->>
4	AR-O-I	\\Alfingsql1\CrystalReports\	RDR2: Order (Items)	☑	<<-->>
5	AR-I-S	\\Alfingsql1\CrystalReports\	INV1: Invoice (Service)	☑	<<-->>
6	AR-I-I	\\Alfingsql1\CrystalReports\	INV2: A/R Invoice (Items)	☑	<<-->>
7	AP-PO-S	\\Alfingsql1\CrystalReports\	POR1: Purchase Order (Ser	☑	<<-->>
8	AP-PO-I	\\Alfingsql1\CrystalReports\	POR2: Purchase Order (Ite	☑	<<-->>
9	AP-GR-S	\\Alfingsql1\CrystalReports\	RPD1: Goods Returns (Serv	☑	<<-->>

Figure 35-44: Report override

Source: Screenshot

To set the other options switch to the corresponding tab and provide the necessary information. The GROUP REPORTS function allow to group reports into a category. Whenever one of those reports is printed all other reports in this group are also printed. The further options are very self explaining.

36 XL-Reporter

The second main report tool for work with SAP is the XL-Reporter. This tool is included in the SAP main package. It needs a working Excel version to work properly. XL-Reporter is basically a add-on that offers advanced reporting and financial analysis for SAP Business One. The main advantage is that it allows making a real-time financial data analysis in any format that is necessary.

36.1 Basic concepts

The XL-Reporter has several different concepts to work with report data. It is necessary to understand this before generating new reports. The next figure shows the XL-Reporters understanding of several dimensions.

- Fact Set   A Fact Set contains the business data which can be queried. Such a query results in measure values, grouped and ordered by dimensions. A Fact Set corresponds to a transaction table in the SAP database table.

- Dimension   A Dimension corresponds to a Master table in SAP

- Light Dimension   A column of a fact table is which is not coupled to a Basic Dimension. It can be used to filter, group and sort a query result

Each Fact Set table consists of several Dimension tables. A Dimension table contains further descriptions and columns that provide detailed information. The Dimension table itself consists of several attributes. Those attributes can be used in the report. An example for this is that the Dimension table contains the Account name and other account information while the Account code is the link between the Dimension and Fact Set table. A Light Dimension is information that is linked directly from the Fact Set table into the report.

PK = Primary Key
FK = Foreign Key

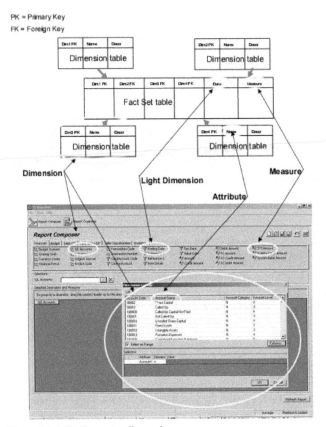

Figure 36-1: XL-Reporter dimensions

Source: SAP Metadata Repository

After understanding those basic concepts we will start to build a profit and loss statement based on an individual example.

36.2 Profit and Loss Statement

This is an example how to create a profit and loss statement with XL-Reporter. Based on these tutorials building different reports should be possible.

36.3 Defining an Excel spreadsheet

First of all a new Excel template which will be used as the standard design for the report has to be built. This is also called a worksheet template. In this worksheet the entire layout, styles, text and other information that is to be included in the report has to take place.

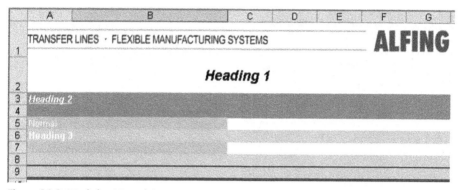

Figure 36-2: Worksheet template

Source: Screenshot

This worksheet shows the settings for each individual header. This could be done individually for each company's preferences. It is important to save the file as an Excel template. This is done in FILE → SAVE AS and selecting .XLT as file extension. The standard template folder should be kept otherwise the template won't be accessible from XL-Reporter. If the report should be used in a network surrounding it is necessary to change the template path within Excel and point it to a network location.

36.4 Creating a Report Definition

Creating a report definition is done in SAP where XL-Reporter has to be started. It can be found in TOOLS → XL-REPORTER. After doing this a new screen will open up. From thereon it is possible to create a new report. This is done in FILE → NEW → REPORT DEFINITION.

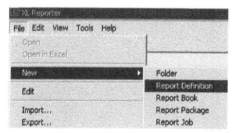

Figure 36-3: New Report Definition

Source: Screenshot

After entering the description the system will ask to assign a template to the report which should be the previously created one. The new report definition is opened automatically with the selected template.

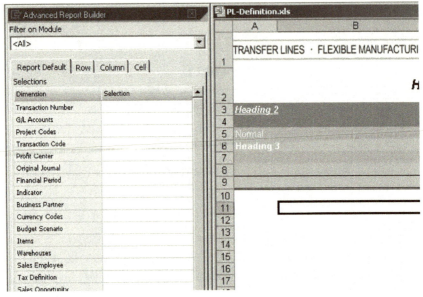

Figure 36-4: Report builder

Source: Screenshot

It shows the report and on the left side the advanced report builder.

36.5 Specifying the Sales Accounts in the report

In our sample report we need the data from the sales accounts. To retrieve the data from the database we must define a selection for the accounts and specify which information for the accounts we want to view in the report. In our case we want a detailed report with the single amounts of each account and not the summed totals. Therefore the account selection should be an expansion and the totals should be summed separately.

In our worksheet we select the row number 5. Afterwards we select the Row Expansion button ⁺Ͼ.

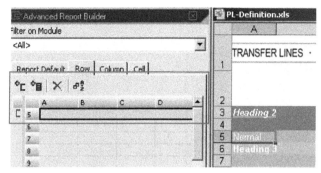

Figure 36-5: Row Expansion

Source: Screenshot

The SELECTIONS area below shows the available dimensions. Clicking on 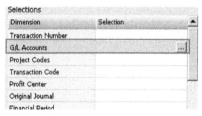 in the G/L Accounts row opens the selection's detail.

Figure 36-6: Selections Area

Source: Screenshot

This will open the Dimension Lookup window.

Figure 36-7: Dimension Lookup

Source: Screenshot

The accounts between 4000.... and 5000.... which equals all the cost of sales accounts must be selected. OK continues applying the selection.

Figure 36-8: Apply selection

Source: Screenshot

36.6 Make dimensions visible

It is possible to locate the selection in the current Excel worksheet. If a cell is selected in the worksheet it does not show any further information about its contents. To make the markings visible select [image] from the XL-Reporter toolbar. [image]. With the markings turned on the different selections will appear in the following ways.

- Expansions on row or column level are indicated by solid drawn lines.
- Summaries on row or columns level are indicated by dotted lines.
- Selections for cells are indicated by more noticeable dotted lines.

The next step will be to specify the dimension attributes to view for the sales accounts.

36.7 Specifying dimensions for sales accounts

The dimensions of the sales accounts specify which information should be displayed in the report. It is necessary to specify the attributes we want to display for each account that we have selected.

Select the cell in the worksheet, in our case A5, and click on formula builder f_x in the XL-Reporter toolbar. The formula builder will appear.

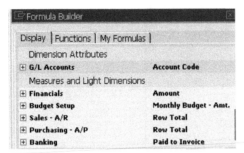

Figure 36-9: Formula Builder

Source: Screenshot

Depending on the selected cell the information displayed can vary. Clicking on the plus sign in front of the G/L Accounts dimension opens the attributes for this field. Double clicking on the attributes moves it to the corresponding cell. This has to be done with all attributes that shall be displayed.

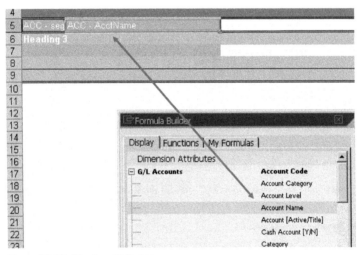

Figure 36-10: Display attributes

Source: Screenshot

The next step will be to add the amounts.

36.8 Adding the amounts to the report

In this sample all data is retrieved from the SAP financials module. For the example the cell C5 and D5 for the amounts contain this information. C5 will display the amount of the current period, while D5 will display the values of the previous period.

Adding the information is done by clicking in the cell and calling the formula builder _fx_ again. In the formula builder the amount that should be displayed in the amount has to be selected. For the example applies FINANCIALS → AMOUNT.

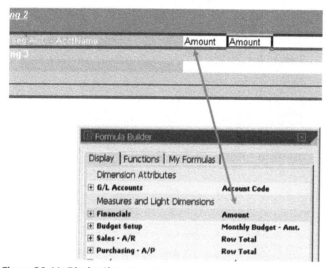

Figure 36-11: Display the amount

Source: Screenshot

The same has to be done for the cell D5. The indicator for the previous period will be set later. There is one issue. The amounts displayed in the sales accounts are counted as negative amounts. To change this behavior it is necessary to multiply the amounts -1 to display them as positive in the report. By clicking on the appropriate cell and going to the formula editor in Excel allows doing this. Multiplying the amount with -1 changes the negative sign into positive.

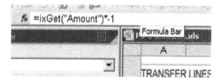

Figure 36-12: Change the amount display

Source: Screenshot

This has to be done with both cells, C5 and D5. Both cells will display then an error which says #VALUE!. This is because Excel is not able to calculate the formula until the report is finished and the data fields populated with the proper amounts.

36.9 Adding a summation line for totals

Row 6 will specify the totals for the sales accounts. Therefore entering a description in the cell B6 and going to cell C6 to add the data is the way to go. Because the account selection specified in Cell C5 is an expansion it is not able to determine the number of rows necessary to sum as total. Next step is going to the formula builder fx and choose the functions tab.

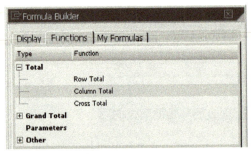

Figure 36-13: Functions tab

Source: Screenshot

Expanding the list TOTAL and double clicking Column Total will enter this total into the cell. This has to be redone with the cell located on the right side. Again the cell itself will show an error.

Figure 36-14: Value error

Source: Screenshot

The next step will specify the cost accounts in the report.

36.10 Specify the cost accounts

Until now only the sales accounts have been specified. The next steps will add the cost accounts into the report.

It follows nearly the same procedure like in the steps before. Selecting row number 7 and going to the Advanced Report builder is the first step. Choosing $^\Phi C$ for the report expansion proceeds. In the selection criteria the G/L Accounts have to be selected and opening the Dimension lookup will allow choosing the appropriate accounts from the list.

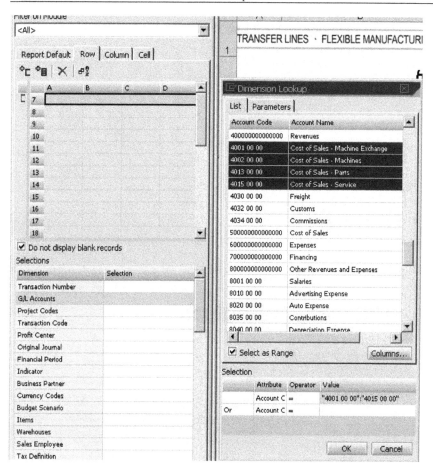

Figure 36-15: Account selection

Source: Screenshot

APPLY saves the selection. The next step is to specify the dimension of those accounts.

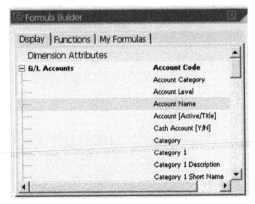

Figure 36-16: Dimension lookup

Source: Screenshot

Open the formula builder and add the G/L descriptions into the column A and B. Afterwards the amount can be added from the list.

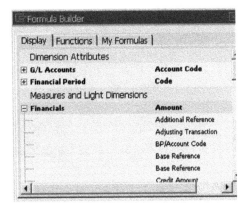

Figure 36-17: Adding amount

Source: Screenshot

After finishing this step the summation formula can be applied calculate the total. The net income can be calculated in the last row. To calculate the net income the standard Excel formula functions can be used which is done by selecting the cell and entering "=C6-C8" or "=D6-D8".

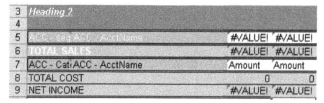

Figure 36-18: Totals

Source: Screenshot

36.10.1 Specifying the periods

Until now the system knows what data should be retrieved from the database. The following steps specify the periods from which the data should be achieved and passed to the spreadsheet. Instead of hard coding the period into the report the usage of parameter allows more flexibility.

The first step is to create the parameter itself which can be used to specify afterwards its contents.

The parameters can be created in the Advanced Report builder by selecting PARAMETERS.

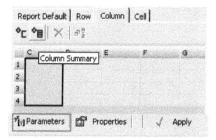

Figure 36-19: Parameters

Source: Screenshot

To enter the details it is necessary to populate the category box with DIMENSION. Afterwards the FINANCIAL PERIOD can be specified in the TYPE field. The ATTRIBUTE box has to be set to CODE. The DEFAULT VALUE has to be left blank. Afterwards a click on the PROMPT box sets the text which shows up during the input. This setups is finished with ENTER and OK.

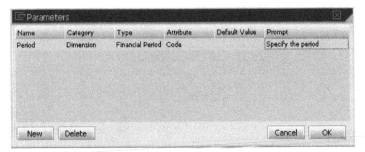

Figure 36-20: Parameters

Source: Screenshot

After this step the parameter is specified and can be placed used within the report.

This is done by selecting the column C in the worksheet. Afterwards the Column Summary 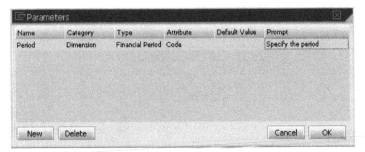 in the Advanced Report builder has to be selected. The selection screen area of the Advanced Report builder will display the dimensions that are available. After clicking the selections column on the right of FINANCIAL PERIOD and the ⊞ button opens the Dimension Lookup window.

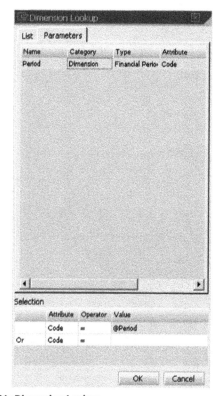

Figure 36-21: Dimension Lookup

Source: Screenshot

In this screen on the Parameters tab the already prepared period parameter can be set. After confirmation with OK and APPLY the selection works in the Advanced Report builder.

This was the period indicator for the current period. Additionally a selection parameter for the previous period will be created. This is done by selecting column D and opening the Advanced Report builder. The column summary ⬛ button will display the available dimensions. Afterwards all previous steps have to be redone until the dimension lookup is reached. Selecting the period field by using the ⬛ button opens the selection window and Dimension Lookup.

Selection			
	Attribute	Operator	Value
	Code	=	@Period
Or	Code	=	

Figure 36-22: Selection

Source: Screenshot

It is possible to select the highlighted criteria which subtracts 12 months from the current period.

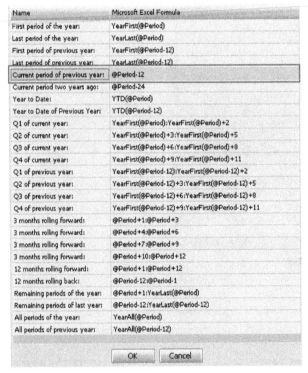

Name	Microsoft Excel Formula
First period of the year:	YearFirst(@Period)
Last period of the year:	YearLast(@Period)
First period of previous year:	YearFirst(@Period-12)
Last period of previous year:	YearLast(@Period-12)
Current period of previous year:	@Period-12
Current period two years ago:	@Period-24
Year to Date:	YTD(@Period)
Year to Date of Previous Year:	YTD(@Period-12)
Q1 of current year:	YearFirst(@Period):YearFirst(@Period)+2
Q2 of current year:	YearFirst(@Period)+3:YearFirst(@Period)+5
Q3 of current year:	YearFirst(@Period)+6:YearFirst(@Period)+8
Q4 of current year:	YearFirst(@Period)+9:YearFirst(@Period)+11
Q1 of previous year:	YearFirst(@Period-12):YearFirst(@Period-12)+2
Q2 of previous year:	YearFirst(@Period-12)+3:YearFirst(@Period-12)+5
Q3 of previous year:	YearFirst(@Period-12)+6:YearFirst(@Period-12)+8
Q4 of previous year:	YearFirst(@Period-12)+9:YearFirst(@Period-12)+11
3 months rolling forward:	@Period+1:@Period+3
3 months rolling forward:	@Period+4:@Period+6
3 months rolling forward:	@Period+7:@Period+9
3 months rolling forward:	@Period+10:@Period+12
12 months rolling forward:	@Period+1:@Period+12
12 months rolling back:	@Period-12:@Period-1
Remaining periods of the year:	@Period+1:YearLast(@Period)
Remaining periods of last year:	@Period-12:YearLast(@Period-12)
All periods of the year:	YearAll(@Period)
All periods of previous year:	YearAll(@Period-12)

OK   Cancel

Figure 36-23: Selection

Source: Screenshot

After confirmation it can be returned to the report itself. The next steps are to display the period indicator within the report. After selection of the cell C2 and choosing the formula builder *fx* the Financial Period will open and allow selecting the code.

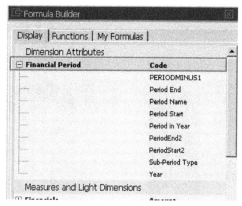

Figure 36-24: Code selection

Source: Screenshot

When the report is running the corresponding periods will be displayed on top of each column.

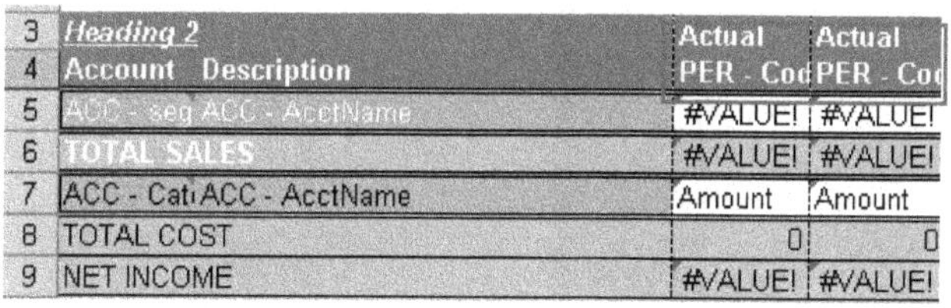

3	*Heading 2*	Actual	Actual
4	Account Description	PER - Cod	PER - Cod
5	ACC - seg ACC - AcctName	#VALUE!	#VALUE!
6	TOTAL SALES	#VALUE!	#VALUE!
7	ACC - Cat ACC - AcctName	Amount	Amount
8	TOTAL COST	0	0
9	NET INCOME	#VALUE!	#VALUE!

Figure 36-25: Period display

Source: Screenshot

Afterwards some additional descriptions for each field can be added into the other cells.

After doing this the report can be saved and run fro the XL-Reporter main screen. Running the report will show up in the following way.

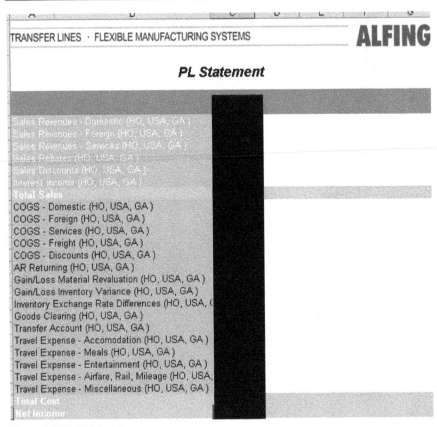

Figure 36-26: Finished Report

Source: Screenshot

The information displayed is not representative. The second period is not displayed due to missing data.

37 List of SQL-Tables

Name	Description
@BCENOTE	Selection Tree Leaf Notes
@BCESETT	Copy Express Standard Setting
@BFEXTDBVERSION	Extension DB versions
@BOEMAIL	BO: Default Email Setttings
@BOEXCEL	BO: Default Excel Setttings
@BOOADM	BO: Outlook Company Settings
@BOODFS	BO: Default Setttings
@BOOSTP	BO: Snapshot Templates
@BOQUOT	BO: Info for Quot/Setttings
@BOSETTINGS	BO: Info for Sync Settings
@BOSTP1	BO: Snapshot Template Queries
@BOSYNCLOG	BO: Info for Sync Log/History
@BOWORD	BO: Default Word Setttings
@NBS_CRSTL_GRP	NBS Crystal Group
@NBS_CRSTL_LN	NBS Crystal Line
@NBS_CRSTL_OVRD	NBS Crystal Overrides
@NBS_CRYSTAL	NBS Crystal One
@SALES_QUOTATION	SALES_QUOTATION Additional
@SQT	SQT Sales Quotation
AACP	Periods Category-Log
AACT	G/L Account - History
AAD1	Administration Extension-Log
AADM	Administration - Log
ACH1	Checks for Payment - Rows - History
ACHO	Checks for Payment - History
ACPR	Contact Persons - History
ACR1	Business Partner Addresses - History
ACR2	Bussiness Partners - Payment Methods-History
ACR3	Business Partner Control Accounts - History
ACR4	Allowed WTax Codes for BP - History
ACR5	BP Payment Dates
ACRB	Business Partner Bank Accounts - History
ACRD	Business Partners - History
ADM1	Administration Extension
ADO1	A/R Invoice (Rows) - History
ADO10	A/R Invoice - Row Structure - History
ADO2	A/R Invoice - Freight - Rows
ADO3	A/R Invoice - Freight - History
Name	Description
ADO4	Documents - Tax - History
ADO5	Withholding Tax - History
ADO6	Documents History - Installments
ADO7	Delivery Packages - History
ADO8	Items in Package - History

ADO9	A/R Invoice (Rows) - History
ADOC	Invoice - History
AFPR	Posting Period-Log
AINS	Customer Equipment Card - History
AIT1	Item - Prices - History
AITB	Item Groups - History
AITM	Items - History
AITT	Product Tree - History
AITW	Items - Warehouse - History
AJD1	Journal Entry - History - Rows
AJDT	Journal Entry - History
AKL1	Pick List - Rows - History
ALR2	Dynamic message data row
ALR3	Dynamic message data row
AMD1	Amout Differences Report Lines
AMR1	Inventory Revaluation - History - Rows
AMR2	Inventory Revaluation FIFO Rows (Archive)
AMRV	Inventory Revaluation - History
APKL	Pick List - History
ARC1	Incoming Payment - Checks - History
ARC2	Incoming Payment - Invoices - History
ARC3	Credit Vouchers History
ARC4	Incoming Payment - Account List - History
ARC5	Reciept log vat adjustment-History
ARC6	Incoming Payments - WTax Rows - History
ARC7	Incoming Payments - Tax Amount per Document - History
ARCT	Incoming Payment - History
ARI1	Add-On
ASC1	Service Call Solutions - History
ASC2	Service Call Inventory Expenses - History
ASC3	Service Call Travel/Labor Expenses - History
ASC4	Service Call Travel/Labor Expenses - History
ASC5	Service Call Activities - History
ASCL	History
ATC1	Attachments - Rows
ATT1	Bill of Materials - Component Items - History
Name	**Description**
ATX1	Tax Invoice - History - Rows
ATXI	Tax Invoice - History
AUSR	Archive Users - History
AWHS	Warehouses - History
BGT1	Budget - Rows
BOE1	Bill of Exchange for Payment - Rows
BOT1	Bill of Exchange Transactions
BOX1	Box Definition - Rows
BTF1	Journal Voucher - Rows
CCPD	Period-End Closing

Name	Description
CCRC	Create New Company
CDC1	Cash Discount - Rows
CFH1	Cash Flow Statement Report - History - Rows
CHD1	Checks for Payment Drafts - Rows
CHO1	Checks for Payment - Rows
CHO2	Checks for Payment - Print Status
CIFV	Inventory-FIFO Revaluation
CIN1	Correction Invoice - Rows
CIN10	Correction Invoice - Row Structure
CIN2	A/R Correction Invoice - Freight - Rows
CIN3	A/R Correction Invoice - Freight
CIN4	Correction Invoice - Tax Amount per Document
CIN5	A\R Correction Invoice - Withholding Tax
CIN6	Correction Invoice - Installments
CIN7	Delivery Packages - Correction Invoice
CIN8	Items in Package - Correction Invoice
CIN9	Correction Invoice - Rows
CLND	Journal Settings
CLNU	Display Definitions - Journal
CPI1	A/P Correction Invoice - Rows
CPI10	A/P Correction Invoice - Row Structure
CPI12	A/P Correction Invoice - Tax Extension
CPI2	A/P Correction Invoice - Freight - Rows
CPI3	A/P Correction Invoice - Freight
CPI4	A/P Correction Invoice - Tax Amount per Document
CPI5	Withholding Tax Data
CPI6	Documents History - Installments
CPI7	A/P Correction Invoice - Delivery Packages
CPI8	A/P Correction Invoice - Items in Package
CPI9	A/P Correction Invoice - Base Docs Details
CPV1	A/P Correction Invoice Reversal - Rows
Name	**Description**
CPV10	A/R Invoice - Row Structure
CPV12	A/P Correction Invoice Reversal - Tax Extension
CPV2	A/P Correction Invoice Reversal - Freight - Rows
CPV3	A/P Correction Invoice Reversal - Freight
CPV4	A/P Correction Invoice Reversal - Tax Amt per Doc.
CPV5	A/P Correction Invoice Reversal - WTax
CPV6	Documents History - Installments
CPV7	A/R Invoice - Delivery Packages
CPV8	A/P Correction Invoice Reversal - Items in Package
CPV9	A/P Invoice - Base Documents
CRD1	Business Partners - Addresses
CRD2	Bussiness Partners - Payment Methods
CRD3	BP Control Account
CRD4	Allowed WTax Codes for BP
CRD5	BP Payment Dates

CRD6	BP's Payer Name
CRD7	Fiscal IDs for BP Master Data
CSI1	A/R Correction Invoice Reversal - Rows
CSI10	A/R Correction Invoice - Row Structure
CSI12	A/R Correction Invoice - Tax Extension
CSI2	A/R Correction Invoice - Freight
CSI3	A/R Correction Invoice - Freight
CSI4	Tax Amount per Document
CSI5	A/R Correction Invoice - Withholding Tax
CSI6	Documents History - Installments
CSI7	Delivery Packages - A/R Invoice
CSI8	A/R Invoice - Items in Package
CSI9	A/R Correction Invoice - Base Documents
CSTN	Workstation ID
CSV1	A/R Correction Invoice Reversal - Rows
CSV10	A/R Correction Invoice Reversal - Row Structure
CSV12	A/R Correction Invoice Reversal - Tax Extension
CSV2	A/R Correction Invoice Reversal - Freight
CSV3	A/R Correction Invoice Reversal - Freight
CSV4	Tax Amount per Document
CSV5	A/R Correction Invoice Reversal - WTax
CSV6	Documents History - Installments
CSV7	A/R Correction Invoice Reversal - Delivery Packages
CSV8	A/R Correction Invoice Reversal - Items in Package
CSV9	A/R Correction Invoice Reversal - Base Documents
CTG1	Installment Layout
Name	**Description**
CTR1	Service Contract - Items
CUMF	Folder
CUMI	User Menu Items
DBCN	Database connection parameters
DDT1	Withholding Tax Deduction Hierarchy - Rows
DGP1	Customer List
DGP2	Expanded Selection Criteria
DGP3	Expanded Consolidation Options
DLN1	Delivery - Rows
DLN10	Delivery - Row Structure
DLN12	Delivery - Tax Extension
DLN2	Delivery Notes - Freight - Rows
DLN3	Delivery Notes - Freight
DLN4	Delivery - Tax Amount per Document
DLN5	Delivery - Withholding Tax
DLN6	Delivery - Installments
DLN7	Delivery Packages
DLN8	Items in Package - Delivery
DLN9	Delivery - Base Documents
DMW1	Query List

Name	Description
DPI1	A/R Down Payment - Rows
DPI10	A/R Down Payment - Row Structure
DPI2	A/R Down Payment - Freight - Rows
DPI3	A/R Down Payment - Freight
DPI4	A/R Down Payment - Tax Amount per Document
DPI5	A/R Down Payment - Withholding Tax
DPI6	A/R Down Payment - Installments
DPI7	Delivery Packages - A/R Down Pymt
DPI8	Items in Package - A/R Down Pmt.
DPI9	Down Payment Incoming - Base Documents
DPO1	A/P Down Payment - Rows
DPO10	A/P Down Payment - Row Structure
DPO2	A/P Down Payment - Freight - Rows
DPO3	A/P Down Payment - Freight
DPO4	A/P Down Payment - Tax Amount per Document
DPO5	A/P Down Payment - Withholding Tax
DPO6	Down Payment Out - Installments
DPO7	Delivery Packages - A/P Down Pymt
DPO8	Items in Package - A/P Down Pmt.
DPO9	Down Payment Outgoing - Base Documents
DPS1	Deposit - Rows
Name	**Description**
DRF1	Draft - Rows
DRF10	Draft - Row Structure
DRF12	Draft - Tax Extension
DRF2	Draft - Freight - Rows
DRF3	Draft - Freight
DRF4	Draft Documents - Tax
DRF5	Draft Documents - Withholding Tax
DRF6	Document Drafts - Installments
DRF7	Delivery Packages - Drafts
DRF8	Items in Package - Draft
DRF9	Document Drafts - Base Docs Details
DSC1	House Bank Accounts
DUT1	Dunning Term Array1
DWZ1	Dunning Wizard Array1 - BP Filter
DWZ2	Dunning Wizard Array 2-Invoice Filter
E874	835874 Report - Final Record
EOY1	End of Year UDOs
FCT1	Sales Forecast - Rows
FLT1	856 Report - Selection Criteria
FML1	Tax Formula Parameter Declaration
FRC1	Extend Cat. f. Financial Rep.
GFL1	Grid Filter Rules
GFL2	Grid Filter Name
H856	857 Report - Record 70
H874	835874 Report - Opening Record

Name	Description
HEM1	Absence Information
HEM2	Education
HEM3	Employee Reviews
HEM4	Previous Employment
HEM5	Employee Data Ownership Authorization
HEM6	Employee Roles
HLD1	Holiday Dates
HTM1	Team Members
I874	835874 Report - Invoices Record
IBT1	Batch Number Transactions
IGE1	Goods Issue - Rows
IGE10	Goods Issue - Row Structure
IGE12	Goods Issue - Tax Extension
IGE2	Goods Issue - Freight - Rows
IGE3	Goods Issue - Freight
IGE4	Goods Issue - Tax Amount per Document
Name	Description
IGE5	Goods Issue - Withholding Tax
IGE6	Goods Issue - Installments
IGE7	Delivery Packages - Goods Issue
IGE8	Items in Package - Goods Issue
IGE9	Goods Issue - Base Documents
IGN1	Goods Receipt - Rows
IGN10	Goods Receipt - Row Structure
IGN12	Goods Receipt - Tax Extension
IGN2	Goods Receipt - Freight - Rows
IGN3	Goods Receipt - Freight
IGN4	Goods Receipt - Tax Amount per Document
IGN5	Goods Receipt - Withholding Tax
IGN6	Goods Receipt- Installments
IGN7	Goods Receipt - Delivery Packages
IGN8	Items in Package - Goods Return
IGN9	Goods Receipt - Base Documents
INV1	A/R Invoice - Rows
INV10	A/R Invoice - Row Structure
INV11	A/R Invoice - Drawn Down Payments
INV12	A/R Invoice - Tax Extension
INV2	A/R Invoice - Freight - History - Rows
INV3	A/R Invoice - Rows
INV4	A/R Invoice - Tax Amount per Document
INV5	A/R Invoice - Withholding Tax
INV6	A/R Invoice - Installments
INV7	Delivery Packages - A/R Invoice
INV8	A/R Invoice - Items in Package
INV9	A/R Invoice - Base Documents
IPF1	Landed Costs - Rows
IPF2	Landed Costs - Costs

Name	Description
ITM1	Items - Prices
ITT1	Bill of Materials - Component Items
ITW1	Item Count Alert
IVRU	Inventory Valuation Utility
IWZ1	Accounts Revaluation History
IWZ2	Inflation Warehouse Filter
IWZ3	Items Last Revaluation Data
JDT1	Journal Entry - Rows
K874	835874 Report - Petty Cash/VAR
L856	856 Report - Record 60
MIN1	Monthly Invoice Report Document Information
Name	Description
MIN2	Item Imformation of MI
MLS1	Distribution Lists - Recipients
MLT1	Translations in user language
MRV1	Inventory Revaluation Information Array
MRV2	Inventory Revaluation FIFO Rows
MSN1	MRP Scenarios - Warehouses Array
MSN2	MRP Run Results
MSN3	MRP Pegging Information
NFN1	Not a Fiscal Sequence
NNM1	Documents Numbering - Series
OACG	Account Category
OACP	Periods Category
OACT	G/L Accounts
OADF	Address Formats
OADM	Administration
OAGP	Agent Name
OALC	Loading Expenses
OALI	Alternative Items 2
OAMD	Amount Differences Report
OARG	Customs Groups
OARI	Add-On - Company Definitions
OASC	Account Segmentation Categories
OASG	Account Segmentation
OATC	Attachments
OBCA	Bank Charges Allocation Codes
OBCG	Bank Charge for Bank Transfers
OBGD	Budget Cost Assess. Mthd
OBGS	Budget Scenario
OBGT	Budget
OBNK	External Bank Statement Received
OBOE	Bill of Exchange for Payment
OBOT	Bill Of Exchang Transaction
OBOX	Box Definition
OBPL	Business Place
OBPP	BP Priorities

OBTD	Journal Vouchers List
OBTF	Journal Voucher Entry
OCBI	Central Bank Ind.
OCCD	Cargo Customs Declaration Numbers
OCDC	Cash Discount
OCDP	Closing Date Procedure
Name	**Descripiton**
OCDT	Credit Card Payment
OCFH	Cash Flow Statement History
OCFP	CFOP for Nota Fiscal
OCFT	Cash Flow Transactions - Rows
OCFW	Cash Flow Line Item
OCHD	Checks for Payment Drafts
OCHF	
OCHH	Check Register
OCHO	Checks for Payment
OCIN	Correction Invoice
OCLA	Activity Status
OCLG	Activities
OCLO	Meetings Location
OCLS	Activity Subjects
OCLT	Activity Types
OCMT	Competitors
OCNA	CNAE Code
OCNT	Counties
OCOG	Commission Groups
OCPI	A/P Correction Invoice
OCPR	Contact Persons
OCPV	A/P Correction Invoice Reversal
OCQG	Card Properties
OCR1	Loading Factors - Profit Center
OCRB	BP - Bank Account
OCRC	Credit Cards
OCRD	Business Partner
OCRG	Card Groups
OCRH	Credit Card Management
OCRN	Currency Codes
OCRP	Payment Methods
OCRV	Credit Payments
OCRY	Countries
OCSI	A/R Correction Invoice
OCST	States
OCSV	A/R Correction Invoice Reversal
OCTG	Payment Terms
OCTR	Service Contracts
OCTT	Contract Template
OCYC	Cycle

Name	Description
ODDG	Withholding Tax Deduction Groups
Name	Description
ODDT	Withholding Tax Deduction Hierarchy
ODGP	Document Generation Parameter Sets
ODLL	Barcode Algorithm File
ODLN	Delivery
ODMW	Data Migration
ODOR	Doubtful Debts
ODOW	Data Ownership - Objects
ODOX	Data Ownership - Exceptions
ODPI	A/R Down Payment
ODPO	A/P Down Payment
ODPS	Deposit
ODPT	Postdated Deposit
ODRF	Drafts
ODSC	Bank Codes
ODTY	BoE Document Type
ODUN	Dunning Letters
ODUT	Dunning Terms
ODWZ	Dunning Wizard
OENC	Encoding Types
OEXD	Freight Setup
OFCT	Sales Forecast
OFML	Tax Formula Master Table
OFPR	Posting Period
OFRC	Financial Report Categories
OFRM	File Format
OFRT	Financial Report Templates
OGFL	Grid Filter
OGSP	Goods Shipment
OHED	Education Types
OHEM	Employees
OHLD	Holiday Table
OHPS	Employee Position
OHST	Employee Status
OHTM	Employee Teams
OHTR	Termination Reason
OHTY	Employee Types
OIBT	Batch No. for Item
OIDC	Indicator
OIDX	CPI Codes
OIGE	Goods Issue
OIGN	Goods Receipt
Name	Description
OIND	Triangular Deal
OINM	Whse Journal
OINS	Customer Equipment Card

Name	Description
OINV	A/R Invoice
OIPF	Landed Costs
OIRT	Interest Prices
OIST	BoE Instruction
OITB	Item Groups
OITG	Item Properties
OITM	Items
OITT	Product Tree
OITW	Items - Warehouse
OIWZ	Inflation Wizard
OJDT	Journal Entry
OJPE	Local Era Calendar
OLCT	Location
OLGT	Length Units
OLNG	User Language Table
OMGP	Material Group
OMIN	A/R Monthly Invoice
OMLS	Distribution List
OMLT	Multi-Language Translation
OMRC	Manufacturers
OMRL	Advanced Inventory Revaluation
OMRV	Inventory Revaluation
OMSN	MRP Scenarios
OMTH	Reconciliation History
ONCM	NCM Code
ONFT	Nota Fiscal Tax Category (Brazil)
OOCR	Loading Factors
OOFR	Defect Cause
OOIN	Interest
OOIR	Interest Level
OOND	Industries
OOPR	Sales Opportunity
OORL	Relationships
OOSR	Information Source
OOST	Sales Stage
OPCH	A/P Invoice
OPDF	Payment Draft
OPDN	Goods Receipt PO
Name	**Description**
OPDT	Predefined Text
OPEX	Payment Results Table
OPFT	Portfolio Definitions
OPID	Period Indicator
OPKG	Package Types
OPKL	Pick List
OPLN	Price Lists
OPOR	Purchase Order

OPPA	Password Administration
OPR1	Sales Opportunity - Rows
OPR2	Sales Opportunity - Partners
OPR3	Sales Opportunity - Competitors
OPR4	Sales Opportunity - Interests
OPR5	Sales Opportunity - Reasons
OPRC	Profit Center
OPRJ	Project Codes
OPRT	Partners
OPTF	BoE Portfolio
OPVL	Lender - Pelecard
OPYB	Payment Block
OPYD	Payment Run
OPYM	Payment Methods for Payment Wizard
OQUE	Queue
OQUT	Sales Quotation
OQWZ	Query Wizard
ORCM	Recommendation Data
ORCN	Retail Chains
ORCR	Recurring Postings
ORCT	Incoming Payment
ORDN	Returns
ORDR	Sales Order
ORFL	Already Displayed 347, 349 and WTax Reports
ORIN	A/R Credit Memo
ORIT	Dunning Interest Rate
ORPC	A/P Credit Memo
ORPD	Goods Returns
ORTM	Rate Differences
ORTT	CPI and FC Rates
OSCD	Service Code Table
OSCL	Service Calls
OSCM	Special Ledger - Analytical Accounting Configuration Rules: Material
Name	**Description**
OSCN	Customer/Vendor Cat. No.
OSCO	Service Call Origins
OSCP	Service Call Problem Types
OSCR	Special Ledger - Analytical Accounting Configuration Rules: Revenues & Expenses
OSCS	Service Call Statuses
OSCT	Service Call Types
OSGP	Service Group for Brazil
OSHP	Delivery Types
OSLM	Special Ledger - Analytical Accounting Report: Material
OSLP	Sales Employee
OSLR	Special Ledger - Analytical Accounting Report: Revenues & Expenses
OSLT	Service Call Solutions
OSPG	Special Prices for Groups

OSPP	Special Prices
OSRD	Batches and Serial Numbers
OSRI	Serial Numbers for Items
OSRL	Serial Numbers
OSRT	Korean Summary Report
OSST	Service Call Solution Statuses
OSTA	Sales Tax Authorities
OSTC	Sales Tax Codes
OSTT	Sales Tax Authorities Type
OSVR	Saved Reconciliations
OTCD	Tax Code Determination
OTER	Territories
OTFC	Tax Type Combination
OTNC	Transaction Category
OTNN	1099 Forms
OTOB	1099 Opening Balance
OTPA	Tax Parameter Attributes
OTPI	Purchase Tax Invoice
OTPR	Tax Return Values
OTPS	Tax Parameter
OTRC	Journal Entry Codes
OTRT	Posting Templates
OTSC	CST Code for Nota Fiscal
OTSI	Sales Tax Invoice
OTXD	Tax Invoice Draft
OUBR	Branches
OUDG	User Defaults
Name	**Description**
OUDO	User-Defined Object
OUDP	Departments
OUPT	User Autorization Tree
OUSG	Usage of Nota Fiscal
OUSR	Users
OUTB	User Tables
OVNM	VAT Report Numbering
OVPM	Outgoing Payments
OVRT	Tax Invoice Report
OVTG	Tax Definition
OVTR	Tax Report
OWDD	Docs. for Confirmation
OWGT	Weight Units
OWHS	Warehouses
OWHT	Withholding Tax
OWKO	Production Instructions
OWOR	Production Order
OWST	Confirmation Level
OWTM	Approval Templates

Name	Description
OWTR	Inventory Transfer
OWTT	Withholding Tax Type
PCH1	A/P Invoice - Rows
PCH10	A/P Invoice - Row Structure
PCH12	A/P Invoice - Tax Extension
PCH2	A/P Invoice - Freight - Rows
PCH3	A/P Invoice - Freight
PCH4	A/P Invoice - Tax Amount per Document
PCH5	A/P Invoice - Withholding Tax Data
PCH6	A/P Invoice - Installments
PCH7	Delivery Packages - A/P Invoice
PCH8	A/P Invoice - Items in Package
PCH9	A/P Invoice - Base Documents
PDF1	Payment Draft - Checks
PDF2	Payment Draft - Invoices
PDF3	Payment Draft - Credit Vouchers
PDF4	Payment Draft - Account List
PDF6	Payment Drafts - Withholding Tax - Rows
PDF7	Payment Draft - Tax Amount per Document
PDN1	Goods Receipt PO - Rows
PDN10	Goods Receipt PO - Row Structure
PDN12	Goods Receipt PO - Tax Extension
Name	Description
PDN2	Goods Receipt PO - Freight - Rows
PDN3	Goods Receipt PO - Freight
PDN4	Goods Receipt PO - Tax Amount per Document
PDN5	Goods Reciept PO - Withholding Tax
PDN6	Goods Receipt PO - Installments
PDN7	Goods Receipt PO - Delivery Packages
PDN8	Goods Receipt PO - Items in Package
PDN9	Goods Receipt PO - Base Documents
PEX1	Payment Results Table - Rows
PKL1	Pick List - Rows
POR1	Purchase Order - Rows
POR10	Purchase Order - Row structure
POR12	Purchase Order - Tax Extension
POR2	Purchase Order - Freight - Rows
POR3	Purchase Order - Freight
POR4	Purchase Order - Tax Amount per Document
POR5	Purchase Order - Withholding Tax
POR6	Purchase Order - Installments
POR7	Delivery Packages - Purchase Order
POR8	Items in Package - Purchase Order
POR9	Purchase Order - Base Documents
PSAR	Frame for Sales Analysis Report
PWZ2	Payment Wizard - Rows 2
PWZ3	Payment Wizard - Rows 3

PWZ4	Payment Wizard - Rows 4
PWZ5	Payment Wizard - Rows 5
PYD1	Payment Terms Allowed in Payment Run
PYM1	Currency Selection
QUE1	Queue Members
QUE2	Queue Elements
QUT1	Sales Quotation - Rows
QUT10	Sales Quotation - Row Structure
QUT12	Sales Quotation - Tax Extension
QUT2	Sales Quotation - Freight - Rows
QUT3	Sales Quotation - Freight
QUT4	Sales Quotation - Tax Amount per Document
QUT5	Sales Quotation - Tax
QUT6	Sales Quotation - Installments
QUT7	Delivery Packages - Sales Quotation
QUT8	Sales Quotation - Items in Package
QUT9	Sales Quotation - Base Documents
Name	**Description**
QWZ1	Query Tables
QWZ2	Query Fields
QWZ3	Query Fields
R874	835874 Report - Import Log Record
RBOX	Tax Declaration Box Report
RCC4	Incoming Payment - Credit Vouchers
RCR1	Recurring Postings - Rows
RCT1	Incoming Payment - Checks
RCT2	Incoming Payments - Invoices
RCT3	Incoming Pmt - Credit Vouchers
RCT4	Incoming Payment - Account List
RCT6	Incoming Payments - WTax Rows
RCT7	Incoming Pmt - Tax Amount per Document
RDN1	Returns - Rows
RDN10	Returns - Row Structure
RDN12	Returns - Tax Extension
RDN2	Return - Freight - Rows
RDN3	Return - Freight
RDN4	Returns - Tax Amount per Document
RDN5	Returns - Withholding Tax
RDN6	Returns - Installments
RDN7	Delivery Packages - Returns
RDN8	Items in Package - Returns
RDN9	Returns - Base Docs Details
RDR1	Sales Order - Rows
RDR10	Sales Order - Row Structure
RDR12	Sales Order - Tax Extension
RDR2	Sales Order - Freight - Rows
RDR3	Sales Order - Freight

Name	Description
RDR4	Sales Order - Tax Amount per Document
RDR5	Sales Order - Withholding Tax
RDR6	Sales Order - Installments
RDR7	Delivery Packages - Sales Order
RDR8	Sales Order - Items in Package
RDR9	Order - Base Docs Details
RIN1	A/R Credit Memo - Rows
RIN10	A/R Credit Memo - Row Structure
RIN12	A/R Credit Memo - Tax Extension
RIN2	A/R Credit Memo - Freight - Rows
RIN3	A/R Credit Memo - Freight
RIN4	A/R Credit Memo - Tax Amount per Document
Name	**Description**
RIN5	A/R Credit Memo - Withholding Tax
RIN6	A/R Credit Memo - Installments
RIN7	A/R Credit Memo - Delivery Packages
RIN8	Items in Package - A/R Credit Memo
RIN9	A/R Credit Memo - Base Documents
RIT1	Interest Rates
RPC1	A/P Credit Memo - Rows
RPC10	A/P Credit Memo - Row Structure
RPC12	A/P Credit Memo - Tax Extension
RPC2	A/P Credit Memo Rows - Expenses
RPC3	A/P Credit Memo - Freight
RPC4	A/P Credit Memo - Tax Amount per Document
RPC5	A/P Credit Memo - Withholding Tax
RPC6	A/P Credit Memo - Installments
RPC7	Delivery Packages - A/P Credit Memo
RPC8	Items in Package - A/P Credit Memo
RPC9	A/P Credit Memo - Base Documents
RPD1	Goods Returns - Rows
RPD10	Goods Returns - Row Structure
RPD12	Goods Return - Tax Extension
RPD2	Goods Return - Freight - Rows
RPD3	Goods Return - Freight
RPD4	Goods Return - Tax Amount per Document
RPD5	Goods Return - Withholding Tax Data
RPD6	Goods Returns - Installments
RPD7	Goods Returns - Delivery Packages
RPD8	Items in Package - Goods Return
RPD9	Goods Returns - Base Documents
RTM1	Rate Differences - Rows
SCL1	Service Call Solutions - Rows
SCL2	Service Call Inventory Expenses
SCL3	Service Call Travel/Labor Expenses
SCL4	Expense Documents
SCL5	Service Call Activities

SCM1	Special Ledger - Analytical Accounting Configuration Rule Conditions: Material
SCM2	Special Ledger - Analytical Accounting Configuration Rule Goals: Material
SCM3	Special Ledger - Analytical Accounting Configuration Rule Additional Calculations: Material
SCR1	Special Ledger - Analytical Accounting Configuration Rule Conditions: Revenues & Expenses
SCR2	Special Ledger - Analytical Accounting Configuration Rule Goals: Revenues &
Name	**Description**
SCR3	Special Ledger - Analytical Accounting Configuration Rule Additional Calculations: Revenues & Expenses
SLM1	Special Ledger - Analytical Accounting Report Lines: Material
SLR1	Special Ledger - Analytical Accounting Report Lines: Revenues & Expenses
SPP1	Special Prices - Data Areas
SPP2	Special Prices - Quantity Areas
SRI1	Serial No. Trans. for Item
SRT1	Korean Summary Report - Rows1
SRT2	Korean Summary Report - Rows2
STA1	Valid Period
STC1	Sales Tax Codes - Rows
SVR1	Saved Reconciliations - Transaction List
TCD1	Key Fields for Determination
TCD2	Key Field Values
TCD3	Tax Code Determination
TCD4	Withholding Tax Code Determination
TCD5	Tax Code by Usage
TFC1	Tax Type Combination - Rows
TNN1	1099 Boxes
TPI1	Purchase Tax Invoice - Rows
TPS1	Tax Parameter Attributes
TPS2	Tax Parameter - Return Values
TRT1	Posting Templates - Rows
TSI1	Sales Tax Invoice - Rows1
TXD1	Tax Invoice Drafts - Rows
UDG1	User Defaults - Documents
UDG2	User Defaults - Credit Cards
UDO1	User-Defined Objects - Child
UDO2	User-Defined Objects - Find Columns
UDO3	User-Defined Objects - Found Columns
UPT1	User Authorization Tree - Extended Permission
VLG1	From To Validation of Recalculation
VPM1	Outgoing Payments - Check Rows
VPM2	Outgoing Payments - Invoices
VPM3	Outgoing Payments - Credit Vouchers
VPM4	Outgoing Payments - Accounts
VPM6	Outgoing Payments - WTax Rows
VPM7	Outgoing Payments - Tax Amount per Document
VRT1	Tax Invoice Report - Rows
VRT2	Tax Invoice Report Grid Info

Name	Description
VTG1	Tax Definition
Name	**Description**
VTR1	Tax Groups
VTR2	Doc. Type Filter
VTR3	Series Filter
VTR4	Tax Groups
VTR5	Tax Groups
WDD1	Documents for Approval - Authorizers
WDD2	Documents for Approval - Terms
WHT1	Tax Definition
WHT2	Withholding Tax Definition - Rows2
WHT3	Value Range
WKO1	Production Instructions - Rows
WOR1	Production Order - Rows
WST1	Confirmation Level - Rows
WTM1	Approval Templates - Producers
WTM2	Confirmation Templates - Stages
WTM3	Approval Templates - Documents
WTM4	Approval Templates - Terms
WTM5	Approval Templates - Queries
WTR1	Inventory Transfer - Rows
WTR10	Inventory Transfer - Row Structure
WTR12	Inventory Transfer - Tax Extension
WTR2	Inventory Transfer - Freight - Rows
WTR3	Inventory Transfer - Freight
WTR4	Inventory Transfer - Tax Amount per Document
WTR5	Inventory Transfer - Withholding Tax
WTR6	Inventory Transfer - Installments
WTR7	Inventory Transfer - Delivery Packages
WTR8	Inventory Transfer - Items in Package
WTR9	Inventory Transfer - Base Documents
OUQR	Query, Formatted Search

Bibliography

[1] **Microsoft Corporation (July 2006):** *SQL Server 2005 Books Online.*
http://www.microsoft.com/downloads/details.aspx?FamilyID=BE6A2C5D-00DF-4220-B133-29C1E0B6585F&displaylang=en (approx. 123 MB)

[2] **Rebecca M. Riordan (January 2005):** *Designing Effective Database Systems.* Addison Wesley Professional ISBN: 0-321-29093-3

[3] **Ken Henderson (October 2004):** *The Guru's Guide to SQL Server Architecture and Internals.* Addison Wesley ISBN: 0-201-70047-6

[4] **SAP (March 2006):** *XL Reporter 2005 A SP01 Meta Data Repository Description.* SAP Press

[5] **SAP (March 2006):** *Using Syntax and Functions in XL Reporter.* SAP Press

[6] **SAP (2005):** *XL-Reporter Online Help.* SAP Library

[7] **SAP (January 2006):** *License Guide.* SAP Library

[8] **SAP (2005):** *SAP Business One Online Help 2005 A .* SAP AG

[9] **SAP :** *SAP Business One Customer Portal.* http://www.service.sap.com

[10] **SAP (May 2005):** *Security Guide MS-SQL-Server.* SAP Library

[11] **SAP (July 2005):** *SAP Business One Add-Ons 2005 Release Notes.* SAP Library

[12] **SAP (January 2006):** *License Guide.* SAP Library

[13] **SAP (November 2006):** *SQL-Server 2005 Upgrade Guide.* SAP Library

[14] **Peck, George (2004):** *Crystal Reports 10: The complete reference guide.* McGraw-Hill ISBN:072231661

[15] **GoToMyPC (2006):** *Go to my PC Online User Guide*
https://www.gotomypc.com/help/index.html

[16] **Wolf, Kowalczyk, Uznik (~2003):** *ShoeFa Studienarbeit.* Fachhochschule Ulm

[17] **SAP (March 2006):** *XL Reporter Metadata and Repository.* SAP Library

[18] **SAP (November 2006):** *Using Syntax and Functions XL-Reporter.* SAP Library